The Joys of National Review 1955~1980

Compiled by PRISCILLA L. BUCKLEY

National Review Books

Dedication

To the men who forged NATIONAL REVIEW
Bill Buckley, James Burnham, Frank Meyer, Jeffrey Hart
To the men who kept it afloat
Bill Rusher, Jim McFadden, Ed Capano
And to that Blythe Spirit
who saw that it came out every fortnight
properly attired
Art Director Jimmy O'Bryan

Acknowledgments

I would like to thank former NR Publisher Wick Allison for encouraging me to undertake this project after my retirement from NATIONAL REVIEW as Managing Editor. But the project would have been stillborn without the help of Publisher Ed Capano, Assistant Publisher Jack Fowler, their staff—Catherine Moraetis, Julie Crane, and Elizabeth Capano—research librarians Russell Jenkins and John Virtes, and Editorial Associate Patricia Bozell, who so willingly and efficiently provided me with the stream of material from the bound volumes of NATIONAL REVIEW which I needed to make the final selections for inclusion in the book. I am also extraordinarily grateful to Arnold Beichman, a long-time contributor and Senior Scholar at the Hoover Institution, and to Professor Thomas H. Hendrickson, Hoover's Associate Director, for inviting me to spend a couple of months in the fall of 1993 at Hoover, where, with the help and advice of a number of Hoover Fellows and Scholars I selected and shaped into final form the material for *The Joys of National Review.*

Contents

Part Two, 1961 to 1965

Part Three, 1966 to 1970

Part Four, 1971 to 1975

Part Five, 1976 to 1980

Introduction

The idea for this book came to me in the summer of 1990 when I was asked to undertake a crash research project for a documentary to be presented at NATIONAL REVIEW's 35th Anniversary Dinner at New York's Waldorf-Astoria on October 5. I had been given two weeks to come up with the raw material and the project was proving unexpectedly tough going. The problem was that day after day, as I flipped through back issues, I found myself derailed from the job at hand by the excitement, the beauty, the *joie de vivre* of material in the back issues, from snippy editorial paragraphs in "The Week" up front, to the final brief book reviews in the back. I found the prose and contents, revisited even years after their appearance, well, dazzling. A profligate display of talent, buried now in the archives.

My initial idea was to resurrect as many of those pieces as could fit in one volume, a quiet demonstration that what had contributed to NATIONAL REVIEW's reputation over so many years as the best-edited and best-written magazine in America was not its opinions but its literary standards.

But of course it would never be possible to disengage the prose from the method. NATIONAL REVIEW was launched to make the case for the rollback and defeat of Communism, and to wage combat with the dominant premises of the liberal establishment. Our writers aimed at those targets, most of the time, and were at their best when scoring against them. I could hardly be persuaded to exclude from this anthology, on the grounds that it was too political, an editorial by Jim Burnham—usually so cool, so analytical—in high outrage at the brutal suppression of the Poznan riots; or a jeremiad by Fritz Wilhelmsen, lamenting Hungary's crushed freedom fighters? Ignore James Jackson Kilpatrick covering the campaign of Hubert Humphrey ("being on the campaign trail with Hubert Humphrey is like spending two weeks in a milkshake machine")?

Accordingly, this volume doesn't seek to be entirely non-political. Its single standard is: good writing. As the distinguished New England novelist and inspired teacher, Mary Ellen Chase, told generations of Smith College English majors a half century ago in her justly famous classes on "The English Novel" and "The Bible (KJV) as English Literature," in judging a work of literature one should ask what the author had in mind to do, how successfully he brought it off, and finally, whether the project had been worth doing in the first place. Pretty good criterion.

Gathered here, in *The Joys of National Review,* are examples of the finest kinds of writings to adorn its pages. Between 1956 and 1980, NR covered seven presidential elections for the most part through extensive profiles of the candidates. The burden of this coverage was done seriatim by the novelist John Dos Passos, critic John Chamberlain, editor/columnist James Jackson Kilpatrick, journalist/scholar Garry Wills (who joined the enemy in 1969), and NR's own Richard Brookhiser, elected senior editor at age 23, less than two years out of Yale. *NR*'s concerns were never exclusively political. Kilpatrick was among the first newspapermen to interview Ezra Pound upon his release from St. Elizabeth's. Theodore S. White, a ranking journalist and historian, pronounced Francis Russell's "Living and Dying in Boston," a mood piece about a random killing, "a permanent part of the American literary and political heritage." A visit to a former Nazi extermination camp by a young American soldier stationed in Germany, then Captain Joe Rehyansky, makes the cut, as do an account by John Lukacs, the historian, of the historic implications of a papal visit to the States, and Francis B. Randall's shrewd observations on post-Stalin Russia and post-Mao China. No editor would leave out the hilarious afternoon Sir Arnold Lunn spent with Evelyn Waugh maneuvering over two bottles of champagne at White's, let alone Hugh Kenner's lunch with T.S. Eliot ("A Stilton Cheese Catechized Upon a Table"). And so much more.

I've included samplings from NR's columnists, Russell Kirk's "From the Academy," Willi Schlamm's "Arts & Manners," Willmoore Kendall's "The Liberal Line," Jim Burnham's "The Third World War," and durable material from the back-of-the-book, essays and book reviews. These were molded and animated by Frank Meyer during NR's first 15 years or so, and expanded and broadened under Chilton Williamson. They included Nika Hazelton's "Delectations," D. Keith Mano's "The Gimlet Eye." They continue to include John Simon's highly praised film reviews and Ralph de Toledano's sparkling music criticism.

Over the years dozens of young men and women have served as editorial assistants at NATIONAL REVIEW and honed their editorial skills on those deceptively simple editorial paragraphs. An ambition was to indite the pointed political paragraph that would lead off the section, or the more *outré*, sometimes outrageous bit of fluff, whimsy, ridicule, or satire that would round it off. This and the short book reviews in the back were the teething rings of young NR editors and contributors. But the older hands relished the sport as well. Professor Willmoore Kendall of Yale set a high standard in the early years ("The attempted assassination of Sukarno had all the appearances of a CIA operation: everyone in the room was killed but Sukarno") and his mastery of the form was ably carried on over the years by Tim Wheeler, Bill Rickenbacker, Arlene Croce, Chris Simonds, and Joe Sobran, among others. It is a rare issue of NR to this day that doesn't carry a Wheeler editorial paragraph. To introduce the five sections of this book, I have used a few such paragraphs, which serve not only to amuse the reader, but to evoke the political atmosphere of the ensuing half decade that makes up a section of the book.

A talented writer in the grip of an enthusiasm is a joy to behold: Bill Rickenbacker on flying, Reid Buckley on bullfighting, Chris Simonds on cars! cars! cars!, Francis Russell on The Apple, Noel Parmentel on Charles van Doren, John Chamberlain on Charles Lindbergh, 14-year old David Johnston on Barry Goldwater, Joan Didion on John Wayne.

The book critic and author, Guy Davenport, wrote of Joan Didion's style in a review of *River Run* that "she has polished her prose too well for her own good. She should put in some tricks with her left hand, or attempt some little impossibilities here and there, so that we could appreciate the smudge." When Joan Didion first wrote for NATIONAL REVIEW, right out of college, her prose, while always careful, was more relaxed, even impish. A couple of brief Didion book reviews have been included.

I was surprised to find that a number of the satirical pieces I had enjoyed at the time do not stand up: the joke was too topical. Jimmy Carter's Killer Rabbit, like Mike Dukakis's tank, have a limited shelf life, along with Bill Clinton's haircut. What does hold up is the evergreen. Northerners have thought Southerners talk funny since before the Civil War: accordingly S. L. Varnado's take-off on the talk emanating from Jimmy Carter's White House continues to amuse. Carter picks up the phone to ask the groundkeepers to do something about the "eyes" (ice) he has spotted on the White House lawn, and Varnado is off and running. In Aloïse Heath's "Seven Keys to Anomie," she shoots Malcolm Cowley full of poisoned arrows, but the real target has been with us since at least Periclean Athens—the intellectual snob. John Keefauver, bravest of the brave, achieves the impossible in making rollicking fun of a discussion of racism ("The Inside-out Black Whites and the Inside-out White Blacks").

I've included a sampling of NATIONAL REVIEW editorial frolics, many of them appearing in Bill Buckley's "Notes & Asides" column: an encomium by Arthur Schlesinger Jr. on the cover of a Buckley book, and what then ensued; an attempt by a fan to get a glossy, autographed picture of WFB; an effort to recast publisher Bill Rusher into a cult hero (dismal failure), and one of Bill Rickenbacker's 18 successive forecasts of the year ahead, the eagerly awaited "Here It Comes" year-end editorial.

Space restrictions are an editor's nightmare. Most of the pieces in *Joys* have been cut to winnow out anachronisms and to make space for other material. The sections that make up *Joys* are each between 16,000 and 20,000 words, which is less reading matter than you get in a single current issue of NR. (Each item, by the way, is introduced by the date of the issue in which it ran.) The book is illustrated with line drawings by Alois Derso, NATIONAL REVIEW's only artist in its first few years. (A review of a book on Mr. Derso's illustrious career appears on p. 87).

Any collection of this kind is bound to be idiosyncratic, the editor's own interests determining what stays in, what doesn't. I include (for instance) a review on Hemingway rather than a superb review on Auden because I tend to be more interested in Hemingway than Auden, and guess this is so of most readers. Another editor mining the nearly 650 issues I explored to complete this project could come up with an entirely different book, but one every bit as distinguished as *Joys*, because the only thing an editor can't do is compile a book from the back issues of NATIONAL REVIEW that is dull or ill-written.

Priscilla L. Buckley
Sharon, Connecticut
March 1994

Foreword

William F. Rickenbacker

It was almost forty years ago and we were young and full of beans and really didn't give a tinker's dam about anything or anybody except maybe our souls and the relation between them and the Mind of God and also maybe the almost equally sacred duty we felt to shake up an Establishment besotted and far gone in statism, sober it up, wipe the drivel off its face, and return it to navigating the good straight course laid out by those heroes, our Founding Fathers. Those folks in high position, we didn't give them no respect at all.

Bliss was it in that dawn to be alive, but to be young was, well, to be green and small. *Urbi et orbi* though we might hope to speak, we were far from mass communications. One day in the early 1960s we were sitting around the little table in Bill Buckley's little office when Bill Rusher stuck his head through the French door from his own cubbyhole to announce with joy, "Write well this week, gentlemen, you are writing for thirty thousand subscribers!" We cheered. About the others I do not know; but, as for me, I secretly resolved that this giddy prosperity should not choke off my flow of animal spirits nor shorten my stride nor dull my sword. Today NATIONAL REVIEW has some 270,000 subscribers, it has put on long pants, and it has ceased raising Hell. I join every devoted reader in applauding its transformation into a graceful and wise maturity. But one may be forgiven, one hopes, if in the time of triumph one looks back with an eye not entirely dry and recalls as vividly as one recalls one's first big serious kiss what perfectly gorgeous fun it was, week after week, to tweak some high and mighty noses. The senses can recall that early office, how it looked, crowded and shabby, with walls doing double duty as billboards for jokes, catastrophes, and wonders; how it smelled, mainly pipe smoke and cigar smoke and secretarial fluids and cheap wine; above all, how it sounded, for even as I write this my ear fills up again with characteristic sound of those early years, the sound of endless laughter.

Laughter. One Wednesday after we had put the issue to bed and were having a wee drappie at the wee table in Bill Buckley's wee office, Bill Rusher entered, thirty minutes late as was his unbreakable custom, tut-tutted us with his stern "Drinking again, eh?" and sat down to join the party. The party, as it turned out, was discussing the works of Charles Dickens, and one editor mentioned that he was going through the entire works. Bill Rusher heaved a great sigh, as of a Hercules only half-way through the Augean stables, and said, with what might have been misconstrued as a touch of self-importance, "Well, I find that after a day at NATIONAL REVIEW I can't get any serious work done in the evening." To which another editor replied, in a casually helpful tone of voice, as if taking a respectful interest in Mr. Rusher's problem, "Well then, why don't you try doing your serious work during the day?" The laughter that greeted that sally must have been heard at Grand Central. Bill Rusher turned quite red, blushing for the first and last time that I have knowledge of, and was unable to speak. Our greatest debater was stumped by the dementia of his colleagues.

Laughter. I popped into Bill Buckley's office one day and found him deep in an interview with a reporter from a major magazine. I offered to back out, but Bill said, "No, stay, we're just finishing up." Sure enough, within a minute or two the reporter rose, Bill rose, we all said adieu, and then as the reporter approached the door that Bill was holding open for him, he stopped, turned, and fired off a perfectly polished barb that he must have spent the entire preceding evening practising and probably tried out several times on his wife. Clearly he thought he had slain the dragon. Dragon Bill, however, scarcely pausing to take a breath, took the reporter's frail jibe, turned it into an unanswerable witticism, and smiled ever so smoothly. The reporter gasped, collected his remaining wit, and managed to say, "Still the *enfant terrible*, eh, Bill?" Bill patted him on the shoulder—a gesture that helped to steer him out the door—closed the door, turned around to me, and said, "I figure I can get away with that_____ until I'm forty."

Laughter. In 1965 or so, John Lindsay ran for mayor of New York, and much of his campaign oratory in the early stage was directed at those nefarious and shadowy monsters, the "power brokers" and the "special interests." This became too much for me. I asked Jimmy O'Bryan to design some nice letterhead in a style that would reek of money and also of an attempt to achieve respectability. He designed absolutely authentic stationery for The Special Interests (Executive Secretary, me) and The Power Brokers (me again), with addresses the same as NR's offices. Next time Lindsay yapped at these fine organizations, the Executive Secretary fired off letters to all nine of the major Manhattan daily publications, very high-toned and pompous letters, explaining that the Brokers and the Interests were very old groups that represented New York's most prosperous families, which were nevertheless "very private people" (the code phrase for crooks), and that a lawsuit would follow any further dragging of these fine families into the mud of vulgar politicking. One or two papers, including the *New York Times*, checked up by responding to the address given and received their authentication. Within a week or two I had word that these letters were being passed about in City Hall and the staffers were having a good laugh at Lindsay's expense. After two or three weeks of this the Lindsay campaign suddenly stopped targeting my fine old organizations. How we laughed!

Yes, we made it fun, as Ronald Reagan said at NR's 35th anniversary banquet, but a light heart can be connected to busy hands and our hands had work to do. Strictly as writers, as workmen busy in an ancient craft, we strove to make our way against the grain and to force our opponents, if we could not bring them to agree with us, at least to admire the way we had with words ("very hand on hip," as Arlene Croce once wrote), and, I think, to envy us not a little (a new writer of ours, I forget who, was identified in some leftish publication, it doesn't matter which, as "one of Bill Buckley's bright boys on East 35th Street"—gloriosky, Zero!).

The 53 authors who appear in this collection include about twenty who were either permanent or frequent members of the cast of characters on East 35th Street. What words you see here were either written on the premises or edited on the premises with, in either case, but one goal in mind: to make each word justify itself, each sentence stand firm, each writer's style come through as clearly individuated as the writer himself.

Opinions could differ. Frank Meyer, you may observe, isn't in this collection, although it is possible to argue that he was a successful stylist even according to the benchmarks set out by Mary Ellen Chase and quoted with approval here by editor Priscilla Buckley, whom I love. Frank did not aim to entertain or astonish but to elucidate, to argue, to exhort, and to do all this in language of high purity and seriousness. Did he succeed in suffusing his prose with his own majestic earnestness? Was this something that was, after all, worth doing? In the mid-1950s, making the wry point that the leftist intellectuals were in the grip of a clinically identifiable mass delusion, Frank summed up a book of political essays with this sentence:

> Every contributor to this collection—Richard Hofstader, David Reisman, Peter Viereck (that sterling conservative), Talcott Parsons, Nathan Glazer, S.M. Lipset, Daniel Bell—blandly ignores the possibility that there could be any real issue of a rational kind in American politics today which would justify the existence of an opposition, and proceeds to a sociological-psychological analysis of the extraordinary fact that there is one.

Cela est bien dit, n'est-ce pas, ma chère?

Besides paying extraordinary attention to matters of style, the 35th Street crew worked a profound change in the use of language in journalism. Gone was the Strunk-White stricture against the use of foreign phrases. Down the memory hole went the fear of long words, unusual words, difficult words, weird words. "Oxymoron," considered dead for centuries, took new life on East 35th Street and has now passed into the Elysian Fields of television commentators, standup comedians, and newspaper editorialists. Other exhumations— "exiguous," "eximious" come to mind—haven't caught on quite so quickly. Latin phrases appeared with dismaying frequency and an aristocratic refusal to translate or explain, driving the egalitarians, populists, and yahoos to paroxysms of helpless rage. Among the many achievements of NR is one seldom mentioned, that its breezy inclusion of Latin as a means of expression seduced dozens, and perhaps hundreds, of people to resume or even to begin their study of that indispensable language. After two or three decades of NR we were reading in the papers that there was a shortage of Latin teachers in the public schools. And that, ladeez and gennulmen, is an open and shut case of *post hoc ergo propter hoc*, thinkeenot?

So welcome to the Big Top, boys and girls of all ages! And now, as the greatest show on earth begins, let your eyes follow the dazzling spotlight to the end of the arena as the fun begins! Yes! Here they come! Here come the dancing bears!

Part One

1956 to 1960

The Week
Selected Editorial Paragraphs

March 2, 1957
Senator Byrd has called for reducing the budget by 5 billion. NATIONAL REVIEW stays, and raises him five.

October 19, 1957
Oyez, oyez, oyez! Now is the time for all good men to gather together the rights with which they were endowed by their Creator, take refuge in those homes that—tradition assures us—are their castles, and bolt all the doors. The United States Supreme Court, following its summer recess, is back in session.

November 22, 1958
"What," asks Gerald Johnson in the current *New Republic,* "would the football think of the game if a football could think?" A good question—but one which is really less pressing than another: "What would a *New Republic* reader think of the *New Republic* if a *New Republic* reader could think?"

Reminiscences of a Middle-Class Radical

John Dos Passos

It's hard to overestimate the revulsion wrought by the first world war in the minds of a generation that had grown up in the years of comparative freedom and comparative peace that opened the century. It's hard to remember in the middle Fifties today that in those years what little military service there was in America was voluntary, that taxes were infinitesimal, that you could travel anywhere in the world except through Russia and Turkey, without saying boo to a bureaucrat. If you wanted to take a job it was nobody's business but yours and the boss's. Of course, as the labor people were busily pointing out, if you worked in a sweat shop for a pittance and happened to starve to death in the process it was nobody's business either. When Woodrow Wilson led the country into the European war, however little we approved this reversal of American tradition, most of us just out of college were crazy to see what war was like. We experienced to the full the intoxication of the great conflagration, though those of us who served as enlisted men could hardly be expected to take kindly to soldiering, to the caste system which made officers a superior breed or to the stagnation and opportunism of military bureaucracy. Waste of time, waste of money, waste of lives, waste of youth. We came home with the horrors. We had to blame somebody.

The reformers we admired, the Bull Moose people, the Progressives from Wisconsin, Eugene V. Debs and the old-time Populists, had tended to blame everything that went wrong on malefactors of great wealth. Capitalism was the bogey that was destroying civilization. Cut the businessman's profits, we said. Production for use. We thrilled to the word cooperative. Industrial democracy was the refrain of our song. In Europe we had picked up some of the slogans of Marxists and syndicalists. We agreed with them that democratic self-government had sold out to capital. Capitalism was the sin that had caused the war; only the working class was free from crime.

Most of us had been brought up in easy circumstances. If we were enlisted men in the army we found ourselves suddenly instead of top dog, bottom dog. An enlightening experience, but we couldn't help some cries of pain. We came home with the feeling that bottom dog must be boss. We must restore self-government at home. If the people had had their way none of these disasters would have happened.

The Revolt of Bohemia

Greenwich Village met us at the dock. American Bohemia was in revolt against Main Street, against the power of money, against Victorian morals. Freedom was the theme. Freedom from hard collars, from the decalogue, from parental admonitions. For Greenwich Village art and letters formed an exclusive cult. The businessman could never understand. It was part of the worldwide revolt of artists and would-be artists and thinkers and would-be thinkers against a society where most of the rewards went to people skillful in the manipulation of money. The would-be artists and writers felt out of it. The revolt of Bohemia was the last eddy in the ebb of the romantic flood that had flowed in various great waves through the literature of nineteenth-century Europe. When artists and writers found it hard to make themselves a niche in industrial society they repudiated the whole business. Greenwich Village was their refuge, the free commune of Montmartre on American soil. *Les bourgeois à la lanterne.*

Greenwich Village wanted freedom and so did the working class. Only the people who worked in factories wanted freedom from certain very definite things, especially from low pay and bad conditions of work. They wanted to be treated as first class citizens the way businessmen were. Greenwich Villagers, mostly the sons and daughters of professional people, clergymen and lawyers and doctors, felt a sudden kinship with the working class. Of all strata of society only the artists and writers and the people who worked with their hands were pure. Together they would overturn the businessman and become top dog themselves. From the alliance between the trade unions and Greenwich Village the American radical was born.

The war had left an aftermath of ruin. Dislocated populations were starving and sick. The apocalyptic vision of capitalism's collapse that had haunted the working people of Europe was coming true. Revolution was the cure. Only a complete new order could bring health and cleanness back into the world. It was ordained by the march of progress. Only the bankers and industrialists and the old feudal hierarchies stood in the way of the millennium. In Russia the Soviets had seized power. To the artists and writers of Greenwich Village the Soviets were a New England town meeting on a larger scale. Self-government come to life again. Through the Soviets the people who did the work of the world would conduct their own affairs. War was ruining civilization. Everywhere the plain people wanted peace. Only the bankers and businessmen had profited by the war. Merchants of death. Down with the bankers and businessmen. With the working class in power, peace would be assured.

From sometime during the spring of 1926 or from the winter before a recollection keeps rising to the surface. The protest meeting is over and I'm standing on a set of steps looking into the faces of the people coming out of the hall. I'm frightened by the tense righteousness of the faces. Eyes like a row of rifles aimed by a firing squad. Chins thrust forward into the icy night. It's almost in marching step that they stride out into the street. It's the women I remember most, their eyes searching out evil through narrowed lids. There's something threatening about this unanimity of protest. They are so sure they are right.

I agreed with their protest: I too was horrified by this outrage. I'm not one either to stand by and see injustice done. But do I agree enough? A chill goes down my spine. Do they frighten me because I'm really among the oppressors, because there is some little mustard seed of doubt in my mind about the value of their protest? Maybe I'm not sure enough that I'm on the right side. Evil is so various.

Whenever I remember the little scene I tend to turn it over in my mind. Why did my hackles rise at the sight of the faces of these good people coming out of the hall?

Was it a glimpse of the forming of a new class conformity that like all class conformities was bent on riding the rest of us?

February 15, 1956

On the Occasion of Eleanor Roosevelt's 74th Birthday and the Publication of Three New Books about Her

James Burnham

I hope that someday somebody *will* write a biography instead of a blurb about Eleanor Roosevelt. ... At her macrocosmic level Mrs. Roosevelt makes all the world her personal slum; and on her flat-heeled shoes she charges her humorless way across oceans and continents as a lesser social service lady pounds the sidewalks of Chicago's South Side or New York's Tenth Avenue.

She carries to its global limit the defining social service trait: an insatiable appetite for sticking one's nose into everybody else's business. With the endemic social service condescension given an international arena, her powerful arms stretch out to wipe the noses, scatter the fleas, sterilize the latrines, brainwash the ideas, and purify the morals of all the unfortunate and benighted whose lives are not organized according to the social service manual. And woe to the unwary man, or woman too, who doesn't say, "Yes, Ma'am" when Mrs. R. states the rules for housetraining the babies. What a rich human pudding this new Welfare World of ours! Just a countless stuffing of misfits, whiners, and shoving minorities— besides the eternal, resigned, and therefore

Eleanor Roosevelt

uninteresting poor—for the Social Service Worker to pull out with her thumb ... Mrs. Roosevelt and the New Deal were made for each other by a preordained harmony, like Leibniz' two perfect clocks that always told the same time. For after all, what else is the Welfare State but the dream, the Utopia (or the nightmare, if you will) of the Social Service Worker?

As for the very occasional old tramp who looks up from his relaxing gutter just long enough to say—as perhaps a few more have thought without saying—"Go lump it, Eleanor," he is consigned to the utter darkness where Richard Nixon, Louis Budenz, and the spirit of Joe McCarthy lie gnashing their teeth.

December 20, 1958

Any Old Hook

Willmoore Kendall

The ideal contemporary American ambassador is a man who flies abroad for the harm of his country. He represents not the nation that accredits him, but the nation to which he is accredited; his task is to enrich that nation at the expense of this (by upping the ante on foreign aid), and bring down the walls of International Misunderstanding (that is, eat humble pie over the shortcomings of his native land, and plead the virtues of his adoptive land). Whether or not he typifies American life and American culture; whether or not he knows anything about the United States, or has even lived here in recent decades, are matters of indifference, or of concern only to persons with outmoded notions about diplomacy. If he has Forgotten English, it is of course desirable for him to re-learn it while he is abroad (else how can he dissipate American misunderstanding upon his return?); but what is indispensable is that he should, like Guess Who I and Guess Who II, speak like an angel in the language of his hosts.

With minor exaggerations for the sake of emphasis, those are the attitudes that underlie the current liberal line on ambassadors and that render comprehensible the particular kind of furor the liberal propaganda machine, spearheaded as usual by the Washington bureau of the *New York Times*, has kicked up over the appointment of Maxwell H. Gluck as ambassador to Ceylon.

Ungluechlich Glueck

A furor was, of course, called for: just as the liberals are as much against Communism as I am, so I am as much against the appointment as they are. But for different reasons: I couldn't care less whether Mr. Gluck really knows the name of the Prime Minister of Ceylon; but I object enormously to his not having sweated up that and other pertinent information the night before (or, as FDR did before his famous pre-inauguration conference with Hoover, at least get it all down on little cards that he could carry in his vest pocket).

I don't mind in the least his not knowing Nehru's first name; but I mind enormously his not having been able to dig himself out of that hole without admitting he didn't know it. I view with indifference his evident ignorance about Ceylon, but deplore his ignorance about America as revealed in his failure to plead the Fifth Amendment on the question about Bandaranaike, and the First Amendment on the question about Nehru (the indicated response: "I'll answer that question, Senator, when you tell me what legislative purpose you have in mind; a simplified spelling statute, maybe?").

I am unconcerned about his being uninformed (Could Jefferson, when he went to France, pronounce La Rochefoucauld? Could Franklin, when he went to France, reel off the Christian names of the King? Did Chester Bowles, when he went to India, know that Nehru is a Communist stooge? Does he, for that matter, know it even now?); but I view with grave concern his being a dope.

Mr. Gluck is clearly not the man to represent the U.S. in Ceylon, the *Times'* reasoning runs; Mr. Gluck is a patronage, that is, shirt-sleeve ambassador; therefore—and how's this for a non-sequitur?—there must be no more shirt-sleeve ambassadors. The Gluck case, in other words, becomes the occasion for a second barrage of the kind of propaganda the machine subjected us to at the time of the Bohlen appointment: ambassadorships must be reserved for permanent foreign service officers; only they are competent to do an ambassador's work; and something—something drastic—has got to be done about the chief remaining argument against the proposed monopoly, which is that only rich men can afford to occupy most of the key ambassadorial posts.

What must be done? Why, let Congress make available to ambassadors the funds they need in order to live it up with the diplomatic crowd in foreign capitals. "The question," writes James Reston from Washington, "is ... whether, as Mr. Gluck has demonstrated, [Congress] ... wants to pay what it costs to get them."

But let me translate: The *Times* wants to level rich men down, and bureaucrats up (how can an oligarchy function without some real plums with which to reward its servants?). It wants, in any case, to keep the embassies in the hands of suitably generous one-worldists, which means keep them out of the hands of men with a stake in—and loving familiarity with—the United States.

And just as any stigma will do to beat a dogma with, any hook—e.g., the Gluck case—will do to hang one on.

August 24, 1957—The Liberal Line

Presidential Politics: Campaign '56

Adlai Stevenson: Patrician with a Mission

John Dos Passos

They were all such nice people. Nice people on the platform. Nice people in the gallery. The audience is made up of just about the nicest people in New York, kind good plump jowly people, well-heeled but not rich, people who in their day have made sacrifices for worthy causes. Looking them over by the way, it doesn't look as if they had suffered great losses by their liberalism. The good cause has triumphed. Many of them are encrusted in the bureaucracy of labor unions, colleges, foundations. Many of them have built up lucrative practices in the law, in public relations, in labor relations. Even so some of them can remember the old days when the cops were beating them on the head with their nightsticks. It's a reminiscent audience; they first banded together as liberals a couple of decades ago to support the idealistic aspects of Franklin Roosevelt's New Deal. It has all come to pass. They have grown gray in the liberal faith. Here is a man who expresses for them its fulfillment. At the sight of Adlai Stevenson smiling from behind the microphone the audience purrs like a gigantic cat.

Adlai Stevenson is a nice man himself. He too is beaming with good intentions. He makes it up to them all for the confusions and heartburnings of the evening. Those rude picketers. He makes them laugh. This is the sort of audience he is really at home with. He treats them to a series of witticisms at the expense of the Republican Administration. He couldn't be more amusing. His delivery is crisp and unassuming. Instead of the greasy pomp of the run-of-the-mill politician, he has humor, the self-deprecatory manner of the accomplished after-dinner speaker. The man is agreeably shy; he doesn't take himself seriously. Through it all there emerges the serious intent. Under the sparkle of the after dinner speech he has serious things to say he does not intend to leave unsaid. What he has to say is exactly what the members of the Liberal Party want to hear. It is just what they've been thinking all along. It's just what they have been thinking for the last twenty-five or thirty years. They listen to him enthralled.

October 27, 1956

Presidential Politics: Campaign '60

The Chameleon Image of John F. Kennedy

John Chamberlain

J ohn Kennedy, junior senator from Massachusetts, is the perfect candidate because he looks conservative, acts with a judicious air, respects what passes for academic *expertise*, is rich without seeming to care for money, defers to the hierarchy of his Catholic Church in spiritual matters without admitting the Pope into his own province of Caesar, draws an apparent line between good and bad labor that is reminiscent of Teddy Roosevelt's distinction between good and bad trusts, and always, in a pinch, votes radical.

The "image," then, consists of a series of overlays, any one of which can be conveniently shuffled to the top to catch this or that voter on the margin. This does not mean that Kennedy is personally insincere, for he creates all the overlaps out of facets of his own character and lets the marginal voter, out of unanalyzed emotional needs, do the shuffling for himself. *Caveat emptor.* The only sincerity in this is that Kennedy is willing to become the beneficiary of the voter's own moronic misapprehensions.

John F. Kennedy

April 23, 1960

Stuart Symington: Everybody's Second Choice

John Chamberlain

T ime marches on, but the theory that Missouri's handsome, courtly Senator Symington has perfect presidential availability does not wither. ...

The case for Symington has the inevitability of something spewed out of a punch card from an IBM machine. First, there is the symbolism: he can write with both his right and left hands and whether you call him a liberal conservative or a conservative liberal doesn't seem to matter. Though naturally left-handed, he plays golf right-handed. Indeed W. Stuart Symington the Third has something for everybody. He was born in Amherst, Massachusetts—but his father, who was a professor of romance languages at the time, came from an old Maryland family of impeccable Scottish lineage. His mother, a Harrison of Virginia, could claim relationship to two nineteenth-century Presidents, William Henry and Benjamin Harrison. A grandfather, the first William Stuart Symington, fought for the Confederacy, taking part in the bloody Pickett's Charge at Gettysburg, and later surrendered his sword as Major Symington at Appomatox. ...

Coming from a border state, with patriotism written all over his defense record, and with a reputation of being both pro-business and pro-labor, Symington has an availability that can only be described as beautiful. But as some esthetician has said (could it have been Walter Pater?) beauty without a touch of irregularity in it is apt to be boring. The trouble with Symington is that his beautiful availability induces no passion in anybody outside of a narrow circle of political pros. Every other Democratic candidate has some group pressing in upon the pros, kicking up enthusiasm and generating both slogans and funds. Humphrey has the ADA-ers, Stevenson the die-hard Eleanor Roosevelt liberals and campus eggheads, Kennedy the Catholics and the academic expertise-merchants, Lyndon Johnson his Southern and Texan "moderates." But Symington is, at best, merely the second choice of everybody—A Number One Number Two Man, as Chancellor Robert Hutchins of the University of Chicago once said of his factotum Bill Benton. And where passion for an individual is obviously needed to give a candidate a first shot at the nomination, the realization that a man is everybody's substitute choice is likely to induce a sober consideration. Can a compromise candidate command the enthusiasm, and the loyalty needed to win the big sweepstakes in the autumn? It is the very flawlessness of Symington's availability that must ultimately doom it, in November if not in July. "Available" types explode no emotional TNT.

May 21, 1960

L. B. J.: Least Popular with the USSR

John Chamberlain

When Jack Kennedy buried Hubert Humphrey's presidential dreams in West Virginia, the White House hopes of Lyndon Baines Johnson, the U.S. Senate Democratic majority leader from Texas, were all but obliterated too.

But when the Summit collapsed in early May, and Johnson, alone among the presidential candidates in either party, responded with a declaration from his viscera that Khrushchev had better stop "being sanctimonious" in "making pious protestations of outraged innocence," every American who had ever heard about Davy Crockett at the Alamo knew that Lyndon was back in business again. Johnson may privately regard the Republican Administration as a bunch of dogs, but he knows that when a U.S. President reaps insults from a snakewhip artist like Khrushchev the only possible self-respecting response is "I don't care if he is a hound, you gotta quit kicking my dog around."

Lyndon Johnson

Against all his drawbacks one compensating factor looks like the Jungfrau: Lyndon Johnson is a man, not an extension of an IBM machine.

This is not to say that conservatives or libertarians should look upon Johnson's candidacy with fond hopes. The man in Johnson has his own principles which stem from the upbringing of a southern "pol" in a particular time and place. He is slightly more conservative than the other Democratic aspirants, who are not conservative at all, and only slightly less conservative than Richard Nixon, which means that a Johnson in the White House would hardly become a Fabian-in-reverse, dedicated to the job of reducing federal aid to the hundred-and-one pressure groups or clipping the political money power of the big unions. But when Johnson stands up in Reno, Nevada, to say, "I am not prepared to apologize to Mr. Khrushchev. Are you? I am not prepared to send regrets to Mr. Khrushchev. Are you?" the domestic aspects of his ADA rating (it's 58 per cent) dwindle somewhat. The point is that Johnson has the coloration of his native Texas, where patriotism, even if it means following a lone star, is still reckoned a virtue.

July 2, 1960

Antigone in Aulis

Russell Kirk

Yes, I know it wasn't Antigone who found herself stranded among the barbarians, but a quite different heroine. Antigone, nevertheless, found herself on trial in the Outer Darkness only a few weeks ago, before a people some thousands of years and miles distant from Thebes; and she came off much more successfully than she did from her old trouble with Creon. It happened thus: a Midwestern teachers' college invited a young English poet and translator to read something to the student assembly. The poet came, and he conquered the Aulians with his translation of *Antigone*.

Any reader familiar with the climate of opinion in our teachers' colleges will appreciate the incongruity of this situation. The classics, if taught at all in such colleges, are taught only with an eye to a dull preparation for lifeless "Latin I" courses in such high schools as still genuflect to ancient language and letters. Nothing is more alien to the presidents and deans—and many members of the faculty—than the higher imagination, poetic truth. How did Antigone slip past these sentinels of the unburied corpse of higher learning?

Well, nine hundred students and staff-members turned out for the occasion; and they sat rapt all through the poet's reading. (The president, deans, and some department-heads shifted restlessly in their seats, I confess, but the students drank *Antigone* in.) A department-head introduced the poet, after the fashion of our educationists, with twenty minutes of pedantic condescension to the audience, in the course of which he misrepresented every important fact in the poet's life. Thus the poet began with a severe handicap, his audience's patience already severely tried; and it took him more than an hour to read his translation. No one snickered; no one left, no one went to sleep.

The great theme of *Antigone* is the conflict between natural justice and duty, on the one hand, and state decree and civil obedience, on the other. In a generation like ours, which has forgotten the natural law and has knelt to Leviathan, *Antigone* takes on a meaning little understood during the nineteenth century when the standard versions of Sophocles were done into English. This pertinence, too, must have touched the prospective teachers when they heard such passages as Antigone's reply to Creon:

> *I never thought your edicts had*
> *Such force they nullified the laws of*
> *   heaven,*
> *Which, unwritten, not proclaimed,*

> can boast
> *A currency that everlastingly is*
> *   valid;*
> *An origin beyond the birth of man.*
> *And I, whom no man's frown can*
> *   frighten, am*
> *Far from risking heaven's frown by*
> *   flouting these.*

Yes, the students heard Antigone out, they applauded most vigorously, and some might have been content to sit there all day listening to Sophocles' mighty lines. Not so, however, the president and the deans and the rest of the hierarchy. The hierarchy were not slow to express their astonishment at the civility the audience had displayed. "Why, I never saw the students so quiet," said the president, rather belligerently, to the professor who had arranged for the program. "You must have beaten it into their heads that they were supposed to be on their good behavior."

I venture to append to this brief relation a humble moral. There is, I think, an enduring human nature, common to the Greeks of the fifth century, to the English of the sixteenth century, and to us. Some qualities of that nature even the worst system of formal education has difficulties in repressing. Of these qualities, among the rising talents of every generation, are a longing for poetic imagery; a dim participation in the tragic view of life; and an aspiration after moral principle. *Antigone* is a great drama because—for one reason—it is humane in the highest sense: that is, *Antigone* exemplifies the educational discipline called *humanitas*, the training of the ethical faculty through the understanding of great literature. Despite all the muddled secular indoctrination in positivism and pragmatism and progressivism to which the unfortunate inmates of our teachers' colleges usually are subjected, truth will get a hearing now and then; the ancient hungers of the imagination are hard to deny; and though the works of Sophocles may be forgotten when the works of William Heard Kilpatrick have become Holy Writ, they will not be forgotten *until* that apotheosis of bathos.

September 8, 1956—From the Academy

15

End of the Masquerade

James Burnham

Your Sergeant Death, as Shakespeare calls him, is a great stripper-off of masks, particularly when he comes revolver in hand. Not all the perfumes of Muscovy can wash the Poznan blood off the Kremlin's face, which behind Stalin's genial pipe or Khrushchev's affable grin, is revealed in the first flash of a security guard's gun to be ever the same grim visage of terror and brutality. Machine guns, bombers, tanks: this is the answer of Communism to the call for bread and freedom.

And as they rolled over Polish bodies the Communist tanks flattened also the soft rhetoric of our George Kennans and Stewart Alsops, our experts and smug journalists, who have been telling us how the Soviet regime has come to be accepted by its subjects, how (in Kennan's servile words) "there is a finality, for better or worse [*sic*], about what has occurred in Eastern Europe." The people of Poznan, clasping hands as they faced the tanks demanding food and decent working conditions and an end to Moscow's rule, and the soldiers who joined them instead of firing on them: these in one day communicated more of the truth about the Soviet Empire than a decade's dispatches by correspondents and diplomats.

The embryo revolt in Poznan was not isolated, but the latest act in a series that extends over the past four years: the slave labor revolts beginning in 1952, before Stalin's death, in the Vorkuta complex; the East German uprising; the large-scale recent fighting in Eastern Tibet; the riots in Tiflis. Every such demonstration proves, contrary to the skeptics, that a policy of liberation is closer to Soviet realities than any policy of containment or coexistence.

Each time that the East Europeans act on the premise of liberation, Washington is taken wholly by surprise. The actors receive no guidance, no aid, no comfort from us. They die, and our officials continue with the latest round of efforts to persuade those who shot them of our peaceful and friendly intentions.

The slave laborers of Vorkuta, the German workers of June 1953, the Poznan citizens of yesterday, prove that they are ready to die fighting their enemy, who is also ours. But by our vacillation—by our emptiness—we condemn them to die in vain. Therefore our cheek also is stained with their blood.

July 18, 1956—The Week

The Meaning of Hungary

Frederick D. Wilhelmsen

Not ten days ago the Hungarian people had done what no one had conceived possible. ... Our political scientists, almost to a man, declared rebellion against the industrialized might of a modern state impossible. There is hardly a political analyst in America who has not been saying for years that revolution behind the Iron Curtain not only could not succeed, but that it could not even get under way. What they forgot was the heroism of a Christian people. What they forgot was that the Faith is not of this world. There are no graves for those of us who are of the Christian West; or—better yet—graves exist solely that we might climb out of them. And Hungary, alone and unaided, rolled back the tombstone of history.

It was perhaps this taunt thrown in the face of dialectical materialism, or was it panic in the Kremlin which saw suddenly that its soft policy of the past year failed to melt like butter the will of decent men but produced only iron and the determination for freedom. ...

This act of Russian Soviet treason was brilliant, magnificent: it was inspired—by hell itself. Today there is a band of corpses, a Soviet rosary, spanning the bridge between Buda and Pest. The frantic calls for help from clandestine radios have ceased. The voice of Hungary is silenced ... Yet they still fight on, the Hungarians.

They have been fighting since before they were Christians, since the days when they came riding into the Danubian valley through the Carpathian mountains from Central Asia in the dusk of the ninth century. And as with all the great migrations, the First Hungarians—members of the Old Turkish race—followed the sinking sun toward the West, sensing in some dumb manner that their future lay in the Lands of the Evening. That they were hurried on by the Finger of Providence can be doubted by no one who sees history in the light of the Incarnation. Their first King, Stephen, received the Crown from Pope Sylvester II. ... A light of Faith in the center of paganism, Hungary poured out its blood through the long Middle Ages and even beyond. That land of Hungary—or, more accurately, the Lands of the Holy Crown of St. Stephen—stood as a shield against the threat from the East. ...

No one understands, really understands, the role of this one thousand-year kingdom, this nation which vested its ruler as late as 1916 in a garment woven by the wife of St. Stephen nine hundred years before, no one really knows this people who does not understand the meaning of the Sacred Crown of St. Stephen. The Hungarians believe that no government can last long that does not possess the Crown, not simply symbolically but physically. ... Until 1945 all Hungarian Courts issued their verdicts "In the name of the Sacred Hungarian Crown." ...

Not ten days ago the image of that ancient Crown, symbol of Hungarian liberty, promise of Hungarian independence, appeared everywhere in the streets of Budapest. Children carried tommy guns and crosses in their hands, the Crown of St. Stephen in their hearts. Let us think long on this Crown, we who protest this morning and who appeal to the President for action in the United Nations. This Crown is capped by a Cross—what else would one expect from such a civilized people, a people which has always considered its national existence one with the mission of Christ? This Cross is bent over at a crazy angle: it appears about to fall ... bent under the Soviet boot. But although bent, not broken. We must, as the Apostle John writes, "harden ourselves in hope." Remember that the Cross always bends: as Chesterton wrote of the early Church, "the heavenly chariot flies thundering through the ages ... the wild truth reeling but erect."

The Cross reels today in Hungary. But reeling it stands. And like all crosses it stands arms outstretched—crying for your help and mine. Holy God, grant us the courage to embrace that Cross.

December 1, 1956

George Kennan

The Coming Struggle for Outer Space

Whittaker Chambers

TV utilized a break in a Braves-Yankees broadcast to amplify the first, skeptical announcement of a day or so before that Sputnik really was up there. Listening to the somewhat breathless confirmation ("it says: 'Beep! Beep!' ") I laughed. Neighbors, who happened to be present, asked why. I could only answer: "I find the end of the world extremely funny." "What's funny about that?" one asked. What could I answer: that men always defy with laughter what they can do absolutely nothing else about? Beyond that, any explanation I attempted would have been as puzzling as my reaction seemed.

As soon as my wife and I were alone, I said: "They still do not see the point. The satellite is not the first point. The first point is the rocket that must have launched it." Of course, the scientists and the military chiefs grasped this obvious implication at once. But it took three or four days for anybody to say so, in my hearing.

In short, the struggle for space has been joined: But this was only the immediate, military meaning. Widen it with this datum: the satellite passed over Washington, sixty miles away. One minute later, it passed over New York. We have entered a new dimension. Like Goethe after the battle of Valmy, we can note in our journals: "From this day and from this place, begins a new epoch in the history of the world; and you can say that you were there."

There is a wonderful passage in the *Journal of the Goncourt Brothers*, wonderful, in part, for its date, which cannot be later than 1896. I shall not be able to quote it exactly from memory, but it goes much like this: "We have just been at the Academy, where a scientist explained the atom to us. As we came away, we had the impression that the good God was about to say to mankind, as the usher says at four o'clock at the Louvre: 'Closing time, gentlemen.' " None of us supposes that this moon means closing time. None of us can fail to see, either, that closing time is a distinct possibility. Again, the point is not that we do not yet have the ICBM fully developed; we will. The point is that the new weapons are, of their nature, foreclosing weapons, and, whether or not they are all presently in our hands, too, they are in the hands of others over whom we have no control. That is what I meant by "end of the world." Only those who do not know, or who do not permit their minds to know, the annihilative power of the new weapons, will find anything excessive in the statement. "Nine H-Bombs dropped with a proper pattern of dispersal" was a figure given me, three or so years ago, as the number required to dispose of "everything East of the

Mississippi River." Whether the figure is accurate to a bomb or a square mile is indifferent. Any proximation of it speaks for itself.

Whatever else Sputnik is or means, the handwriting that it traces on our sky writes against that attitude the word: Challenge. It means that, for the first time, men are looking back from outside, upon those "vast edges drear and naked shingles of the world" which Arnold reached in imagination. In imagination which is the creative beginning of everything (God Himself had first to imagine the world), the one indispensable faculty that has brought man bursting into space from that primitive point of time he shamblingly set out from. That breakthrough (all political considerations apart) touches us with a little of the chill of interstellar space, and perhaps a foreboding chill of destiny—a word too big with unchartable meanings to be anything but distasteful to our frame of mind. For it is inconceivable that what happens henceforth in, and in consequence of, space, will not also be decisive for what happens on the earth beneath. In short, Sputnik has put what was useful and effective in method and dissection once more at the service of imagination. It is the war of imagination that, first of all, we lost. It is in terms of imagination that the Russians chiefly won something. The issue has only been joined. Nothing is final yet. But it is joined in space, and it is at that cold height that henceforth we will go forward, or go nowhere. There is no turning back.

Whittaker Chambers

Before this illimitable prospect, humility of mind might seem the beginning of reality of mind. As starter, we might first disabuse ourselves of that comforting, but, in the end, self-defeating, notion that Russian science, or even the Communist mind in general, hangs from treetops by its tail.

November 2, 1957—Letter From Westminster

Ronald Knox, R I P

Ronnie Knox's circle was so select and circumspect at Eton, Oxford or amongst English writers that few in America will fully enjoy Evelyn Waugh's biography (*Monsignor Ronald Knox*, Little, Brown). Ronnie was tiptop scholar of his generation in Latin and Greek and Biblical English, but he was a satirist, a detective novelist, and a wit. Though he had no elocution, the Church used him like a prima donna in the pulpit. He became a recluse and translated the Vulgate Bible in ten years. It would have made St. Jerome's lion sit up and paw his admiration. Ronnie was shy and refused to be a lion, hence his refusal of tempting offers in America and of visits to Rome. As the rebirth of Newman in thought, diction, and, oddly enough, features, he was afraid that the Vatican would change his headgear or the color of his buttons. He accepted an Apostolic Pronotaryship which is one of the consolation prizes the Church deals out to failed bishops.

He came from an Anglican Bishop's litter (but what a brood!), including an editor of *Punch*, an atheist Fellow of Kings, Cambridge, a High Church priest, and finally Ronnie. If Newman shook Oxford with a single tract, Ronnie convulsed it with a parody of Dryden's satire *Absalom and Achitophel*, only Ronnie called it *Absolute and Abitofhell*. And so through life. He believed that Catholic propaganda should be made by humor and satire. He resembled Swift but poured oil, not vinegar. He made no enemies, for his hobby was collecting friends. His beautiful collection of Eton and Oxford friends was massacred by the First War. He never recovered and avoided a career.

I can remember him at Eton in 1902. The smallest boy in the Fifth Form Select. I sat beside him but I never addressed him a word out of snobbery, for I was an Oppidan and he was a scholar wearing a gown like a gaberdine! But he had his uses when the terrible Headmaster Warre, looking like a Cyclops in his glasses, sometimes threw the door open, and forty terrified boys in tails rose praying inwardly they would not be called to construe the Greek. The form master, also frightened, always called on "Knox minor" who could give a reading of Sophocles with a look of innocent assurance, and we all breathed again.

Oxford was a long triumph. There was no prize trophy he could not win, no society he could not address in paradox, no dinner he could not convulse. He was a polished Chesterton—a Chesterton without guile and a Belloc without anger.

Trinity made him a Chaplain, which was like putting a jester into a surplice. He developed the sport of teasing bishops and carried experiment and eccentricity in the Church of England until there seemed little of England, or even of the Church as understood by Anglicans, left. He and his friends used a

Book of *Uncommon* Prayer. But it was all good fun and kept religion at the universities amongst many who had a mocking spirit or taste for practical jokes. An amusing photograph shows the future Monsignors Knox and Vernon Johnson at Caldey Island in 1910, but they might be two runaway schoolboys on Coney Island.

It is rather impudent to puff or push Ronnie to the American public. It would be a glaring exemplar of "caviar for the general." But perhaps NATIONAL REVIEW would enjoy a little ecclesiastical caviar. Take alone some of Ronnie's titles. They read remote from the pastoral job and they bewildered many good prelates—*Studies in Sherlock Holmes, Let Dons Delight, The Mass in Slow*

Monsignor Ronald Knox

Motion or *Reunion All Round.* This last was a perfect parody of Swift at his most mocking logicality. There was no sect he did not present for reunion with the Church of England. It was based on Mallock's parody of the great Dr. Jowett in the *New Republic*, where Jowett accepts tolerantly (almost godlikely) the negation of God if only held conscientiously. And of course Ronnie was thinking of Shaw's broad definition of British bishops as part of a great Moslem Empire and therefore free to have several wives!

Much of Ronnie's writing reads like schoolboys at play. He seemed to be quenching his bitter grief for losses in the wars. Suddenly he dried his tears and quelled his laughter and sat down for a ten years' grind. Chapter by chapter he produced an English Bible. He said that he translated the Gospels as though they had just been discovered in scrolls or papyrus for the first time and he had turned them into language fit for the *Daily Mail*. As it was, Presbyterian ministers, though not caught by the sacred name of Knox, read his version because it gave many an idea what St. Paul's Epistles meant.

To admirers outside the Church it seemed that a first-class mind (perhaps a mixture of Porson and Calverly), had been set to translate a portentous Latin piece into Schoolmasters' English. Within the Church controversy has arisen to what extent, like Newman, he was discouraged and baffled. It now appears from Mr. Woodruff's review that—though Cardinal Bourne hoped to use him to turn St. Edmunds, an old-fashioned seminary, into a striking school like Eton or Winchester and failed—Cardinal Griffin encouraged and God-sped the new Bible with generosity rarely shown a convert.

—Sir Shane Leslie
February 13, 1960

A Conversation with Ezra Pound

James Jackson Kilpatrick

On April 18th, the Department of Justice dismissed a 13-year-old indictment against Ezra Pound, and a week later the authorities at St. Elizabeth's Hospital in Washington placed this aging poet on an outpatient status. On the afternoon of April 30, Pound drove to Richmond in the company of Harry Meacham, president of the Virginia Poetry Society, and for a little more than two hours we talked together in the oddly chaste and dulcet surroundings of the Rotunda Club here.

Ezra Pound

This account of that causerie—it surely was nothing so formal as an interview—should be qualified at the outset: We did not talk serious politics. It is useless to talk serious politics with Ezra Pound. He is the last statesman of a lost cause—a cause lost a thousand years ago—and most of his enemies are dust. Talking with him, it is difficult to separate his live antagonists from the dead ones, the Rothschilds of 1750 from their counterparts two centuries later; and there is this problem for the ignoramus, meaning me, that when Pound touches a subject he does not so much touch it as embrace it. His mind is a river that holds ten thousand years of sand, but it deposits little sediment in washing over the untutored listener. Coleridge once remarked that the best poetry is that which is only generally, and not precisely, understood; and what I am groping to say is that I do not understand Pound even generally. Acknowledging that he is "anti-Semitic," I venture the positive assertion that Pound's anti-Semitism never will inspire the faintest urge in anyone to put a torch to a synagogue; a less effective rabble-rouser could not be conceived: The rabble would not understand a word that he says.

I offer this impression also: if words have any meaning left, Ezra Pound surely is no lunatic; and if it is true, as Dr. Overholser says, that Pound's condition has not changed since he entered St. Elizabeths' in 1946, then Pound was not lunatic then. Obscure, yes; eccentric, yes; full of apparent confusion, yes. But crazy, no.

He was twenty minutes late arriving for our appointment. The party had left Washington on time, but had stopped midway for a sandwich, and Pound's dentures had proved inadequate for Howard Johnson's corned beef. They had taken their time to inspect the countryside—Rip Van Winkle absorbed in the neon mountains of Route One—and Pound had found all the traffic incredible.

"All the time I was in the bughouse," he remarked, "I kept saying there were 160 million nuts outside, but I didn't realize what the poor devils were up against."

He shakes hands with the hard grip and strong forearm of a man who has played much tennis, and he dominates a room as if his armchair were downstage center. He wore an open-necked shirt of a particularly god-awful magenta, tails out, and a pair of outsized slacks with the cuffs rolled up. A black coat, flung cloakwise over his shoulders, completed the costume. If the description sounds theatrical, it is intended to suggest that there is in Pound a good deal of the actor, a good deal, indeed, of the ham. His bearded face, mobile, is the bust of some morning-after Bacchus; but it is seldom in repose. He sits on the lower part of his spine, head supported on the backrest of the chair, eyes closed; his restless hands are forever searching for glasses, or plucking pencil and notebook from a breast pocket, or shaping ideas in the air. Now and again, he bolts from his chair like some Poseidon from the deep, and his good eye—his right eye—is suddenly shrewd and alive.

On Education

He began to talk generally of education. From everything he could read (he hated to read, reading was abominable, nothing but pulp came from publishers anyhow; Bowen's *Coke* was a masterpiece; it was a travesty upon the name of education that he was seventy years old, and in his second kindergarten, before he discovered Coke's *Institutes*)—from everything he could read (he read nothing any more, none of the contemporary poets, how can any contemporary criticism of contemporary works amount to a damn?)—from everything he could read, the schools are full of bilge. College freshmen should be required to know two languages, at least one of them inflected, and should be obliged to take analytics; and they should study U.S. history, not by way of Tocqueville and "Sandbag," or Toynbee (Toynbee is flapdoodle), but rather by way of Adams, Van Buren, and Benton. It is nonsense for illiterates to be teaching the future when they know nothing of the past.

I single out these observations from a torrent of conversation, much as one plucks a recognizable rooftop from a flood. Pound no sooner launches one thought than he embarks upon another, and I summarize his critique of today's classrooms as one collects miscellaneous fishes after some volcanic churning on the ocean floor. He was thus, in his own fashion, treating current poetry by commenting upon the Italian foreign office in the days of Mussolini, when he sensed that he had lost me altogether.

"I really do have an orderly mind," he said abruptly. And then in a penetrating sentence: "I only want to make certain my interlocutors know the beginnings." Then he was off again, into the causes of war, the suppression of historic truth (of one historian, banished to obscurity by the educationists, Pound had an epitaph: "Poor fellow, he committed accuracy"), the corruptions of the Federal Reserve Board, the usury rates of Byzantium, the reasons why he has not translated a particular Chinese writer, the enduring characteristics of the Manchu Dynasty, the old days in London with Ford Madox Ford. It was wonderful to eat something hot; he had forgotten what it meant for food to be hot. At Rapallo there are surf rafts, and one floats on a blue sea. Had he mentioned that Hemingway once sent him a shark's jaw, the grave of the unknown sailor?

Again the pause, the bright and searching eye. "I don't have a one-track mind," he apologized.

Reading this over, I doubt that I have said much of anything new about Ezra Pound. I can remember, as a child, a certain ballroom adorned by a multi-faceted chandelier, formed of a hundred tiny mirrors, which revolved slowly in the glow of colored spotlights. Pound's mind spins and refracts in the same way. Or to shift the simile, his speech is like the focusing of a ground-glass camera: The subject is always there, but now it is blurred, now sharp, now vaguely defined. He loves talk, and this mistress may yet prove his undoing, for his tongue is unbridled, and sly, deceitful men will ride his improprieties for all the embarrassment that can be drawn from them. And Pound, to recall his criticism of Eliot, also is hurt by the company he keeps; he swims with the grand abandon of an ancient shark, but a host of parasitic pilot fish ride on his back. So far, he is not disposed to shake them off.

That Pound, as an American citizen, made some imprudent broadcasts from Italy during the war years, is plain enough. By nice legal definition, perhaps these exhortations gave enough curious aid and comfort to the enemy to constitute treason to the United States, though two hours with Pound are enough to prompt grave doubts on this score; one envisions Bill Mauldin's Buck and Willy listening to Pound on the shortwave.

Whatever these sins may have been, they are long past; the nation has forgiven worse offenders. Pound now has served twelve years as a political prisoner in a land that prides itself on political freedom, and it seems to me good that at long last, this old Ulysses will go back to Rapallo, there to lie in a raft on the infinite sea, and gaze at the infinite sky.

May 24, 1958

Seven Keys to Anomie

Aloïse Buckley Heath

"Who Are the Intellectuals?" Malcolm Cowley asked the readers of *The New Republic* at some length a couple of weeks ago. Who are the "freely speculating minds," he inquired, with the disciplined urgency of a man who suspects that unless he finds out he may shortly be reduced to talking to himself. He knows *what* intellectuals are, all right: they are distinguished from other people by "a special *attitude*"; they are persons "open to ideas," they also "differ among themselves on every conceivable issue."

He knows what intellectuals do, too, or at least some things. One thing intellectuals do, says Mr. Cowley, is nominate Adlai Stevenson for the Presidency. (Which, for my money, means that intellectuals think Adlai Stevenson is an inconceivable issue, and I think so too.) Another thing Mr. Cowley says intellectuals do is, in 1934, as Roosevelt's lieutenants, successfully apply "the ideas of John Maynard Keynes, which, after 20 years have also been accepted by many of the leading Republicans"—accepted not, one assumes, because the leading Republicans are intellectuals, but because "the intellectual commonplaces of one generation become the political commonplaces of another."

In the "intellectual community" whose personnel Mr. Cowley seeks, there is, he says, "a division of function." There are those who "expound" and there are those who "willingly listen" (and I anticipate with considerable pleasure a follow-up article in *The New Republic* to be entitled: "Who Are the Intellectuals Who Willingly Listen?"). "Note," Mr. Cowley continues, inaccurately, I fear, "that the two roles may be exchanged. Professor Smith, who has been suggesting a new American policy in the Middle East, steps down from the platform and listens while Professor Robinson expounds the Dead Sea Scrolls; then Robinson listens in turn while Professor Braun develops a new theory of city planning." Anybody who reads this paragraph carefully can see the flaw in Mr. Cowley's illustration. Professor Robinson actually is *not* a "willing listener"; he only listens to the others so that they will listen to him, and you can see his point, because, frankly, Professor Smith and Professor Braun don't know beans about the Middle East or city planning. (I really don't know why Mr. Cowley even mentioned those three. Simply everybody calls them the Scratch-My-Back Club.)

I hope that nothing I have said suggests that Mr. Cowley is indulging in a rhetorical question when he asks, "Who Are the Intellectuals?" Conservatives, as we all know, positively wallow in what is known as non-constructive criticism, but no liberal would feel qualified to voice a dislike of your blueberry pie unless he could suggest an extra 2 tbs. shortening and perhaps a little less sugar; nor would Mr. Cowley ask who the intellectuals are unless he knew how to find out.

Present of a Pony

The social psychologists, who have been working on the authoritarian personality and "what they call anomie, sometimes defined as a state of indifference resulting from blank discouragement," are just the boys to spot all those faceless intellectuals. Mr. Cowley suggests that they be identified by means of seven questions (supplied by himself), the answers to which would be graded by comparison with a list of "typically intellectual answers to the questions." The typically intellectual answers which characterize typical intellectuals would, I assume, be established by a preliminary canvasing of the people who nominated Adlai Stevenson and of Roosevelt's lieutenants in 1934.

For any of NATIONAL REVIEW's readers who are interested in making Cowley's Intellectual Register, I herewith present his questionnaire, along with a list of typically intellectual answers, which I just happen to know because I just happen to be typically intellectual, even if Mr. Cowley doesn't know who I am.

1. *"What are your degrees, from which colleges or universities?"*

Don't worry about the degree on this one; anything from B.A. on up will do, unless your degree is in science, in which case you must have a Ph.D., and it must be in physics. Your college is the real test here; the only acceptable alma mater is either: a) a private college or university in the East, *or*, b) a state university in the Middle or Far West, *or* c) the University of Grenoble, but NEVER d) *any* college or *any* university *anywhere* in the Southern half of the United States unless you are William Faulkner (and *I* don't think you are).

2. *"Whom did you vote for in the last two presidential elections?"*

Intellectuals diverge widely on this one, so you can be pretty much on your own. Any one of the following four answers is correct: a) Adlai Stevenson, Adlai Stevenson; b) Adlai Stevenson, Norman Thomas; c) Norman Thomas, Adlai Stevenson; d) Norman Thomas, Norman Thomas. (Actually, if you want to go into the nuances of the thing, in 1956 Norman Thomas was less intellectual than in 1952 and Eisenhower had become much, much more intellectual, but let's not take any chances.)

3. *"Do you often read any of the following magazines? [With a list appended.]"*

Simply check any magazine with a circulation of 25,000 or under except NATIONAL REVIEW. After NATIONAL REVIEW, write: "???" or "!!!" Either is acceptable.

4. *"If you drive a car, what is the make and how old is it?"*

The typically intellectual car is a) if expensive, old, or b) if new, inexpensive. If you are fool enough to answer, "Cadillac, 1957" you will almost certainly flunk; a 1929 Rolls Royce, on the other hand, is perhaps the *most* in intellectual cars and may easily net you a 20 point bonus.

5. *"Do you spend much time looking at TV?"*

If you think you've passed all the other questions, it might be safe to branch out into a little whimsy here. In any case, the following answers, personality-geared, are all good: a) "Never"—straight-type intellectual; b) "Only Milton Berle"—droll-type intellectual; c) "Any soap opera"—sarcastic-type intellectual. If you have *any doubts at all* about the other questions, however, give the first, or straight-type answer.

6. *"Do you believe that the United States should continue testing hydrogen bombs?"*

Here again, any one of three answers rates maximum score: a) "Absolutely not!"; b) "Certainly not!"; c) "No." (Now are you beginning to see why it's so difficult to pinpoint intellectuals?) You should firmly resist the temptation here to say: "No, but ..." or: "No. However ..." This kind of garrulity is almost as unintellectual as saying yes.

7. *"Which of these attitudes toward racial segregation is closest to your own?* [With an appended choice of opinions.]"

Ignore all those choices of opinion, which are simply traps. Write diagonally across the list, in very large black letters: "UNDER NO CIRCUMSTANCES!!!" and then underline it twice. This is a highly typically intellectual solution to the problem and it saves thinking about all those choices, which is so time-consuming. And if you remembered everything I told you, you're in! "The passing grade," Mr. Cowley reassures us, "would be 70 or 80, not 90 or 100; for intellectuals differ among themselves on every conceivable issue." And when you think of all those different colleges and cars, you can see his point.

April 13, 1957

On Oscar Hammerstein

William S. Schlamm

In *Oklahoma!* Mr. Hammerstein (for he, evidently, is the ideologue of the firm, while Mr. Rodgers simply writes the very singable tunes) still finds it in his heart to praise the proverbial virtues of the poor but honest American. In *South Pacific* he was already sufficiently disillusioned to teach a lesson or two on racial equality. In *Carousel* his disgust with the easy millions he was making drove him to adore the starving thief. I skip the intervening period to get to the point of today's report—namely, that Mr. Hammerstein has arrived at praising, in *Pipe Dream*, the virtues and the simple innocence of the bordello.

Pipe Dream is based on the novel *Sweet Thursday*, by John Steinbeck, one of our guaranteed lusty authors, and it tells the story of how the pains of the respectable life can be cured by dedicated bums, and how true love can be saved through a madam and her staff (which, as the girls so tactfully sing in a Christmas carol, is busy only after eleven at night).

Mr. Hammerstein, no doubt, has wandered to Mr. Steinbeck's Cannery Row because he craved "realism." All handymen who have the knack of writing perfectly usable operetta libretti sooner or later dream of "realism." It's like the clowns who want to play Hamlet. Now the operetta is a perfectly legitimate art form— but precisely so long as it *resists* "realism." For it is the true operetta's indigenous contempt for the pedestrian laws of gravity that gives it its impish elegance, its gay abandon, its absurd delight. Gilbert's sophisticated pursuit of nonsense made the Gilbert & Sullivan operettas an undying joy. The *mondaine* contempt Offenbach's libretti writers felt for their reality made his music dance down the ages.

But the contemporary libretto writer is driven by the devil of "social consciousness"; and though his job is exclusively to enchant us, he insists on giving us lessons. Now entirely aside from the fact that I, for one, refuse to be taught by Mr. Oscar Hammerstein II (who has the philosophical profundity of a Gimbels floorwalker), the one thing that is even more boring than a message-drama is an evening of *sung* messages. Mr. Hammerstein's lyrics in *Pipe Dream* are sometimes excruciatingly didactic and he begins to bore me.

Besides, if Mr. Hammerstein intended to buy "realism," Mr. Steinbeck sold him a bill of goods. Mr. Hammerstein is an innocent boy from Broadway, who simply doesn't know his way around the wickedly complex world, and somebody should tell him that a madam is frequently an objectionable person. Also, I'd like to testify that some of the nicest girls I have known, in my time, I met *outside* bordellos. In short, there is hardly anything phonier than the assumption that bums are honorable and whores decent. Compared with that kind of message a Horatio Alger story is the epitome of honesty, and an old-fashioned operetta a monument to realism.

When he wrote the book for *Pipe Dream* Mr. Hammerstein, I am willing to bet, thought of the *Dreigroschenoper* (Kurt Weill's and Bertold Brecht's *Three-Penny Opera*) which, indeed, achieved some extraordinary effects by exploiting the human material of thugs and slatterns. But the *Dreigroschenoper* triumphed because they were *not* "realistically" used. Rather, they functioned as stylized metaphors in a savage satire. But in *Pipe Dream*, Mr. Hammerstein is audibly crowing that here, at last, he has introduced "real" people into musical comedy. Mr. Hammerstein, in short, does not know a thing about operettas; he merely wrote a few good ones while he was young, dumb, and hungry.

December 21, 1955—Arts & Manners

Reviews by Joan Didion

On John Wayne in *The Alamo*

Wait. About 45 minutes into *The Alamo*, a man appears on that immense Todd-AO horizon. He smiles. He moves his shoulders a little. He says "less-go" or something like it; who cares what he says? He goes riding through the tall grass down to San Antonio, right off the top of the screen, and you are, if you are like me, lost, lost forever. It is John Wayne. It might be Clark Gable, appearing in a white linen suit amid the flaming ruins of Atlanta to carry Scarlett home to Tara; it might be the purr of an American plane—always distinguishable from Axis planes, which had engines that whined—coming in overhead just as the rations ran out in a World War II movie. From then on, the ball game's over.

At least it was for me. I wept as Wayne told his Mexican *inamorata* How A Man's Gotta Live. I wept as he explained why Republic is A Beautiful Word. I wept through the siege of the mission; there was no use in my companion's trying to amuse me by pointing out that it had just come home to Richard Widmark, although the problem had been under discussion on screen for some three hours, that "WE NEED MORE MEN!" I was inconsolable by the time the battle was done, and Wayne lay on the cold cold ground, bleeding as no one has bled since Janet Leigh in *Psycho*. The last white woman walked out of the Alamo then. She had soot on her face, and she was carrying her child, and she held her head high as she walked past Santa Anna into the sunset. So conspicuous was my sniffling by then that you could scarcely hear the snickers from my neighbors, a couple of young men from *Esquire*, both of whom resembled Arthur M. Schlesinger Jr.

They don't make 'em like Duke on the New Frontiers.

December 31, 1960

On C. P. Snow's *The Affair*

C. P. Snow, whose novels read as if they were the products of a collaboration, over sherry, between Anthony Trollope and a speechwriter for Adlai Stevenson, once explained that he writes the way he does because the "wicked, absurd social attitudes" implicit in the way his contemporaries write had helped to bring "Auschwitz that much nearer." (This hallucination, that novels *make things happen*, is common among people who write them.) Mr. Snow's own novels are as far from

Auschwitz as they are from Agincourt; they constitute instead the literature of the National Health Service, and celebrate a world of committees, compromise, decisions, and revisions, a world in which Civil Service Hamlets Behave Well in Difficult Situations.

July 2, 1960

On Françoise Sagan and Flannery O'Connor

For her fourth novel, Miss Sagan has called out the regulars: the Older (than Miss Sagan) Woman, the Older (than that) Man, and the Younger (than anybody) Man. The woman and her younger lover brood upon their affair (so "Parisian, so common") while the older man dallies, understandably, with less pensive women and foregoes brooding to run his trucking business, an aberration regarded by Miss Sagan and her heroine as evidence of distinct mental cruelty, if not clear perversion. This interesting plot-line is developed in its totality in 127 pages, each containing such observations as "ash trays break only in novels and films," or "she leaned against him, slid her hand under his shirt, felt the warmth of his skin against her palm. He was alive." (Neither he, she, nor Miss Sagan ever present any convincing excuse for his being so.). ... Miss O'Connor whose merciless style and orthodox vision were established by *Wise Blood* and the collection of short stories called *A Good Man Is Hard to Find*, again focuses upon the problem of redemption in *The Violent Bear It Away*, an allegorical novel in which a 14-year-old Tennessee orphan named Tarwater wars with his compulsion to become a prophet: "the Lord out of dust had created him, had made him blood and nerve and mind, had made him to bleed and weep and think, and set him in a world of loss and fire all to baptize one idiot child that He need not have created in the first place and to cry out a gospel just as foolish. He tried to shout 'NO!' but it was like trying to shout in his sleep." A difficult, perilously stylized book, *The Violent* is at every point controlled by Miss O'Connor's hard intelligence, by her coherent metaphysical views of experience, and by the fact that she is above all a writer, which is something different from a *person who writes a book*—and somebody ought to explain the difference to Miss Sagan.

April 9, 1960

Assorted Commentaries

Hugh Kenner on Style
(from a review of *Letters from Hilaire Belloc*)

Belloc's picturesque bigotries, his devotion to wine, his pessimism, his unfailing assurance, his doubtful histories, these are celebrated enough. That in his most casual dealings with the English language he was incapable of setting down three sentences without distinction is a circumstance lost on publicists who suppose "style" to be a lacquer for what you have to say and a useful substitute when you have nothing to say. Americans in particular have been encouraged to mistrust anything called "style." Like the embroidered weskit, it marks a man who is habitually up to no good, or at least is unlikely to inform us reliably that the hoss thieves went thataway.

On the contrary, a man who speaks truth gracelessly betrays not disregard for *bon-ton* ceremonial, but ignorance of the *location* of the truth he speaks. Without style, the habit of truth leads to fanaticism; style disposes, subordinates, separates, and arrays. On this principle might be based a comprehensive education in the art of dealing with torrents of prose, an art essential to twentieth-century survival.

April 25, 1959

Colm Brogan on the British Press
and the U-2 Affair

When the U-2 affair blew up, the English weekly review, *The Spectator*, bluntly asked which side were we on, making it clear that the question was no mere rhetorical flourish, but was seriously addressed to the multitude who, according to *The Spectator*, just stopped short of dancing in the streets to celebrate a setback for our principal ally at the hands of our principal enemy. Just how large were the jubilant multitudes I would hesitate to guess, but we certainly had a handsome display of *Schadenfreude*.

Perhaps even worse, we had an outburst of plain, unadulterated funk. Journalists and writers of letters to the editor could hardly control their trembling fingers as they typed out their horror at the malignant and insensate provocation offered by the Pentagon warmongers to a man of such acute sensibilities as Mr.

Khrushchev. Many were the pious signs of relief that Mr. Khrushchev had kept his statesmanlike head and emerged purified and strengthened from his dark night of the soul.

July 2, 1960

Roger Becket on Leonard Drohan
(*Come With Me to Macedonia*, by Leonard Drohan, Knopf)

"*What* a novel!" cries the jacket, and on the blurb Mr. Knopf himself declares, "I cannot remember when I have laughed so much." The author's intention, apparently, was satire—the affectionate sort— and heaven knows his subject (office life in the government bureaucracy) is waiting for a white knight. But Leonard Drohan is not his name. His ineptitude, in fact, is so thorough, so unflawed, so flatly jejeune, that a few bits are almost worth reading for themselves. Page 35: "There was no question abut it, Georgina was all woman. ..." Page 36: "Sometimes, in moments like this, Humphrey wondered how his life was going to turn out." There are 344 pages.

September 14, 1957

Boo Hoo: The U.S. Weeps for Charles van Doren

Noel E. Parmentel Jr.

(The scandale de la saison *of fall 1959 was the revelation that Columbia English instructor Charles Van Doren, of the Van Dorens, who had kept much of the nation tuned to NBC's* Twenty-One *quiz show for weeks with his dazzling display of erudition, had in fact been coached by the producers of the show. Van Doren, who first denied the charges in a grand jury investigation, subsequently changed his story.)*

When crying Charlie Van Doren, the Eggheads' Bill Rosensohn, finally got around to testifying before the Harris Committee, there wasn't a dry eye in the house. Make no mistake: puling, mewling, perjured pedagogue or no, he wowed 'em. It was the sudsiest performance to open in Washington in many a moon, rivaled in utter unctuousness only by the Dick Nixon and Checkers Show, and drew rave notices.

The spectacle of a congressional committee being had by this maudlin fake was not enough: it was followed by the soppiest collection of public tributes since the death of Lou Gehrig. People who ought to know better suckered up like marks on the midway. Dave Garroway broke up in the middle of a Method rendition of "Friends, Romans, Countrymen," and had to be helped off the set. Ed Sullivan quoted Shakespeare and Cervantes and, as an afterthought, threw in the *Rubaiyat* of Omar Khayyam. It was quite a week for Charlie. He was compared to Julius Caesar, Nathan Hale, Shoeless Joe Jackson (a canard on Joe, a man of considerable charm), Roger Casement, Herbert Hoover, St. Paul, and Nat Holman. (Charlie's own taste modestly ran, in an interview with *Newsweek*, to Oedipus Rex—"Some explosion had taken place in me, too ...")

"Don't forget," quoth Hy Gardner, "Lillian Roth came back." (Indeed she did, and in time to be on hand for the Fix.) Everyone got into the act, whatever his politic. Jack Paar and Dorothy Kilgallen chimed in, along with the *New York News, Mirror,* and *Journal-American*. Swarmy Charlie, expecting mixed reviews at best, had taken the trouble to send tender *billets doux* to some of the New York press. They hit hard, and went right along with The Weeper, Sincerely Regretting in every edition.

How did this noxious weakling become a folk hero overnight? The situation begins with the incredible gullibility of the American public, a national state of mind which is aided and abetted, encouraged, perverted, subverted, and finally skewered by what is cynically called "the communications industry." The power exerted over the public mind by the television industry, and ultimately, the advertising agencies, enables stumblebums to don pancake makeup and emerge as first-raters.

A Liberal Household

That kind of alchemy happens to be an old Van Doren family custom. Congenitally tender-minded, this tribe of scribblers and prattlers has gone further with less than any family in recent history, not excepting the Trapps. Carl was an overrated historian; Mark is an inconsequential poet and critic, with the basic instincts of a flack. He is a kind of left-wing Mr. Chips, once in the news for some hanky-panky in the Hiss-Chambers case; an all-around Nice Guy. Both these luminaries married ladies with some influence in literary *kaffe klatsches*, and both played the game to the hilt. Through this parlay of incessant scribbling, literary log-rolling (all Van Dorens are inveterate book reviewers), and Seventh Avenue approach to culture, the family has prospered. Dan Enright and Henry Luce tapped them for America's Great Families. We've come a long way from the Lowells and *God Save the Mark*.

November 21, 1959

Remembrance of Oats Wild

Robert Phelps

L ast week, at a friend's house, I heard six or eight old barrelhouse piano rolls. They were the sort nickelodeons used to bang out in bars, and I myself, aged ten, used to pump out on my aunt's player piano. Now they have been reverently recreated on an instrument especially rebuilt for the purpose, recorded with scrupulous high fidelity on a glossy LP, and issued with nostalgic program notes.

The same day, I began to look through this fascinating collection of Mississippi River poetry-in-the-raw, and it was the curator's touch on both— barrelhouse and folklore—that reminded me how abruptly, as a nation, we have grown up and are suddenly *nel mezzo del cammin,* entering our middle-age.

When a nation is young, heedless, lusty, it begets what we later call its folklore: ballads, tall tales, heroic legends, myths. It's all done in the heat of the moment, unintentionally, and the results, like family by-blows, have no legitimate status. Time passes. The begetters grow up, become self-conscious, law-abiding, prudent, consolidated. Then the wild oats are remembered, nostalgically, the way people dance the Charleston today; and finally scholars like B. A. Botkin gather, tidy up, and edit it all for the rest of us to read and ponder over.

The present collection (*A Treasury of Mississippi River Folklore,* Crown) is wonderful, though considering the quantity of folklore that has drained into the Mississippi Valley these past two centuries, I don't know how it could have been otherwise. Unlike the Deep South, New England, or even the Far West, where Mr. Botkin has panned for previous anthologies, the Mississippi region, stretching as it does from upper Wisconsin to the Gulf of Mexico, is incalculably rich in variety: ethnic, economic, topographic, climatic.

Nevertheless, no aspect of human life as risked, hunted, haunted or just plain lived within this vast area seems unrepresented. There are tales of cardsharpers, river pirates, boat races, zombies, of rivalries, revenge, courage, terror; of the moods and menaces of the river itself; of the "St. Louis Blues," Uncle Tom's Liza, Jim Bowie, yea, even the ubiquitous Congressman Davy Crockett "hisself."

But dominating all the more spectacular details is the deep, inexplicable effect of eternally flowing water on the imagination and bloodstream of everyone who lives on or near it. As one reminiscing lady told Mr. Botkin, "When we lived in Quincy, every night the whole family would just get up from the supper table and say, 'We'll just go out and look at the river.'"

It isn't any wonder that the most universally appealing book in American literature is still the one Mark Twain wrote about two boys drifting down the same river on a raft; or that one of T.S. Eliot's most beautiful poems remembers how its mysterious

> *... rhythm was present in the nursery bedroom,*
> *In the rank ailanthus of the April dooryard,*
> *In the smell of grapes on the autumn table,*
> *And the evening circle in the winter gaslight.*

January 25, 1956

Part Two

1961 to 1965

The Week
Selected Editorial Paragraphs

April 8, 1961

Available at the Government Printing Office: pamphlet entitled "Tea Drinking in 18th Century America: Its Etiquette and Equipage." Will you have cream and sugar in your harbor?

June 3, 1961

Having looked and looked for the New Frontier, we finally spotted it last week when the negotiators foregathered in Geneva to seal the fate of Laos. It's 500 miles closer to us than the Old Frontier.

October 7, 1961

Running the rounds in lollipop circles: a comic book on Caroline Kennedy and Jack and Jackie. A high point in the slop occurs when the President is entitled the "Conqueror of Pain." He didn't conquer pain; he nationalized it.

January 30, 1962

In the Never-Never world of Kwame Nkrumah, he has only to say, Let It be Done and Lo It is Done; Let This be Truth and Lo It is Truth. Let all wisdom, all knowledge, all science have been born in Africa, said Nkrumah, and Lo a painter appears and Behold on the walls of the Archives in Accra, vast murals show: Africans teaching Mathematics to the Greeks; Africans originating the Science of Medicine in the ancient empire of Ghana; Africans originating the Science of Chemistry in the ancient empire of Ghana; Africans teaching the Greeks the Alphabet; Africans (this time in Egyptian garb) discovering the Secret of Paper. And if you don't believe this is possible, just remember—the Africans invented Nkrumah.

July 17, 1962

Having banned schoolroom prayer, the Supreme Court lifted the ban on the transmission of pornographic material through the mail. Children should be obscene and not heard?

August 14, 1962

THE WORLD WE LIVE IN: Saudi Arabia, which is pressing for freedom for oppressed people of Portuguese Angola, recently announced the appointment of a new director for slave affairs.

May 7, 1963

THE BANG! POW! OOOF! AGGGHHH! THEORY OF HISTORY DEPT. (From an article by Eric Goldman, professor of history at Princeton.): "One time about to board a plane for Chicago, my eye fell on a copy of Mickey Spillane's *Kiss Me Deadly* and it dawned on me that for years I had been talking about American culture without ever having read one of its most popular spokesmen. Well, I read Mr. Spillane, snarling sentences, kicks in the stomach, cult of action and all, and I understand the persistent strain of McCarthyism in American life as I had never quite understood it before."

December 17, 1963

The editors of NATIONAL REVIEW regretfully announce that their patience with President Lyndon B. Johnson is exhausted.

June 15, 1965

Item. Calvert's Whiskey calls back $30,000 worth of advertising because an Indian civil rights group objects to the use of a warbonneted chief and the word "firewater." *Item.* The NAACP threatens a boycott if the Chrysler Pavilion at the World's Fair doesn't do something about the Bill Baird puppet show, which has four purple pistons singing a parody of "Dry Bones," which goes: "Dem nuts, dem bolts, dem pistons ..." *Solution*: Change the "dems" to "damns." Change the firewater to grape juice. Change the purple pistons to purple cows. Change the purple cows to pink elephants. Change the Indian to Aunt Jemima. Change Aunt Jemima to Aunt Jeremiah. Change tomahawk to Uncle Thomas Hawk. Change boycott to mancott. Never give up.

July 27, 1965

Now that we have had a nice close look at the tuberosities of the planet Mars, let's get back once again to the main question. Is there intelligent life on earth?

A Stilton Catechized Upon a Table

Hugh Kenner

Every critic should be required to present his credentials. Mine culminate in this: that I was once the witness to a full-dress performance of the Critical Act: not a Pateresque extravaganza nor an epigram fired from the hip, but an expert paradigmatic demonstration, no phase omitted. It was performed on November 19, 1956, at his Club in London, by a Man of Letters who will not mind remaining anonymous.

When we had dealt with the jugged hare (which was perhaps neither jugged nor hare; I was never sure) the Critic addressed his mind to our next theme. "Now, will you have a sweet; or ... *cheese?*" Even one not conversant with his letter to the *Times* on the declining estate of Stilton would have understood that the countersign was *cheese*. I said, Why, cheese; too lightly, I fear. One does not crash in upon the mysteries. There was a touch of reproof in his prolongation of the ceremony: "Are you sure? You can have ice cream, you know." (In the Club!)

I said, No, cheese. He then said, "Very well. I fancy ... a fine Stilton." He despatched the waiter for Stilton, and then imparted the most momentous confidence of our interview: "Never commit yourself to a cheese ... without having first ... *examined* it."

The Stilton lay, or stood, on a board, encumbered with a sort of swaddling-bank, girded about with a cincture, and scooped out on top like a crater of the moon. It was placed in front of my mentor. With the side of his knife-blade he commenced tapping the circumference of the cheese, rotating it before him, his head cocked in a listening posture. I will not swear that he was listening. He then tapped the inner walls of the crater. He then dug about with the point of his knife amid the fragments contained by the crater. He then said "Rather past its prime. I am afraid I cannot recommend it."

The Stilton vanished. In an awesome silence we awaited the substitute offering. It was a board upon which stood half a dozen assorted cheeses. Some were identifiably cheese only in context. One resembled sponge cake spattered with chocolate syrup, though I believe it was not. Another, a pockmarked toadstool-yellow, exuded green flecks. The Man of Letters took up again his knife, and each of these he tapped, he prodded, he sounded. At length he segregated a ruddy specimen: "That is a rather fine Red Cheshire ... which *you* might enjoy." I did not enquire into this decision.

His attention was now bent on the toadstool-yellow specimen. This he tapped. This he prodded. This he poked. This he scraped. He then summoned the waiter.

"What is that?"

Apologetic ignorance of the waiter.

"Could we find out?"

Disappearance of the waiter. Two more waiters replace him.

"?"

"   "

He assumed, at this silence, a mask of Holmesian exaltation:

"Aha! An Anonymous Cheese!"

He then took the Anonymous Cheese beneath his left hand, and the knife in his right hand, the thumb along the back of the blade as though to pare an

T. S. Eliot—the "Man of Letters"?

apple. He then achieved with aplomb the impossible feat of paring off a long slice. He ate this, attentively. He then transferred the Anonymous Cheese to the plate before him, and with no further memorable words proceeded without assistance to the consumption of the entire Anonymous Cheese.

"Analysis and comparison," this man wrote some forty years earlier, "Analysis and comparison, methodically, with sensitiveness, intelligence, curiosity, intensity of passion and infinite knowledge; all these are necessary to the great critic." I leave as an exercise to the reader the correlation between these phrases and the remarkable demonstration with the cheeses.

But many, the mail indicates, prefer Kraft, the quality of which you need not really care for, but which it is safe to count on; guaranteed by the package, squared off in a glutinous slab. We are grown as sensitive to certain empty niceties of print as to nuances of packaging: paucity of capital letters or spareness of punctuation are worrisome. It is very comforting to look at a page like this one, laid out in three uniform columns; very upsetting to find a lot of white space around the words (though meditation, which many poems imitate, is often the equivalent of much white space around the words). *Vers libre*, fifty years ago, occasioned much distress among occasional spectators of the poet's craft; but it seems unlikely that metrical complexity worries any casual reader of verse today so much as he is worried by the mere look of the page. He insists on *seeing* the structure, or he will fold his honest arms and assert that none is present.

This point is far from trivial, though criticism has had little or nothing to say about it. Mr. Robert Creeley, writing of wooden figures (NR, February 11)—

> *In*
> *the act of making them*
>
> *it must have been*
> *so still he heard the wood*
> *and felt it with his hands*
>
> *moving into*
> *the forms*
> *he has given to them,*
>
> *one by singular*
> *one, so quiet,*
> *so still.*

—is *using* the surrounding silence of the paper to complement the studied, spare gravity of appreciation which is what the poem enacts. A voice (and we hear a voice, feeling its way) is counterpointed by the visual reticence, the refusal to putty out five foot lines.

Prufrock (1910) was perhaps the first major poem to be typewritten by its author, and verse for the past half century has been learning to use for expressive purposes its own typographical decor. Dante would have wondered at this, but then Homer would have wondered at Dante.

April 22, 1961

The Last Apple

Francis Russell

The apple reddening at the tip of the bough, the very last, that the pickers overlooked or could not reach.

Sappho

So gawky is any translation. No one can capture the autumn enchantment of Sappho's last apple in English, any more than one could translate the bloom of Housman's orchards into French. The apple is the most classical of fruits and at the same time the most magical. In the Babylonian story of creation an apple tree was the precursor of the Garden of Eden's Tree of Life. Although in the Bible Eve took from the neighboring tree of the knowledge of good and evil an unnamed fruit "good for food" and "pleasant to the eye," nevertheless the Jewish and Christian traditions have always held that it was an apple she gave to Adam.

At the western rim of the world the three daughters of Hesperus guarded the golden apples of the sunset on the glimmering tree that had sprung up to mark the nuptials of Zeus and Hera. Hippomenes used the three apples that Aphrodite had brought him from the temple garden of her own island of Cyprus to tempt Atalanta from her fleetness. Paris, choosing beauty above riches and glory, gave Eros's apple of discord, inscribed "For the fairest," to the goddess of love and so brought on the Trojan War. It was Hercules's eleventh labor to steal the apples of the Hesperides.

In the earlier decades of this century the McIntosh, developed a hundred years ago from seedlings grown wild in Canada, became the favorite American apple. As an apple it is innocuous. It has a fragrance, a certain bloom when picked, but it is too even-skinned, too unsubstantially pretty, its flesh too white and commonplace in favor. Compared with the Baldwin, that rough-skinned product of the granite-seamed Massachusetts earth, it lacks character. One associates the Baldwin with those Currier & Ives lithographs of the New England autumn, the happy pickers, and the orchard trees bent down under the weight of the apple clusters. The McIntosh suggests the supermarket.

Best of all American apples is the Hubbardston, a name so forgotten today that it means nothing even to horticulturists. Outwardly it looks much like a Baldwin although there is a glimpse of gold behind its crimson. The flesh is very firm, honey-tinted, and with a juice-sustaining blend of tartness and sweetness and appleness that I have found in no other apple in the world except the outwardly puny Cox's Orange Pipin, and even there to an inferior extent.

Why this superb fruit has been allowed to disappear I do not know, but undoubtedly there are low commercial reasons for it. Possibly one cannot grow as many to a tree or an acre. The Hubbardston may be more difficult to pack, slower to open. It does not have the high-colored prettiness of a centerpiece.

I know a gnarled and decaying apple tree in Scituate, Massachusetts, that in spite of all neglect still brings forth a small crop of Hubbardstons each year. No one, except the tent caterpillars in the spring and myself in the autumn, ever visits it. It is never pruned, never dunged, never sprayed, and those apples that do not fall of their own accord are left to hang there until they are beaten down by the winter storms. Every September I go there to pick myself a basketful of them. They are all more or less wormy, and one has to nibble round the worm-holes. But as I stand under the tree in the long sunlight cautiously munching one Hubbardston after another, glancing up at the few remaining red and gold globes among the bare branches, I think that this old tree—purged of its insects and dead timber—would flourish most fittingly in the magic garden at the edge of the Western world.

December 3, 1963

Hemingway's Code

Jeffrey Hart

Somewhere in our minds, rescued from time, most of us have an ideal Paris in which people like Hemingway and Joyce, Scott Fitzgerald, Ezra Pound, and Ford Madox Ford, sip cognac at the Dome, or walk by the Seine among the bookstalls, or meet at Sylvia Beach's bookshop. It is the Paris of the early Twenties, where so many of the great books and poems of our time were being written. Hemingway evokes it in *A Moveable Feast* in what, in its special way, is one of his most moving and beautifully written books.

We find that Paris here, but also Hemingway himself, at a time when he was living a kind of ideal literary life, very poor, and sometimes even hungry, but confident of his powers, learning from books and from Pound and Stein, alive in all his senses, and writing his early stories—sometimes writing at a cafe table, sometimes in his chilly room, sometimes at the Voralberg in the Austrian Alps where he went with his new wife on skiing excursions. Though he writes of all this forty years later, he can make one feel how it was, then, to experience Paris for the first time:

> We had oysters and *crabe Mexicaine* with glasses of Sancerre. We walked back through the Tuileries in the dark and stood and looked through the Arc du Carrousel up across the dark gardens with the lights of the Concorde behind the formal darkness and then the long rise of lights toward the Arc de Triomphe.

Hemingway can be devastatingly funny, too, or just and affectionate, as to Pound, or cruel, as to Wyndham Lewis, but even the malice of a man as intelligent as Hemingway is redeemed by the fact that it often rises to insight. His longest section, on Scott Fitzgerald, is a small masterpiece, a strange mixture of the outrageous and the marvelous, darkening at moments with the awareness of Zelda's insanity:

> Zelda was very beautiful and was tanned a lovely gold color and her hair was a beautiful dark gold and she was very friendly. Her hawk's eyes were clear and calm ... when she leaned forward and said to me, telling me her great secret, "Ernest, don't you think Al Jolson is greater than Jesus?"

A book as good as *A Moveable Feast*, contradicting as it does all those theories about the decline of Hemingway's powers, is bound to return attention to his actual achievement, and if one is to think seriously about Hemingway, the natural way would be with what is most distinctive and memorable about him, his style.

Hemingway once remarked that what is best in American writing derives from the prose spoken by Huck Finn, and when we listen to Huck's language, earthy, circumstantial, "uneducated," it is easy enough to see what Hemingway valued in it and learned from it. Yet we cannot understand the full meaning of Hemingway's comment unless we remember, as Lionel Trilling pointed out, that Huck's prose is a kind of "moral symbol." It presents itself as the antithesis of the language of another character in the book, the Widow Douglas, and, implicitly, criticizes what she embodies—the pious, the respectable, the well-intentioned. Huck, in contrast, sees the world as it really is. "And Woodrow Wilson"—I quote from Trilling—"was Hemingway's Widow Douglas."

On the one hand, in 1917, there was the rhetoric of good intentions, all the talk of a war to end wars, self-determination, and a world safe for democracy; but on the other, the facts as experienced by the men who actually went there. Now we know from Charles Fenton's valuable book on Hemingway's early years, and from stories like "The Doctor and the Doctor's Wife," that Hemingway's home town, Oak Park, Illinois—upper middle-class in character, its liberal Protestantism just at the point of dissolving into sentiment and moralism—was precisely the sort of place that would be most susceptible to Wilsonian moralism and uplift. As a matter of fact, according to one of his friends in the ambulance corps, Hemingway arrived in Italy "extremely conscious of the war as a 'crusade for democracy,' and burning with a desire to have a share in it."

This rhetoric of good intentions invited, at the very least, correction through exposure to fact, and the prose style shaped by Hemingway's war experience aims at the presentation of such fact—or, more precisely, by its special procedures, it recalls us to an awareness of the *importance* of fact:

> They shot the six cabinet ministers at half-past six in the morning against the wall of the hospital. There were pools of water in the courtyard.
>
> Everybody was drunk. The whole battery was drunk going along the road.
>
> I knew that I was hit and leaned over and put my hand on my knee. My knee wasn't there.

Notice how a fact is used to puncture rhetoric—a typical device—in this beaut about the Spanish Civil War:

> Gaylord's was the place where you met famous peasant and worker Spanish commanders who had sprung to arms from the people at the start of the war without any previous military training and found that many of them spoke Russian.

But if Hemingway's style calls attention to the importance, even the primacy, of fact, it does a number of other things as well. He is forced to complicate Mark Twain's attack on respectable cant because the experience with which he deals is so much more drastic. It may be useful to put the matter in sociological terms. Mark Twain had attacked the middle-class uplift of the Widow Douglas by bringing to bear upon it what we might call Huck Finn's lower-class facts, presenting them in an earthy, deliberately "uneducated" style. Similarly, Hemingway brings to bear on Wilsonian uplift the facts carried by the vocabulary of infantrymen, prizefighters, newspapermen, and gangsters. But the experience of those facts is so painful that mere *presentation* is not enough. It is not enough to recognize that the rhetoric of Woodrow Wilson or the moral expectations of Oak Park, Illinois, stand in an absurd relationship to the world as it is.

There must be a way of meeting, or, if you will, of enduring, those facts. And so Hemingway combines his lower-class vocabulary with a discipline that is essentially aristocratic, involving as it does the use of manners—most importantly, British irony and understatement—to deal with such emotions as terror and disgust.

If this sense of the uses to which a code of manners may be put has a literary source, we may look to Kipling, whom Hemingway admired intensely. At any rate, Hemingway brings into American literature, perhaps for the first time, what is recognizable as the classic *Tory* strategy, to be found in Swift and Yeats, which combines upper and lower against middle, noble and peasant against those paradoxical cousins, the climber and the moral idealist.

The story is well known of how Hemingway received over two hundred wounds from machine gun and mortar fire on the Italian front in 1918, yet it is manifest that the trauma of the war was more than physical. "I can remember feeling so awful about the war," he told an interviewer in 1950, "that I couldn't write about it for ten years. The wound combat makes in you, as a writer, is a very slow healing one." The war was a moral trauma, indeed a moral revelation. It presented him with a range of experience that was beyond the grasp of respectable, progressive America. And he saw that because respectable, progressive America habitually employed idealistic abstractions to protect itself from the facts of the war, it was also helpless in dealing with the kind of experience epitomized by the war but prominent in the rest of life as well.

The disciplined irony and understatement of Hemingway's prose, then, is his equivalent, as a writer, for the various codes and disciplines his fictional characters employ in their encounters with experience. The codes of the bullfighter and the big-game hunter may indeed be taken as exemplary, but only if we remember that the wild beasts Hemingway confronts are inside his head.

The code, though, won't always do. Malcolm Cowley was right when he described Hemingway as one of the "haunted and nocturnal" writers, akin in temper to Hawthorne and Melville, for a careful reading of his work reveals that though he knows the value of discipline he also knows its limits. The surgeon in "Indian Camp" does not listen to the screams, and the "clean well-lighted place" has the power to hold *nada*, nothingness, at bay—but the *nada* and the screams are *there*, part of actuality, just as death is always there, sharpening the edges of Hemingway's words, forcing things to be themselves because they cannot possibly be anything else.

The sharpness of the edge between existence and non-existence: perhaps that is why Hemingway was so much drawn to Spain, where every hill and building is sharply itself in the dry air. Still, the sustaining discipline is always a contingent thing, subject to circumstances. Hemingway's own discipline, the way of meeting experience that we see reflected in his prose, almost, but not quite, got him through his experience. But the fact that in 1961 he could not get through it would not have come as a complete surprise to him.

June 2, 1964

Death One Afternoon

F. Reid Buckley

Not in years had he visited Spain. But the rubicund giant with bullish shoulders and noncommittal eyes lifted anticipation from the level of pure spectacle to the promise of something more lasting than two dusty hours balanced bloodily between horns. That broiling afternoon in August of 1959, the southeastern Andalusian seaport of Málaga was in ferment. Two previous encounters had shown that Luis Miguel Dominguín, the great matador from Madrid, and Antonio Ordóñez, the challenger from Ronda, meant to fight out the question of supremacy.

Many had expected Dominguín, twelve years uncontested *Número Uno*, publicity-seeker and womanizer, to fold, funk under the murderous pressure. Two weeks earlier he had been gored, and badly. But the aging professional was digging his heels into the sand. He did not mean to relinquish his crown to the younger man whose bright flame had sparked superlatives from the critics most convinced that the arena was in hopeless degeneracy.

The specter of death had entered the duel, no doubt about it, and death-loving Spaniards at sidewalk cafés talked about nothing but the coming *mano-a-mano*. Sipping the sweet Málaga wine, they related over and over again how Manolete, the incomparable, had been pressed by the brash young Dominguín into the horns that killed him. Poetic justice, felt the more savage, if Ordóñez returned the favor. And present in Málaga to immortalize a drama that might outdazzle anything in bullfight history was the American genius Spaniards considered the world's greatest living writer.

Beard and hair were white now. The dignity of age had settled on his powerful physique. That square skull had been fashioned by nature to support laurels, and had been heaped high. Perhaps nowhere more than in Spain are the writings of Ernest Hemingway admired. The starkness of his prose, so translatable, is aped by aspiring authors. His fatalism strikes deep Iberian chords. He fought on the wrong side during Spain's apocalyptic war. No matter. *The Sun Also Rises*, known as *Fiesta* in Europe, captured the Spanish imagination. The Franco press did not stint praise. Humble people swallowed him in crowds. His was a compelling romance—the old warrior of letters returned to the scenes of his youth, come to observe the soaring star of Ordóñez, son of the bullfighter he had used as the matador prototype for *The Sun Also Rises*. Hemingway had never subscribed to the mystical devotion for Manolete. He had stated publicly his admiration for the skill of Dominguín.

How would he react to the passionate Andalusian art of Ordóñez, who was another Manolete come alive?

Style was the man, in the case of Ernest Hemingway. His style was his philosophy. It is important to note the difference in style between Dominguín and Ordóñez. Dominguín stood for Castilian sobriety. He was, superlatively, a *domador*. In triumph after triumph, beginning with autumn of 1958 and including his first encounter with a sluggish Ordóñez, he displayed his superb domination of the brute beasts. But  Ordóñez fried him in their second encounter. Fully as accomplished as Dominguín, a hot, southern beauty invested every motion, so that blood throbbed in eardrums and the hearts of young women palpitated. Beside him, Dominguín seemed as cold as an academy. Antonio Ordóñez possesses the tragic sense.

This was the rubber match. "Now we will see," was the attitude of the multitudes who shoved to their seats on the baking stone of Málaga's *plaza de toros*. The bulls were brave, powerful, noble—vital to the culminating thrust of the sword. The rivals fought as neither had ever fought before. There were no faults. Soon there was no strength left in the audience for the booming *olés*. Within minutes, the most ignorant tourist realized that he would not experience an afternoon like this again.

Ordóñez unfurled his *verónicas* with that leisured intensity that gripped everybody in a suspense of held breath, to explode at the end of a sequence in a roar that shook the stadium. Thousands yanked themselves to their feet with his first flourish of the short red death cape. He crooked his head and shoulders in that peculiar posture that gives him his special *salero*, teasing the bulls through pace after pace, drawing them as if his muleta were a magnet and the horns steel nubs hypnotized. Men hugged each other. One old fellow sat and shed tears. When Dominguín received his second bull, the old aficionado simply shook his head, incapable of absorbing more.

Dominguín did not disappoint his adherents. He limited himself to the purest expression of his art, carrying himself with an erect confidence that is alone pleasing to the eye. He did not bend to the bulls with the thrilling hunger of Ordóñez; he stood like a marble, feet planted, and demanded obedience from the bulls. In one grand consummation, he burned out his resources. The second bull tossed him; charged for the kill; missed transfixing him by millimeters. Dominguín staggered to his feet. He waved his peons off. He waved Ordóñez away. Doubled over, clasping his groin, he waited a moment. He straightened his graceful body. He cited the bull. The bull attacked. Feet rooted, almost

53

indifferent, Doming'in executed five consecutive *naturales*, classic passes of extreme danger and difficulty, the most perfect passes in that long afternoon of skills wrought to perfection.

Who received the laurel? It was a choice of excellences. But Ordóñez is an artist, an artist in the first rank of the tragic tradition.

I do not think of that on my way up to Domingúin's hotel suite. He was lying in bed, his followers hovering anxiously as a doctor took the raw lips of the round deep wound in the groin and pressed them together manually, needle flashing in and out of the flesh. Luis Miguel was very pale. He said to me, "It was a good fight, I think. The crowd was pleased?"

He was as dead, I realized, as Manolete.

Ernest Hemingway walked up. One hand gestured idly towards the wound. He said a few words I did not catch. Domingúin answered softly. Hemingway nodded.

Ernest Hemingway lingered in the parlor a moment, face sunburned, whiskers very white. He wore slacks and a faded umber-red shortsleeved sport shirt. He smelled of animal smells, the wine he drank such gargantuan lots of, the garlic he chewed, the sour mash of the sweat under his armpits—a hoary monolith in that roomful of nervous sycophants, withdrawn, perhaps ever suffering. I have asked myself since, did he then decide to favor Ordóñez in his article for *Life*? It was an act of courage, if so. Hemingway had witnessed, and acknowledged, superior art.

Why did he kill himself? It seems indecent to add another speculation. A mutual friend tells me his facial cancer had spread all over his body. He could no longer fish and hunt and drink: his pleasures. But I have wondered often, did Hemingway recently read over *Fiesta*? Was he struck by what a dead novel it is? A tiny portion of his work will live forever. He did what he could with his unillumined, *domador's* art, his pruned and often boorish (and sometimes majestic) prose. But Ordóñez whom he ended hero-worshipping, belongs to a rank above the Domingúins of literature. Was Hemingway brought to realize the limitations of his talent that gold and glorious afternoon?

September 9, 1961

Varus, Varus, Where Are My Legions?

James Burnham

In prison: General Challe, General Zeller, Generals Nicot, Bigot, Gouraud. Under indictment: Generals Vanuxem and Crèvecoeur. Gone underground: General Salan, General Jouhaud, General Gardy. Resigned: Generals Pouilly, Beaufre, Souard, Huré, and (two weeks ago) General Olié, chief of the General Staff—following the example of his predecessor, General Ely. In public and unbending opposition to the regime: France's highest ranking soldier, Marshal Juin. Reassigned: General Massu, Generals X, Y, Z. ...

Summoned before the Special Military Tribunal for perfunctory trial, and sentencing to two, five, ten years of jail or concentration camp: hundreds, literally hundreds of colonels, commandants, majors of the army and air force. They stand erect, heads proudly high, France's noblest decorations and the ribbons of her most bitter struggles across their tunics. The Tribunal still sits, after all these months, and these officers daily pass before it, each making his brief, straightforward, never cringing but often deeply puzzled declaration.

"The defense of the integrity of the nation is the *raison d'être* and first duty of the splendid profession of soldier, which I chose for my own"—it is Colonel Vaudrey speaking to the Tribunal, but it could as well be any of his comrades. "For me, military discipline is not an end in itself, and I cannot even conceive it except in the service of honor and my country— words embroidered in letters of gold on the silk of our flags. ... For this, Mr. President, I am ready to answer."

"I had the great honor"—Colonel Groussard is speaking as witness in behalf of Commandants Bléhaut and Monchonnet—"to be in command at the 1939-40 St. Cyr [the French West Point] graduation. Commandants Bléhaut and Monchonnet were members of that class. From the moment they left school, they were launched into war. For twenty years they have served, in Europe, in Africa, then in Asia and again in Africa. ... You realize that these are two elite officers, who for twenty years have served their country with the finest spirit of sacrifice and unblemished loyalty."

These officers and men, whose entire lives have been dedicated to honor and country—who have proved that dedication in Gestapo torture chambers, at Dienbienphu, in the terror-haunted alleys and deserts of Algeria—are being punished for what crime? The generals, because they disobeyed, or are alleged to have disobeyed, the commander-in-chief? (But weren't they taught at Nuremberg that soldiers may not obey an immoral command?) The colonels and majors and paras because they *did* obey their superior officers?

Charles de Gaulle

We do not yet quite have our own Indochina and Algeria—though we have had our Korea, and now our Laos and our Cuba. We do not yet have our Special Military Tribunal, but is it absurd to suggest that its doctrine is presaged in the Fulbright Memorandum, and its procedure foreshadowed in the rude, unprecedented, shamelessly publicized steps by which General Edwin Walker was relieved of his command—on the instance of a vile journal nourished in that same cesspool of the Left? "From high command to private first class," reported the *New York Times* military analyst, Hanson Baldwin, after a firsthand survey, "the army in Europe has been deeply disturbed by the case of Major General Edwin A. Walker. Officers of all ranks, particularly the senior ones, deplore the manner in which the case was handled and feel that some fundamental elements of military justice and fair play were violated." The officers knew, of course, that "the Walker case" was not an isolated incident, but a symptom in a mounting series.

"Varus, Varus, where are my legions?" Augustus is said to have cried when the news reached him that elite XVII, XVIII, and XIX legions, under the feckless command of Quintilius Varus, had been annihilated by Arminius in the Teutoburg forest. By that slaughter the whole history of the world was altered, for Rome and the limits of Latin civilization had as a consequence to fall back to the west bank of the Rhine. When Charles de Gaulle and John Fitzgerald Kennedy call in desperate need, will their legions still be there to answer?

October 7, 1961—The Third World War

The Violation of Arthur: A Frolic

William F. Buckley Jr.

Just after Mr. Kennedy's inauguration, I met with Professor Arthur Schlesinger Jr., historian and dogmatic theologian for Americans for Democratic Action, in public debate in Boston on the subject of the welfare state. It was on that occasion that Mr. Schlesinger, countering some point or other I had made, announced that the "best defense against Communism is the welfare state." Now everybody expects that professors will say foolish things from time to time, but Professor Schlesinger had just then taken leave of Harvard to accept a position as special assistant to the fledgling President of the United States, so that a great deal of publicity was given to that remarkable statement. And those who felt a decent interval would surely be allowed to elapse before an egghead academician would presume to press such homeopathic nonsense about how to deal with Communism on practical men of exalted station, must have sobered on witnessing the Professor's grand entry into the lecture hall, twenty minutes late, escorted by screeching police cars—it obviously hadn't taken long for Mr. Schlesinger to acquire princely habits.

And along with them, it is my sad duty to report, he seems to have lost—an occupational risk for humble folk who suddenly find themselves supping with the great—whatever sense of humor he once possessed. It is reported, by a close observer, that during his fifteen years at Harvard that humor actually surfaced thrice. Alas, it is, I gather, down now, for the very last time; and I for one am very sorry to see it go.

Schlesinger had been accustomed to such fawning audiences as he regularly came upon at Harvard and elsewhere in the academic world, where they preach academic freedom and practice liberal indoctrination; and was quite visibly disconcerted on discovering from the audience's reaction that one half of those present were quite adamantly opposed to his views and those of the New Frontiersmen. Under the circumstances, he thought to curry the opposition's favor by handing me, as their spokesman of the evening, a most redolent bouquet. Quoth Arthur: "Mr. Buckley has a facility for rhetoric which I envy, as well as a wit which I seek clumsily and vainly to emulate." The crowd (or my half of it) purred with pleasure. As an old debater, I knew exactly what he was up to, and determined, when my turn came to rebut, to say something equally oleaginous about Arthur. But I had only fifteen minutes, before getting up to speak, during which to compose a compliment, and I guess my imagination failed me. ... I forget.

And indeed I forgot about the whole incident until a couple of months ago when I received a letter from a lady in Boston who had been there that night. She cited Mr. Schlesinger's creampuff to illustrate his exemplary "fairness to the opposite political camp." It happened that at just that moment I was supposed to furnish my publishers with some quotations for the jacket of my new book, *Rumbles Left and Right.* I thought it would be mad fun to include the words of Arthur Schlesinger—you know, sort of the literary oxymoron of the year.

Well, sir, you'd have thought this was the biggest swindle since the Donation of Constantine. A few weeks ago, while minding my own business, I received a frantic telegram from my publisher announcing that Arthur Schlesinger, having seen the blurb in an advertisement for my book in NATIONAL REVIEW, demanded to know where and when he had said any such thing about me. I wired back: *My office has a copy of original tape. Tell Arthur that'll teach him to use unction in political debate but not to take it so hard: no one believes anything he says anyway.* Needless to say, I sent a copy of the telegram to Mr. Schlesinger, with the postscript: "Dear Arthur: I am at work on a new book which, however, will not be completed until spring of 1964, giving you plenty of time to compose a new puff for it. Regards." And then, on the upper lefthand corner of the letter, properly addressed to Mr. Schlesinger at his august quarters (The White House), I wrote, "Wm. 'Envy His Rhetoric!' Buckley," with my return address.

That, apparently, did it. Before even Arthur could say "I-believe-in-Free-Speech," the firm of Messrs. Greenbaum, Wolff and Ernst let it be known to my publisher and to NATIONAL REVIEW that they would demand an apology—or Schlesinger would sue. Now there is a very good case to be made for everyone apologizing who has ever quoted Arthur Schlesinger; but isn't it droll to be asked to apologize *to* Schlesinger for quoting *from* Schlesinger? Messrs. G. W. & E. have solemnly announced that I have "invaded Mr. Schlesinger's privacy." (Someday I may be prompted to write about Mr. Schlesinger's complex views on privacy, with which I am acquainted at first hand.) A most interesting complaint, considering that Mr. Schlesinger's words had been uttered before an audience of 1,500 or so, before television and radio and before members of the press and the wire services. For someone who wants what he says to be kept private, and as I say, all the world should cooperate in securing Mr. Schlesinger's privacy, that's a strange way to go about it, wouldn't you say?

Though I dunno, lots of things about Schlesinger seem strange, and I intended to have a very interesting time with Messrs. Greenbaum, Wolff and Ernst going into some of them. Ernst, by the way, is the great Morris Ernst, the free-speech specialist who so strongly believes in free speech that now his firm threatens an injunction to keep my *Rumbles* from being published, and

NATIONAL REVIEW from being distributed, unless I apologize to Schlesinger for exercising my right of free speech by quoting Schlesinger.

Ah well, it is a mad world. But I shall certainly put in for next year's Freedom Award. On the grounds that the more time Schlesinger devotes to me, the less time he has left over to devote to public affairs. Who else has clearer title to the public benefactor?

You may quote me, if you like. I promise not to sue.

April 9, 1963—Notes & Asides

Presidential Politics: Campaign '64

Hubert Humphrey: Prairie Philosopher

John Chamberlain

Hubert H. Humphrey of Minnesota has always had a secret weapon: his opposition seldom takes him seriously until it is too late.

At the risk of being invidious, let us begin with his looks. His brow is broad, one might say Roman, his chin is strong, but there is something about the curve from nose to chin that is soft, a concave interval between the convexities that suggests an almost baby-food blandness. It is not until the senator swings into real oral combat that the whole face becomes something stronger—and, to conservatives and old-fashioned liberals, something decidedly dangerous.

Hubert H. Humphrey

Many people have been surprised by Humphrey. Who would have thought to see an ADAer one heart-beat from the Presidency? Back in 1960 the pollsters in Wisconsin were surprised when he whittled Jack Kennedy's lead to proportions that could be claimed by Humphreyites as at least a moral victory for their man. Before that there was Nikita Khrushchev, who obviously tried to use the touring ADA senator when he invited him to the Kremlin for a little chat that lasted eight and a-half hours. Looking at it one way, Khrushchev was well recompensed for the time he spent with the country boy from the American Middle West; at least the message Humphrey brought home to Eisenhower, that Khrushchev would like a bid to visit the United States was, worse luck, acted upon. It was not until some time after the famous interview that Khrushchev realized he had been a trifle too gabby with Humphrey, whose own gabbiness can be altogether disarming. In the course of his frankness, Khrushchev had made some slighting remarks about the super-Marxism of Mao Tse-tung's agrarian program—and after Humphrey had passed the remarks on, the response from Peking was jolting. Thus Humphrey, by sowing discord, was manifestly one of the architects of the current split in the Red world. The lad from Minnesota had Khrushchev as a peg upon which to hang a reputation for being a first-class reporter in America's interests.

In the U.S. Senate Humphrey has been a continual surprise. His bills are defeated, but they pop up again. His amendments, turned down in a first formulation, come back in other guises. He put over cloture in the civil rights struggle as no other majority leader has succeeded in doing. Dick Russell is still amazed.

September 8, 1964

Tears for the Grand Old Party

Clare Boothe Luce

Come, Republicans, all legitimate heirs of Abraham Lincoln and Theodore Roosevelt! Come, let us the loved ones mourn the demise of the Grand Old Party.

Come, fellow liberals, moderates, midstream breast-stroke swimmers, all who fought for Willkie, Vandenberg, Eisenhower, Rockefeller, Lodge, and Scranton—(please, Harold, let go of our sleeve!)—and for Stassen. ...

Here are the hearses—all Cadillacs. Our line forms on the left for the funeral march, our cortège is small, but distinguished. Let no foot falter, no knee buckle, as we mournfully meander towards the mausoleum, the Cow Palace. (Please, everybody, remember to bring your own Kleenex.)

O sorrow unfathomable, O grief unutterable, O stark, bleak withers-wringing woe! We are going to bury the Grand Old Party!

Ah, the doom—crack!—the gavel falls: *"The 28th Convention of the Republican Party is now called to order."*

Who is to blame for this bitter, senseless, soul-searching tragedy? Be honest: we cannot blame the Press, they howled like banshees, wailed like air-raid sirens: "Stop Goldwater." They warned us, the Washington commentators, the panelists, the pollsters, the widely syndicated readers of political entrails, the ink-stained St. Georges of democracy, growing pale, shaking like men with the ague.

Ah, tolls now the first death knell: *"Alabama casts its 20 votes for Senator Barry Goldwater."*

Do you remember, last year (when, omigod, there was still time!), what beads of sweat appeared on the Jovian brow—Walter Lippmann's—dank dripping from laurel leaves, they too, trembling like aspens? Oh, he abjured us, for our own sakes, he Lippmann, for three decades the dear daily companion of our breakfast juice, the Peer of Pundits, the King Canute of Columnists, the Plato, the Philosopher King of Journalism—he told us that this would be suicide. He told us this ... thing ... could never happen.

Ah, again the funereal bell: *"California casts 86 votes for Senator Barry Goldwater."* We cannot blame the Democrats. They, too, the New Frontiersmen, sought to save us. All highbrows, all intellectual Alpinists, all biographers of the late John F. Kennedy, all Harvard, Princeton, Yale men, even Cornell and Dartmouth men, all people with higher-than-average IQ's and whiter-than-snow white collars, all told us this grave was yawning.

Again the knell of doom: *"Illinois casts 58 votes for Senator Goldwater of Arizona!"*

Now is the moment of truth—too late have we faced it. Barry, caught at last with his Conservative pants down, all his Extremists showing, will be buried beside Alf Landon under the Johnson landside in November.

Ding-dong ... ding: *"Michigan passes, while it polls the delegation."*

O fateful creed, conservatism, this stale smell, this senile, démodé, putrescent, outworn, archaic, antediluvian, reactionary, *Square* cause! (But who would have thought the feeble old thing had so many ballots in it?)

Ask not for whom the bell tolls: *"Ohio proudly casts all its 58 votes for the Senator from Arizona."*

(Sorry, Senator Javits, we're fresh out of Kleenex ...)

No, we've none but ourselves to blame. Conservatism will be rejected, repudiated, thrown out, buried full forty fathoms deep, out on the lone prairie, in a nameless grave—a chewed-up, battered, bloodied, ten-gallon hat its only marker ... marking, too, the final disappearance of the old Frontier (except, of course, on television). Yes, this is the Conservative score, Goldwater's fate, and the funeral of our Party. The funeral too, alas, of our brave little band of Liberals.

The shroud is measured: *"New Jersey casts 40 votes for the next Republican President, Barry Goldwater."*

(Just use your sleeve, Senator Javits—the cameras are still focused on the fight in the Michigan delegation.)

Ah, it's Goldwater over the dam, and the Grand Old Party dammed, doomed, done in, kicked in the ... kicking the bucket. Oh, how did this unutterable thing ever happen? What timidity, indifference, what cowardice, what failure of nerve, what—what's that you say? Of course, you've got it—we were betrayed!

June 30, 1964

I've Been Working on the Doorbells

David Johnston

I am a fourteen-year-old boy. Among other things, I am a Goldwater supporter. I worked hard to see the Senator's election, but I was never able to, nor was anyone else.

Let us reconstruct the first week of September 1964. One week was remaining until school would start for a new year. I had decided to be a conservative Republican the day after the Senator's nomination. I had always been and will always be a Republican. It was on this day, a Tuesday, that I had received my campaign materials from the Republican Headquarters in Stockton, California.

The package consisted of five Goldwater buttons, two "Viva Barry," seven "Goldwater '64," and one "Democrats for Goldwater" bumper stickers.

I immediately put a "Viva Barry" sticker on my binder and attached a Goldwater button to my shirt. Since my mother is a Goldwater-hating Democrat (aren't all liberals?) I could not go near her with my Goldwater button or I would have been disciplined. Since she didn't see my binder, I was safe in that respect.

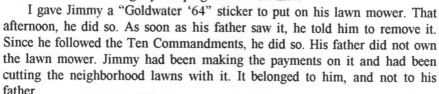

Barry Goldwater

When school started, two of my best friends, who wish only to be known as Jimmy and George, agreed to take on the difficult task of assisting my campaign for the Senator.

I gave Jimmy a "Goldwater '64" sticker to put on his lawn mower. That afternoon, he did so. As soon as his father saw it, he told him to remove it. Since he followed the Ten Commandments, he did so. His father did not own the lawn mower. Jimmy had been making the payments on it and had been cutting the neighborhood lawns with it. It belonged to him, and not to his father.

I gave George a "Democrats for Goldwater" sticker, which he quickly attached to his binder. (He was then a Democrat, but I have since converted him.) Since his mother would not let him take anything home in connection with Goldwater, his binder had to stay at school.

The Goldwater pins, naturally, caused a great deal of commotion around the school. The majority of the students supported Johnson. When we asked them why, most would answer, "Because our parents do." So naturally, our pins were frequently torn off and flattened.

The disrespect for our pins, which were, after all, our private property, did not discourage us; it made us even stronger Goldwater supporters.

After school had been in session for a few weeks, a Republican Headquarters was opened in town. One day we asked a teacher who wants to be known only as Mr. K. if we might go to the Republican Headquarters during the noon hour.

He said that although he didn't like Goldwater, he admired our interest in the campaign and would therefore let us go.

Since that was the first day it was open, they had some cakes there. We each had a few pieces. We then picked out about fifty Goldwater-Miller buttons, a like amount of Goldwater-Miller bumper stickers, and some books such as *None Dare Call it Treason*, by John A. Stormer. We also ordered some large pictures of Goldwater with a caption underneath which said, "In your heart, you know he's right, Vote for Barry Goldwater." These came a week later at which time we hung them up in our classroom.

Mr. K., who gave us permission to go whenever we wanted, as I mentioned before, had not supported Goldwater. But after we gave him some books and pamphlets on our candidate, he did support Goldwater, and on November 3, he voted for him.

The next morning at recess, three big boys, all Johnson supporters, started chasing us. We ran into the hall and kept running until a teacher, whom I shall not mention, stopped us. Our pursuers kept coming at us.

This teacher as they were ripping off our Goldwater pins and tearing our shirt buttons and pockets off was standing there watching. I cannot remember for sure if they kicked us or not, so I shall not include that. We asked him to tell them to stop, but he replied to this effect:

"It serves you right!"

They finally quit and we returned to the playground. George, a frequent user of profanity, muttered a few of his favorite words. Then the bell rang.

We financed our campaign through donations of money, half of which we sent to Barry Goldwater's campaign fund and the other half of which we used to buy Goldwater '64 bubble gum cigars which we distributed throughout the school.

The cigars made us mad one time. We had seen bubble gum cigars which said "All the Way with LBJ" on them, but we had never seen any with something about Goldwater on them. We went to the dime store and looked under the box of Johnson ones, and sure enough, there were the Goldwater ones. We argued for a while with the owner of the store about equal space for the candidates. He couldn't do anything about it since we bought all of the Goldwater ones that day.

The day before the election, I gave out Goldwater literature to all of the teachers at the school and the workers who worked there.

On election day, our class voted. Senator Barry Morris Goldwater defeated President Lyndon Baines Johnson by a vote of fifteen to fourteen, respectively.

Election night was awful. I had predicted that Goldwater would carry all of the South except possibly Texas, all of the West except Hawaii, Nevada, and California, and all of the Midwest except Michigan. He didn't.

I stayed up until I had to go to bed. Then I planned my defeat statement, which I would tell to all victorious Johnson supporters.

The next morning, I followed the usual routine, and as soon as I left the house, I put on my Goldwater pin. Someone saw it.

He said, "I thought you said Goldwater would win."

I responded to his remark and all others like it by saying, "I would and I'm sure Senator Goldwater would also rather lose with good principles than win with crummy ones."

August 24, 1965

At Home with Sir Alec

Colm Brogan

(*To understand Britain's new Prime Minister Sir Alec Douglas-Home, Colm Brogan believed it might be well to understand the kind of family he comes from, as exemplified by his brother William.*)

William Douglas-Home's war experience was somewhat unconventional. At a time when the German army was crumbling to defeat, he was ordered to attack a French town. William had other ideas. He knew there were many French civilians in the town, and he believed the German commander could be persuaded to surrender to save innocent life. So he flatly disobeyed his order and rode in a jeep towards the German position, carrying a pair of white underpants tied on a stick as a flag of truce. He was turned back, but he took no part in the attack.

Afterwards he almost insisted on being tried and was duly sent to prison. Alec visited him in Wormwood Scrubs and burst out laughing when he saw his brother in this highly unusual environment. William put his experience to good account. He wrote a serious play about prison life called *And Now Barabbas*. It was a great success. He followed this with a light political comedy called *The Chiltern Hundreds* which was a bigger success and also did very well as a film.

Then disaster fell. He brought on another comedy called *Aunt Edwina*. Of this effort it may be enough to say that *Aunt Edwina* became the trade name for any play of unadulterated corn. The gallery kept up a fusillade of booing and shouting, but when the final curtain fell on the first night, the author stepped forward and fired back at the gallery. It was widely admitted that he got much the better of the exchanges. The same thing happened every night. When the last curtain fell, the dauntless author appeared behind the footlights and hurled defiance at critics and audience alike. He spent all the money he had made from his previous successes to take *Aunt Edwina* from theater to theater. He even sold his car to raise funds. The good ship *Aunt Edwina* finally sank in a theater in Croydon, but she went down with flags flying and guns blazing. On the last night, as on the first night, the author took his very militant bow.

This was remembered some years later when John Osborne came to an even worse cropper. Osborne had made a lot of money out of *Look Back in Anger* and *The Entertainer*, plays that I thought were grossly overpraised. Then he wrote a musical called *The World of Paul Slickey*. It came to London after a provincial tour, and opened at the large Palace theater. It is my unending regret that I missed the first night. This time it was not merely the gallery that booed.

The stalls were booing as well. Elderly brigadeers in evening dress were standing up, purple in the face, shaking their fists and shouting at the stage. There was even a demonstration on the pavement outside. This was John Osborne's moment of truth. How did he meet the challenge? Did he take the stage like William Douglas-Home and fight back? Did he sacrifice his own money to keep the play going?

Alas, no. After the first night there was a customary party. Osborne who was producer as well as author did not even look in. The notices were uniformly hostile, and in a few days Osborne took himself off to Capri, leaving the ship to sink.

Virtually all those connected with the Progressive Theater are left-wing, but even they had to admit that when it came to facing adversity and defying opinion the aristocratic Douglas-Home had some quality that was conspicuously lacking in the lower middle-class Osborne.

December 31, 1963

A Layman's Hope for the Vatican Council

Evelyn Waugh

I believe that I am typical of that middle rank of the Church, far from her leaders, much further from her saints, distinct too from the doubting, defiant, despairing souls who perform so conspicuously in contemporary fiction and drama. We take little part except where our personal sympathies are aroused, in the public life of the Church, in her countless pious and benevolent institutions. We hold the creeds, we attempt to observe the moral law, we go to Mass on days of obligation and glance rather often at the vernacular translations of the Latin, we contribute to the support of the clergy. We seldom have any direct contact with the hierarchy. We go to some inconvenience to educate our children in our faith. We hope to die fortified by the last rites. In every age we have formed the main body of "the faithful" and we believe that it was for us, as much as for the saints and the notorious sinners that the Church was founded. Is it our voice that the Conciliar Fathers are concerned to hear?

As the service proceeded in its familiar way I wondered how many of us wanted to see any change. The church is rather dark. The priest stood rather far away. His voice was not clear and the language he spoke was not that of every day use. This was the Mass for whose restoration the Elizabethan martyrs had gone to the scaffold. St. Augustine, St. Thomas à Becket, St. Thomas More, Challoner and Newman would have been perfectly at their ease among us; were, in fact, present there with us. Perhaps few of us consciously considered this, but their presence and that of all the saints silently supported us.

No doubt there are certain clerical minds to whom the behaviour of the laity at Mass seems shockingly unregimented. We are assembled in obedience to the law of the Church. The priest performs his functions in exact conformity to rules. But we— what are we up to? Some of us are following the missal, turning the pages adroitly to introits and extra collects, silently speaking all that the liturgists would like us to utter aloud and in union. Some are saying the rosary. Some are wrestling with refractory children. Some are rapt in prayer. Some are thinking of all manner of irrelevant things until intermittently called to attention by the bell. There is no apparent "togetherness." Only in heaven are we recognizable as the united body we are. It is easy to see why some clergy would like us to show more consciousness of one another, more evidence of taking part in a social "group activity." Ideally they are right, but that is to presuppose very much deeper spiritual life in private than most of us have achieved.

If, like monks and nuns, we arose from long hours of meditation and solitary prayer for an occasional excursion into social solidarity in the public recitation of the office, we should, unquestionably, be leading the full Christian life to which we are dedicated. But that is not the case. Most of us, I think, are rather perfunctory and curt in our morning and evening prayers. The time we spend in church—little enough—is what we set aside for renewing in our various ways our neglected contacts with God. It is not how it should be, but it is, I think, how it has always been for the majority of us and the Church in wisdom and charity has always taken care of the second-rate.

December 4, 1962

Pope John, Pacem in Coelis

The manifestations of sincere grief over the death of Pope John are unparalleled in human memory. What has happened appears to be the solemnization of the old saw that all the world loves a lover: all the world loved Pope John, because he was one of the most convincing lovers of all mankind the world has ever known, and no one, anywhere, lived under the shadow of the doubt that Pope John loved *him*. That is why Catholics right and left, Protestants high and low, Jews orthodox and reform, Hindus, Moslems, Confucianists, atheists aggresive and supine, democrats, monarchs, despots, totalitarians, have joined the chorus of praise, making expressions of requited love, for the simple peasant who, carrying the heaviest crown on earth, went bravely to death, after trying hard, for five years, to teach the world how to live.

What is, of course, arresting about the phenomenon of a world united for perhaps the first time in history, is that no such unanimity met the death of Jesus Christ. Whom after all, Pope John struggled merely to imitate, following the injunction of Thomas à Kempis—never supposing he could wholly succeed, being man, not God. Nor does such unanimity, even after two thousand years of reflection, extend to the appreciation of Christ, Who is still widely reviled, widely despised, universally profaned. The reasons why are complex, but one of them is that Christ, in harder accents than his most recent steward, seemed to be calling for a life based largely upon definition, on a purposive discrimination between good and evil, in the art and science of which He was, of course, the Divine Teacher; whereas the Pope, although of course in thought, word, and deed an obedient servant of the definitional structure of Christianity, dramatized a very different quality, an ecumenicism so lofty that from its high position the particularities of every individual sinner were lost, the distinctive shadows of his profile gone; and so, although the Pope could loathe evil, evil, under his reign, appeared to be a disembodied thing, the kind of thing all of us could join together in loathing with the confidence that we were never being asked to loathe something about ourselves.

Christ loved all men because He made them, and because they have it within their power to redeem themselves; John loved all men without apparent qualification, and his exuberant, sometimes even fussy, goodness, fashioned the thought of two historical encyclicals which excited the altruistic instincts of mankind without, however, settling any of those grim problems which, because that's the way the wheel was cast, survive the death of this great man.

One time, three years ago, when Henry Cabot Lodge was our ambassador to the United Nations, he found himself pleading, before the Security Council, for the release of American aviators who had been shot down for allegedly overflying Soviet territory. "I ask you, gentlemen," said Lodge addressing the Soviet delegation, and pointing to the anxious wives of the crew who were looking down from the galleries, "I ask you, gentlemen, to open up your hearts, and let the men you hold prisoner come back to their wives." Gromyko looked at Lodge as though he had gone quite mad. Nothing so preposterous had been urged upon Gromyko since, as a boy, he had been called upon to celebrate the Czar's birthday. *Quod licet Jovi, non licet bovi.* Pope John, in *Pacem in Terris,* asked the leaders and the people of the world to do exactly that, to open up their hearts; and when doing so, spoke with a heart so pure that the world was caught—temporarily—by surprise. Not long after *Pacem in Terris* came the Italian elections, and the apparent rebuke to the Pope. One million more Italians voted the Communist ticket.But those million new adherents, and even many of the oldtimers within the Party, might yet, *might*, we said, might yet prove to have a leavening influence on the Communist Party itself, a healthy influence, deriving from a conscience Pope John helped to awaken.

Will it happen? Will John's goodness melt ideology's heart?

We fear not. We fear, rather, that his efforts will have proved vain, that his political sense will prove to have been invincibly innocent, that his strategical coordinates were awry, that the enemy's cynicism will triumph over his altruism. We expect that only a return to the life of definition will equip us to resist the enemy as resolutely as the Pope resisted his adamant disease. But, paradoxically, in renewing the fight, and recovering our strategical balance, we can get sustenance from the valiant performance of the Pope, the human being. We can remember to keep our hearts open, to encourage the enemy whenever he shows any sign of moral or rational stirring; we can remember to have infinite faith in the infinite powers of the Definitive Ally; and to be joyful, and humble, in our personal lives.

—William F. Buckley Jr.
June 18, 1963

Franny, Zooey, Seymour, and Marvin

William H. von Dreele

Ever since they made me read *Moby Dick* at that lousy prep school, I've had a thing about whales. I mean they're so goddam *big*. And I got the feeling old Melville really liked whales, too, which is more than you can say for that phony, Hemingway. (Oh, Hemingway liked whales all right—after they'd been *knifed* or *shot* or *kicked* to death by some expatriate American queer.)

Last week when I was having lunch with Marvin I said, "Do you know the whale may become extinct like the Great *Auk*, fer chrissakes?" And when Marvin said, "So?" boy, you can bet I was pretty goddam peeowed. I think this world is run by a bunch of phonies, too, but you've got to feel *some*thing. I mean, at some point you've got to be sin*cere*.

"The blue whale's got flippers that would cover my mother's whole lousy *living* room, wall to wall, and we're killing them off. What do you say to *that*, Marvin Glass?"

Marvin just kept eating his sardine sandwich and looked at me kind of funny. "*You're* Glass," he said. "My name's Wolff." He was right, but you get kind of batty in this writing racket, especially with young punks like John Updike breathing down your neck. I guess I should drop Marvin. All he's interested in *any*way is Sal Mineo movies, and this really depresses the hell out of me sometimes.

I told Marvin about the time I was in the dentist's office and I picked up this square mag called *The Norwegian Whaling Gazette*. It had these *whales* on the cover, see, and I'm *in*terested. It's printed half in Norwegian and half in English. I started reading the Viking bit out loud, real Ingmar Bergman, and some of the creeps looked at me like I was some kind of nut. *"Her finner vi hanner, hunner og unger her foregar parring og fodsel."* Crazy stuff like that.

Marvin looked at me kind of funny, too. "For a former Quiz Kid, you're one helluva drag," he said, covering the sardines in his onion roll under a big blob of catsup. "How's Seymour?"

"Seymour's dead," I said. "Didn't you read my piece in the *New Yorker*, Marvin?" (I had already *said* Seymour's dead in a short story, to say nothing of those 25 goddam pages in the *New Yorker*, fer chrissakes.)

"I only look at the cartoons." This made me go cata*tonic* right there in Schrafft's, which didn't bother Marvin, that phony. But I mean, what's a writer gonna *do*? Stanley Edgar Hyman says I should develop more goddam *themes*, and that's easy for *him* to say but I'm *me*, and besides, what would The College

Generation say? They treat me like I'm some kind of religious *sym*bol, which maybe I should keep pushing if I could get out of these lousy New England *woods* and back to East 79th Street, but I don't know if I can *stand* New York anymore with all those goddam min*ori*ty groups.

Marvin pushed his plate away and wiped his hands on the tablecloth, the *slob*. "Sorry, Buddy, but I can't read your stuff anymore. I get tired of everything important happening in the bathroom."

"Can't read it," I said, going all the way with the Bette Davis pop eyes. "They put me on the cover of *Time* magazine and Marvin Glass says he can't *read* me?"

"*You're* Glass, my name's Wolff," Marvin said, walking out the goddam revolving door. Which is why I'm on whales now. I figure they're a good change of *pace*. If Rachel Carson can make people worry about the health of these nutty *robins*, I'm gonna make people *sick* over *whales*.

July 16, 1963

America: Imagination and the Spirit of Place

Charles Tomlinson

How does one speak of it—of "America," that is? To begin with, there is essentially no "it." America as *it*, was the invention of the great anonymizers—admen, speculators, road-engineers, builders of home sites and filling stations. This *it* has been growing of late, has filled in the foreground and is threatening all that lies beyond. But essentially *it* is not America, but the American's way of escaping from the identity of his continent—from local America.

In local America one may look for evidence of those several Americas we are in danger of losing and that variety of human types we shall lose with them. For as certainly as we begin to lose the spirit of a place we begin to lose the spirit of its people. The shapeless suburbia that is replacing city, small town, and village throughout the states creates the mould for a certain kind of human being, as standardized as his setting. And it is difficult to see what the writer is to do with such a setting. Novels about it seem as flat as the reality. They lack social stiffening, solidity, and texture. Confronted by a world of standardized dreariness, the artist has often retreated inward. A young abstract expressionist explained to me that he aimed "to escape the limitations of visual reality." Looking at the face of his native American city, I saw what he meant. The escape has extended into literature. Where, for example, is the South of Southern Gothic? Certainly not in the United States. Where are the deserted parks of Wallace Stevens' poetry? They are in the France of Paul Verlaine. America, as men have made it, too frequently fails to nourish the eye, the spirit, the imagination.

Traveling, say, in California, one becomes hungry for a renewal of the most basic past achievements in the present scene—a renewal of the imaginative energy, for example, that raised those simple yet lovely ranch houses in Marin County, with their white compactness, their neighborly spacing of houses and barns, and their wise attunement to the needs of the surroundings, spelled out in sharp, clean palings or in the wind-break of the trimmed cypress-hedge. One finds elsewhere a similar intuitive bridge between men and their setting in the scattered artifacts of earlier American culture—and they differ miraculously according to the specific locality they represent and, yes, *interpret*. One finds this intuitive bridge in the snake fences of New England; in the white churches, their unstained glass permitting the elms outside to cast a decoration of shadows and branches over their frighteningly pure interiors. One finds it in the shapeliness of Litchfield and Washington, Connecticut, or, with a different emphasis, in the adobe pueblos and on the plazas of New Mexico and the splendid modern houses of Sante Fe. The Connecticut towns stand out from their greens candidly, sharply. The structures of New Mexico blend with the red desert of their setting. Yet both consummate a relationship, the first by contrast, the second by a kind of mute sympathy. Both take to themselves the aura of "the lived and living things that share our thoughts," to borrow a phrase of Rilke's. They offer the poet a hoard of rich and ramifying images and they have been justly celebrated. James and Hawthorne both turn to the architecture of New England for symbolic currency and, to speak of lesser spirits, Willa Cather and Frank Waters to that of New Mexico. Marianne Moore and Elizabeth Bishop do likewise with the settlements of the northeastern seaboard.

The artifacts of setting draw out its life. They are the gracious complements of nature itself. And the writer, or the painter, feels his kinship with them: their action is analogous to his own. For he, also, among other things, can release the spirit of place, confirm and extend it, give it meaning in his work. He, like the snake fence and the pueblo wall, builds an intuitive bridge to environment. Poet, painter, architect—the work of all three must, as D.H. Lawrence expresses it, "flicker with a spirit of place." They have been the great deniers of the *it*—of the single America that utility is giving us. They speak on behalf of the many-sidedness of the continent itself.

One thinks, for example, of Winslow Homer coming to terms with the weather of the Maine coast, living with it, accepting it. "Night before last it was twelve below zero," he writes and: "My nearest neighbor is half a mile away—I am four miles from telegram and P.O. and under a snow bank most of the time." That laconic, self-sufficient, uncomplaining tone is the authentic voice of America.

Winslow Homer has another vision of America besides his solitary acceptances of sea and forest, of snow and breakers. It is a vision not unlike that of Twain's *Huckleberry Finn*, a vision again of independence, independence of the genteel taboos, a feeling for creative innocence. The poetry of water life: the river, boats, air, loafing at Marblehead—Homer captures without nostalgia the sweetness of such liberty. His youths in straw hats moon under the chiaroscuro of trees, the sun falling against the white planks of a house and lying across the fish-shaped wedge of a drooping hat brim, solidifying and not dissolving the object it touches. This American light, hard, clear, acidic, "The scratching of a slate pencil," as Gaston Probert describes it to Mr. Dosson in Henry James' *The Reverberator*. It lacks the limpid in-between tones of an English summer light. And beneath it boys wade, they lie on the Gloucester rocks, they carry home clams. They are the protagonists in an anecdote, crass perhaps but unsentimental, a hard, dry yankee light defining them. Yet side by side with the dryness, the hardness, there is a plasticity of response. This plasticity, that often flows out of a level terrain of banalities, again recalls Twain. He wrote only one *Huckleberry Finn*, along with much that is second-rate.

But in Twain's river, as in Homer's best pictures, locality reasserts itself and it is locality bathed in a moral temperament, and in an unconcern that is as free of the taint of success as the idiom of the book is free of gentility: "Soon as it was night, out we shoved; when we got her out of the middle we let her alone ... then we lit pipes, and dangled our legs in the water and talked about all kinds of things—we was always naked, day and night, whenever the mosquitoes would let us ..." If that is innocence, it is not the innocence of a Kerouac with its rootless sensationalism, but an innocence grounded in place and in language whose grain lies close to the grain of common experience.

Twain's Mississippi is a dream of possibilities—of freedom from the Calvinism and Puritan will that came so early between the American and his natural sympathies. It is as if the geographical vastness of America had lain waiting through the centuries for some adequate consummation, for a sympathy commensurate with its variety, for a sensitivity that would outlast the mere desire to dominate.

"One must indeed be incurably optimistic even momentarily to dream such a dream." The voice is that of the architect, Louis Sullivan, reflecting in his *Kindergarten Chats* on the early potentialities of Chicago. He also, like Twain, had sensed, as it were, a demand for fulfillment in the inarticulate spaces. "One must indeed be incurably optimistic. ... Yet the Lake is there ... and the Sky is there above it; and the Prairie, the ever-fertile prairie is awaiting. And they, all three, as a trinity, are dreaming—some prophetic dream ... " Sullivan had the civic imagination that would have made the Lake before Chicago serve the city as the rivers of Paris, Florence, and Pisa serve theirs.

It is difficult to sense anything of Sullivan's prairie in Chicago today, insulated against it, as it is, by a littered, shapeless exurbia, but the sky is immense and the lake an unquenchable presence. The apartment houses of Mies van der Rohe, those antiseptic, impersonal hives that overlook it, have misunderstood the nature of the lake altogether. Even on a wintry Sunday, with its beginnings in fog, you can sense there something of the forces that inspired Sullivan's vision. For behind the multi-laned highway which mutes back the immensity of the waters, which has done all that can be done to nullify them, there is an esplanade to walk along. The rest of the city will be driving ten abreast down the highway. You will have your dream almost entirely to yourself. A mana lingers on here, explodes joyful at Oak Street Beach, where the breakwaters on either side set up a contrary motion of currents, so that breakers rush onto the beachlines from three directions, colliding, canceling one another, crashing together in midair, corkscrewing, leaping apart, all very gay as they stream with light. The power of space gathers as the afternoon passes. The sun disappears behind the skyscrapers that now mirror their length over the water in olive-green darkness. A gold drives out the silver of the water lights, then in turn is driven out by a pure dove-grey striped by the shafted reflection of arising moon.

What is the reciprocation these intricate splendors seem to be demanding at every point in the American scene—from the lake at Chicago to the deserts of the Southwest and the coast of the northern Pacific? The critic, Hugh Kenner, has formulated the hope when, writing on Lincoln, he speaks of "an enlightened culture as leisured as the landscape." Until Americans learn to understand their surroundings at the deepest, the most patient level, that culture will never be achieved or one's incurable optimism justified. Instead of a union of the civic imagination and the natural fact, there will be an ever deepening schism between suburb and wilderness, an abyss that imagination has failed to span.

August 12, 1961

Unfinished Business

James Burnham

The front page of the August 18 issue of the West Berlin newspaper, *Bild Zeitung*, consisted of the photograph of the East German boy, Peter Fechter, dying at the foot of the Wall. The caption read: *Vopos let refugee bleed to death. Amis look on.* "Vopos" are the East German "people's police," or militia. "Amis" is German slang for "Americans."

Of course, there was nothing else these individual soldiers could or should have done, except to stand passively watching the death agony of this unknown, unlucky boy. The impotence of those Amis was one more consequence of the defining impotence of their leader: from his failure to respond when, a year before, almost to the day, the Wall made its first probing appearance.

On that morning of August 13, 1961, Berlin's Wall was a trivial enough entity, physically speaking; and even today it is physically not very formidable. But the physical wall has never been important, never anything for modern machines and explosives to take seriously. "The Wall" that properly bears the capitalized initial is compounded of spirit and will, not of matter. It is a wall rather like the wall of fire that Wotan drew around Bruennhilde: which no physical weapon but only a fearless heart could breach.

It cannot be too often repeated: Who said A, must say B. This is the first law of politics, and the hardest to comprehend; and President Kennedy and his ideologues do not, evidently, comprehend it. The Wall was the first term in a linked series. Its first meager stones smashed, by necessary implication, the political structure upon which the Western position in Berlin and the corridors is based. Having accepted so much, how can they oppose—except with words, of which they have a-plenty, or unconvincing gestures like these pointless mobilizings—each further small step, or slice? They cannot; they do not.

Those who fail before A try to conduct themselves as if A had never been. For this or that reason, we could not handle A. But A is over the dam. Now we confront B, or, rather J, K, and L. This time things are to be different. We shall draw the line, stand firm before K and L.

It doesn't work that way. K and L are only secondary consequences of J; J, of I and H; and the whole series, of A. You cannot stop K and L for long. To hold there you must turn back, and painfully, slowly, retrace the series: right back until, with a thousand times more difficulty than at the first chance you meet A's still persisting challenge. In Berlin, that means you must face and conquer, the Wall. Failing that, your position must continue, slow or fast, to crumble.

September 25, 1962—The Third World War

Music: Two Reviews by
Ralph de Toledano

The Cult of Judy

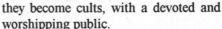

There are some performers who have it, really have it. By some sort of empathy, they reach out over the footlights and merge with the audience. They may be hard and disciplined in their effulgence (Alla Nazimova in her raddled sixties could make Ibsen come alive—and the audience saw her as young and vibrant) or quietly aware of their excellence (Pablo Casals at the cello transcended the moment of music, and will as long as he can put bow to strings). Or, again, they may be outgoing emotion, yet one with their art. Then they become cults, with a devoted and worshipping public.

Ralph de Toledano

Whatever this quality of communication is, it makes a magic which is a great gift for those of us who cannot do, but must watch. The performer who has it ceases to be himself. He is possessed of his audience, even as his audience is possessed of him. This is what makes a cult. And this is what Judy Garland has, what lifted her from the young girl who so appealingly sang "Over the Rainbow" in the *Wizard of Oz* to the joyous, tragic, tears-to-the-eye-bringing singer of America's living popular ballads. It is unnecessary nowadays to say, "Judy Garland." The "Judy" is sufficient, as storming, cheering, shaken, and deeply moved Americans who have heard her in concert can attest. Judy is a cult. Even before she opens her mouth to sing, she has made her point.

The record companies have recognized this and now fill the shops with encyclopedic collections of her recordings. Columbia has put her in its Hall of Fame series. Decca has preserved on vinylite her pacing of those evocative songs from Gershwin's *Girl Crazy*. The catalogue is long. But compelling as all of this may be, it does not match Capitol's two-record album of her triumphant

Carnegie Hall concert—"live and complete," the sleeve says—a concert repeated in sixteen cities, which left the usually glib critics groping for adjectives and feeling the inadequacy of their clichés of praise. Had those fortunate enough to be in that staid and wonderful hall had their way, Judy would be singing encores to this day.

The twenty-six songs that made up program and encores had been polished to smoothness by hundreds of fine popular singers. The body in which the music was created could not match those of the slick and tightly-gowned singers of songs who inhabit the night clubs and the TV screen. The face would not have won any beauty contests. Judy put on weight during the period of her nervous breakdowns and the chaos of her personal life. What is left of the figure, she encased in a formless silk coolie jacket. But this served to emphasize the wonderful quality of her face—the very short, reddish hair, the widely-set warm eyes, and the expressive mouth that quivers from comedy to tragedy.

This is lost in the recording. But the fact that the appeal is purely aural adds a new dimension by shutting out the distractions of the physical personality. The listening ear and mind become aware that Judy holds back nothing. She gives every song—whether it be "Stormy Weather," "For Me and My Gal," or the Al Jolson favorites—everything, and takes everything from it. It is then that the heart discovers the secret of Judy Garland's singing. She has found the eternal verities buried in sweet or maudlin, rowdy or vulgar, melodies that the philosophers of Tin Pan Alley have given her. The full-throated open voice, in overstating its penance, has in fact paradoxically reduced it to an essence.

Among the popular singers of today, there are those who phrase more perfectly and instinctively than Judy: Peggy Lee, who brings mastery and subtlety and impeccable taste to everything she studies; Ella Fitzgerald, with that tremendous Negro ease and instinct, who knows always how to lag behind the beat and then anticipate it; Peggy King, who made a career imitating Judy, found her own significant style, and then threw it all away; Marlene Dietrich, who made a virtue of her vocal inadequacies by adding a sardonic dimension to the songs she made hers. There are singers who can make each popular song an exercise in controlled sensibility.

But there is none like Judy to cut to the quick of our emotions, to become the symbol and the song itself, to make the "bravos" of a shaken audience real and meaningful. This is what gives the cult of Judy its validity. This is what makes Capitol's recording of the Carnegie Hall concert a candidate for the archives of popular song. Each of us weeps for the loves he has lost and the loves he will never have. Each of us rejoices in the loves he has held back, real and significant. The tear and the laugh, the ebullience and the sadness—these are her contribution to an audience which forgets the limitations and, as it hears or sees, thinks it has burst through to the *dinglichkeit* of the sacred and profane in Judy's singing. That "Over the Rainbow" should be her theme song has its poetic justification. That's where she carries us.

August 28, 1962

A Matter of Listening

Sviatoslav Richter does not play the piano; he assaults it. When his fingers strike the keyboard, it is not a transference of musical impulse; it is the Kronstadt sailors marching on the Winter Palace. Among those listeners who want more bang for their buck, the effect is electric. The impact of so much released energy is visceral. But when the last note has ceased to vibrate and calm is restored, the questions remain unanswered: Is this music or muscle? Is it interpretation or kinematics? They are asked after every new Soviet musician breaks out of prison for a Western concert tour.

In Richter's recording of Beethoven's F Minor Sonata (RCA Victor LM 2545), all the elements of the Soviet style are apparent. The *Appassionata* is as involuted a piece of music as you can find in literature of the pianoforte—and it eludes far more introspective pianists. In Richter's thunderous performance, there are wrong and missed notes, excessive dynamics. His disregard of indicated tempi is so blatant that Samuel Chotzinoff, in a commentary printed on the jacket, tacitly apologizes for it. But oddly enough, though Richter comes on like Genghis Khan, he makes it. The drive which lusts so stridently for the final chord carries everything before it. There comes to mind Virgil Thomson's description of what, in writing about Toscanini, he called the "wow technique." "No piece has to mean anything specific; every piece has to evoke from its hearers a spontaneous vote of acceptance." A little breathlessly, the hearer says "Wow!" after experiencing Richter's *Appassionata*. What matters is attack—if we use the word, not in its technical musical meaning, but to denote the synthesis of instrumental technique and accommodation to the score. Richter's playing is rousing, satisfying, but kinematic. You can almost hear his teacher admonishing him with the Russian equivalent of "Give it lots of pedal, boy."

October 9, 1962

Marks of Identity: Graham Greene's
A Burnt-Out Case

Joan Didion

Among the boys in the back of the book, an admiration for Graham Greene has become ever so slightly *infra dig*. The smart money has leaked the word: Greene is "a master craftsman" who manages to turn out "well-tooled" novels despite his regrettable dialectical deficiencies. (Just as Scott Fitzgerald, not so very long ago, was a master craftsman who manages to turn out "well-tooled" novels despite his regrettable inability to come to grips with the Tennessee Valley Authority.)

What makes the boys regretful is not simply their belated ruling that Greene is not after all a "great Catholic novelist" (a notion no less absurd than that of a "great Low Episcopal novelist," or of a "great Trotskyist novelist"); it is their uneasy suspicion that he never intended to be. One can name dozens of novels indelibly informed by Christianity—*Sanctuary*, for one. But where *Sanctuary* is about redemption, *Brighton Rock* and *The Heart of the Matter* are about human concern with redemption: another game entirely. Christianity is part of the *donnée* in a Greene novel; like heat on the west coast of Africa or V-1 raids in London, belief or the lack of it colors a decision, moves a scene, effects the dénouement, emerges as nothing more or less than one of the facts of the matter. There is simply a Cross on the landscape, and its apparently gratuitous appearance disappoints all those who have bought their tickets under a misapprehension that a miracle play is on the bill. Well made, they murmur, distinctly cheated but still game.

At his best, and his best is certainly *Brighton Rock*, Greene is a brilliant novelist precisely because he makes things so well, because he generates the kind of structural excitement that Flaubert gave to fiction, because he has an instinct for the novel that includes a certain sense of what people remember and how they dissemble and how they give themselves away. Like Parkis, the improbable eye in *The End of the Affair*, Greene takes an avid interest in what Sarah Miles and her lover ordered for lunch. They had pork chops; as Parkis explains, "They might be marks of identification, sir, if frequently indulged in." Greene knows all the marks of identity, knows for example that what Helen Holt in *The Heart of the Matter* thinks or does not think about the borrowed furniture in her Nissen hut tells more about Helen Holt than anything she or her passport could possibly say. (It is the kind assigned to junior officials; one imagines it—perhaps wrongly—to be rattan, with the faded, featureless, indelible look of rented summer cottages.) When Greene is good, he is very good, exhibiting the same sure feeling for fiction that Scott Fitzgerald sometimes exhibited (think of Tom and Daisy Buchanan eating that cold chicken in *Gatsby*, think of Pinkie and Rose on their wedding day in *Brighton Rock*); when a Greene novel is good, everything works.

March 25, 1961

Book Briefs

*D*issent, Summer 1961 ($1). *Dissent*, an orthodox little Leftward Ho, came up not long ago with a New York, N.Y., issue, soft on the heels of its spiritual big sister, *Esquire*. Since both editors and contributors were culled from as fine a posse of circuit riders as ever cadged a Guggenheim, the pieces range from the obvious to the ordinary, all in the tone of Eureka, none leavened by humor—save such presumably unintentional bits as short stories which begin "Me kill Daddy-Wong-Wegs." *Dissent* digs Harry Ashmore, Beats, Murray Kempton, Miscegenation (sans clergy), Off-Broadway, Psychiatry, Public Housing, Mort Sahl, the Village, and putting down such bad guys as Amos n' Andy, Meyer Davis, the Police Department Narcotics Squad, Finks, Joe McCarthy, Mississippians, and Robert Moses. Sample some scripture: you'll find old Dan Bell pushing a "social calculus." Hear out the drama critic of the *Village Voice* on the *New York Post*: "She's our mama, that's what counts. She is the good indignant mama of New York City as the *New York Times* is its good gray papa." Meet Irving Howe, grand kleagle of the editorial board: "One hot night in Indiana I had a bitter quarrel with Alfred Kazin." That single line encapsules the final parochialism of this gallant little band of dissenters, hopelessly out of touch with America. Anybody else, one hot night in Indiana, might have encountered Bill Jenner, Elmer Davis, Paul McNutt, George Ade, Booth Tarkington, Herb Shriner, Wendell Willkie, Paul Dresser, James Dean, Bo McMillen, Lew Wallace, Bob Ingersoll, Dr. Kinsey, or even Dan Wakefield. Only Irving could have bumped into Alfred Kazin.

—Noel E. Parmentel Jr.
March 27, 1962

*P*aris on the Seine, by Blake Ehrlich (Atheneum). Mr. Ehrlich, an American journalist with long experience in Paris, apparently knows literally all there is to know about that lovely city. He has managed to cram most of it into this charming volume, which takes the form of a leisurely stroll down the Seine along the historic quais. Pausing here and there to admire a bridge, a square, or an old house, he casually tells us its whole story—which often stretches back across four  or five blood-spattered, bejeweled, heroic centuries. A minor masterpiece, absolutely *de rigueur* for Parisophiles and strongly recommended to everyone else.

—William A. Rusher
November 19, 1963

Taken Care Of, by Edith Sitwell (Atheneum). Needless to say, it's superb. From her description of a magnificently miserable childhood in the great English tradition to her calm closing expectation of the coming day when "all will be over, bar the shouting and the worms," Dame Edith told it all the way it seemed to her—which is perhaps the only way to hear it worth the listening. Her autobiography is a pleasure-garden laden with such dainties as a meeting with Marilyn Monroe ("I cannot imagine anyone who knew her trying to take a liberty with her"); recollections of Dylan Thomas, Roy Campbell, Paul Tchelitchew, and other divine madmen; bemused peepings into the circular literary world of London in the Twenties; and animadversions upon the intrusions of a shabby age. As promised in her preface, she is sharp with D. H. Lawrence (who "looked like a plaster gnome on a stone toadstool in some suburban garden"), Percy Wyndham Lewis, and various parasite nobodies. The occasional digressions on her approach to her craft and on the fallen state of modern criticism are models of lucidity. *Taken Care Of* recalls a life lived with discriminating gusto, and seen in the unique Sitwell through-stained-glass-clearly fashion it is an unrelieved pleasure, and it is too brief. Photographs.

—*C. H. Simonds*
June 15, 1965

An Odd, Sad Waif

Priscilla L. Buckley

Two Hungarians struck up a conversation in Lausanne one winter evening in 1922 and, as Hungarians will, when Hungarians meet, they talked the night through. That, says Emery Kelen, was the start of "our thirty-year partnership." ("Our thirty-year war," snorts Alois Derso.) At any rate, they were to become the pictorial biographers of the League of Nations ("our girl of Geneva") doing for the League what Queen Mathilda had done for the Battle of Hastings at her loom so many centuries before. The Kelen-Derso entente (cordial or not) didn't break up until after the Second World War when Emery Kelen became television director of the United Nations while his partner, Alois Derso, opted instead to continue as an artist and in due course became NATIONAL REVIEW's chief, most popular (and for the first three or four years) only regular illustrator. (In consequence of the choices Emery Kelen now lives in the country, is semi-retired, and finds time to write first-class books such as *Peace in Their Time*, while Derso continues poor, and unretired—and available to NR's editors, provided they don't call before 3 PM.)

In 1922 the young Derso was already famous. It was a day when major international journalists, such as Jules Sauerwein of *Le Matin*, traveled to conferences, not with their typewriters, but with their typists; and Derso, *Le Matin*'s cartoonist, cut a mean figure. He went around gloriously bedecked in a loud checked overcoat that swept to the ground like a monocled *Graf-Baron*, Kelen recalls. "With his long upper lip and demonic smile, he gave the impression of a cardinal contemplating heresy."

They had different styles of working (and of living). Kelen's subjects sat for what were almost formal line portraits. Derso, when he finally got up, circa 4:00 PM, would "prowl around the Lausanne Palace Hotel, head cocked, melancholy eyes riveted to his model. After a while he'd get labor pains, borrow my pencil, scuttle to a quiet corner of the bar, and scribble profiles over every piece of paper within reach." Sometimes Derso would make a hundred sketches before selecting one he liked. "He walks around today," says Kelen, "with ten thousand portraits in his head, a morgue of caricatures."

Between them, Derso and Kelen sketched the story of the League from her start as "an odd, sad waif, born on the wrong side of the two-party blanket and abandoned by her Uncle Sam on the Quai Wilson" to her end, at Munich, when "this girl of ours ... had grown short sighted. Her nose was red from weeping; for she was a maid betrayed. ... The people had turned against the League and our girl was doomed."

In *Peace in Their Time*, an extraordinarily vivid, witty, and well-written book which Mr. Derso insists must be in large part the work of Kelen's charming English-born wife, Helen, because, "frankly Kelen's Hungarian-German-goulash-English is only a little better than my Hungarian-French-goulash-English," Emery Kelen has placed his artist's eye in the service of his pen. His word portraits are memorable. Secretary of State Frank Kellogg, he tells us, "was a little old man who looked like a little old woman who resembles a little old man. ... " And "... slim and trim, [Austin Chamberlain] stood and walked square-shouldered, as if he had swallowed a coat hanger ... [his nephew Neville] could not laugh, and if he smiled, the smile ran down the tips of his wilted mustache like the juice of a bitter melon." "[Sen. Claude A. Swanson's] mustaches needed a good clipping, but his frown did not, as it was already clipped to his face by a pince-nez lest it slide off his beaky nose." Two stout women rolling down the Quai Wilson with heavy strings of Venetian beads look to Kelen "like a couple of overflowing barrels of pirate treasure just fished out of a lake"; a Polish priest "whose name was a bottleneck of consonants ... read while he ate, using his thin nose as a pointer. ..."

Alois Derso: Self-Portrait

To Kelen, the irreverent incidents and sidebars that more serious historians hastily sweep under the rug beg to be told, and tell them he does. Did you know, for instance, that the first time Sir William Tyrell (later ambassador to Paris) made his mark diplomatically it was in arranging the ransom of Lord Curzon's trousers, which had been kidnapped by a disgruntled valet? ... or how French Foreign Minister Aristide Briand got the last word at Mère Léger's restaurant when Gustave Stressman tried to grab the check: "I'll pay for the lunch," said Briand, "you can take care of the reparations"? Or that certain fiscal inconsistencies in Gandhi's style of living finally brought forth this frosty comment from one of his most devoted followers, Mrs. Naidu: "People have no idea how much it costs to keep the Mahatma poor!"?

Emery Kelen emerges here as a man of peace, a believer in the ideals of the League: but he leaves the heavy-handed moralizing (he couldn't be heavy-handed if he tried) to others as he tells what happened to Miss Geneva from her highpoint in Locarno down to the day that Chamberlain betook himself to

Munich, umbrella in hand, and it was all over for "our girl." "All she had to her name were a few Nobel prize winners, some sugar daddies, two caricaturists, and a wisp of an olive branch." In *Peace in Their Time* the talents of Derso and Kelen are reunited a last time in tribute to an old flame, who, as old flames so often will, ended life pretty much as she started it, "an odd, sad waif."

March 10, 1964

The England of Jeeves

Anthony Lejeune

What riles the young angries of the Left is that P.J. Wodehouse has not changed. The world he writes about, the world of the Drones Club and Blandings Castle and Piccadilly Jim, was always a fairyland but it was never their fairyland. He writes about the upper classes without class-consciousness. He writes about love as though Freud had not been invented. He writes without ambiguity.

What a stylist he is. With what effortless economy he makes his effects. Bingo Little comes up to Oofy Prosser in the club and says he's looking for someone to lend him five pounds. "Very hard to find, that type of man," replies Oofy coldly. What more is there to say?

Or: "Good Lord Jeeves! Is there anything you don't know?"

"I could not say, sir."

Or—Jeeves and Bertie again: "In these days of unrest, Jeeves," I said, "with wives yearning to fulfill themselves and husbands slipping round the corner to do what they shouldn't and the home, generally speaking, in the melting pot, as it were, it is nice to find a thoroughly united couple."

"Decidedly agreeable, sir."

"I allude to the Bingos—Mr. and Mrs."

"Exactly, sir."

"What was it the poet said of couples like the Bingeese."

" 'Two minds with but a single thought, two hearts that beat as one,' sir."

"A dashed good description, Jeeves."

"It has, I believe, given uniform satisfaction, sir."

Mr. Wodehouse's literary opponents are quite right in a way. He and his creations have no place in the world of social consciousness and dustbin drama. Bertie Wooster would find little to say to Jimmy Porter or Lucky Jim. He would not enjoy the plays of Bertold Brecht or Shelagh Delaney.

But Bertie is far from the vapid wastrel some people have taken him for. He is highly percipient in his own field. Some of Jeeves' quotations may be new to him, but, during his stretches at Malvern House, Eton, and Oxford, quite a lot of knowledge stuck. The names of Schopenhauer, Edgar Allan Poe, and Chekhov are on the tip of his tongue; so are the names of Tallulah Bankhead and Jack Dempsey. He understands about affairs of the heart. He even speaks French quite well.

More important, he is kind, generous, and loyal to a fault. "The code of the Woosters," he once explained, "as is pretty generally known, renders it impossible for me to let a pal down. Mine not to reason why." He is a chivalrous and, on the whole, eminently sensible Englishman. A world made up of Bertie Woosters would not be at all a bad world to live in. A world made by John Osborne for Jimmy Porter would be intolerable.

June 3, 1961

Part Three

1966 to 1970

The Week
Selected Editorial Paragraphs

May 3, 1966
That Great Come and Get It Day has, we see by a handbill, come and gone, and we only hope they got it. The Committee of Welfare Families of the Lower East Side announced a "Public Meeting for Welfare Clients" and posted this information: "The law says: welfare *must* give you ... Beds, Linoleum, Dressers, Blankets & Sheets, Curtain-Window Shades, Bathroom Mirror, Pots & Pans, Dishes, Silverware, Kitchen Table—one Chair for Each Child—Towels & Linen, Lamps & End Tables. Raincoat." Raincoat? Obviously, to keep from being battered to death by pennies from Heaven.

June 28, 1966
God is Dead Note Down Under and Slightly Sideways: Wellington, New Zealand, May 8—The Anglican Church of New Zealand has decided to omit the Ten Commandments in the modern-language version of the Communion service because "they do not express the Christian emphasis on love and grace."

September 20, 1966
Disarmament talks recessed in Geneva after seven months of fruitless negotiation. Disarmament months recessed in fruitless after seven talks of Geneva negotiation. Negotiation disarmed to talk less and seven fruits were recessed in Geneva. And everybody received his lease for January.

June 13, 1967
Couldn't we move Israel to North Vietnam and let Nasser blockade the harbor at Haiphong?

February 27, 1968
Albany, Feb. 12—The Assembly, overridding Republican protests, voted today to require public schools in the state to hold memorial services each year on the birthday of John F. Kennedy, May 29. Well, so long as they don't pray, it's legal. Pray to God, that is.

August 13, 1968
May we be struck dead, so help us, cross our hearts and hope to die, the *New York Times* of July 29, 1968, on page three, column two, paragraph six, used the word "ultraliberals." But when we resumed reading, wouldn't you know it, the *Times* contrived a context that robbed the word of all its joy. The Soviet Union, in its dealings with Czechoslovakia, is insisting on the removal from leading government positions in that country of the "ultraliberals." So we can relax after all: God's in his heaven, and the *New York Times* hasn't really recognized the existence of an ultraliberal.

September 10, 1968
Or how's this: we could bring the boys back from Vietnam, send the Chicago police force to the DMZ, and hold the Democratic National Convention in Prague ...

November 19, 1968
The AMA has reported an outbreak of Spiro Angina among Democratic politicians. The ailment is a mild cardiac strain brought on by overuse of the lower metaphor, "only a heartbeat away."

June 30, 1970
Good morning, worry-warts. Today we're going to worry about yogurt. All flavors of yogurt—plain, strawberry, mandarin orange, Dutch apple, whortleberry, onion, camembert, chocolate, and fish. Seems if you eat nothing but yogurt for an extended period—yogurt by the metric ton—you will, so help us Ralph Nader, develop cataracts, provided of course you're a laboratory rat at Johns Hopkins which in itself is something to worry about. Them's the findings, and we mustn't dispute findings, so eat your chicken soup before they find out *it's* bad for you.

September 8, 1970
Who dows what we'd do without the U.S. Food ad Drug Adbidistratiod? Id adother bold bove to protect us frob ourselves, it's withdrawd fifteed bradds of dasal spray frob the barket, od the groudds that they really dod't do ady good. Praise the Lord ad pass the Kleedex.

Pleasures of a Birdman

William F. Rickenbacker

One horrible morning in January we took off in complete darkness even though the official time was dawn. Low clouds scudded across Ashiya, the temperature was 32°F, snow and rain were falling at once, the wind was gusty, everything seemed cold and wet and dark. So we pounded down the runway through the slush and got airborne and tucked up the wheels and climbed into the bituminous void and were lurching through the snow flurries when suddenly the blackness and the turmoil ripped down away from us and we rose into the spotless azure of morning. The clouds below us fell away into a rose-drenched oriental carpet. There, to the east, poised on the edge of the orb, the great bronze sun bids welcome.

Bluie West Eight was a tilted strip at the head of a cul-de-sac fjord in southwest Greenland. One morning at about 2:30 we took off for Scotland but before we headed out on course there was one small detail to take care of, namely a piece of ice two miles tall. So, in the moonlit morning, we circle over the patch of water at the head of the fjord, patiently lifting the transatlantic gas load we have just taken on board. Fifteen minutes after takeoff we are ready to approach the ice cap. The lights of Bluie West are still beneath us as we head out towards the pallid prehistoric rampart of ice. It glides beneath us, a continental mass of frozen dull refulgence, the graveyard of a thousand expeditions, a vast and silent and mortal trap.

For subtlety of color there is nothing to match the waters of a coral atoll in the Pacific. I think Kwajalein in particular, with its vast lagoon, a climax of green mounted in a halo of foaming blue. To be sure, there are sharks—was it Wilde who thought no pleasure perfect without a dash of danger?—and from the air one may yet pick out the wreck of a Japanese supply ship, or the empennage of a stout Grumman buried in the sands. But the imperceptible shift of color from the peridot purity of the beach in the lagoon to the oceanic blue— how does that happen? Who can paint it? And who can see it but the birds and their imitators?

Surely the sheer beauty of the earth, seen from above, is one of the greatest pulls in flying. But there are pleasures other than the purely aesthetic. To have the opportunity to study the earth from a modest altitude (say, 5,000 feet above the surface) is to be able to lay eye on historical forces, sociological trends, geological events. Fly from the East Coast to the West and watch what happens to the size and shape of the farms. Note where the land comes under the influence of the section-line surveyor. Dred Scott is mixed up in that.

Come to a river athwart your course—the Delaware, the Mississippi, it does not matter—and see how it thwarted the first settlers. A road leads to the river and then a town forms at the edge of the river and the town spreads upstream and downstream as if this flow of human energy were piling up, piling up against the river-obstacle until the energy bursts over the river on a great bridge or under the river through a tunnel. Then the town stops growing upstream and downstream and grows across-stream.

From a few thousand feet up, the western desert yields a narrative older than human life in the hemisphere. You can see streambeds that have been dry for twenty-thousand years. You can spot a bed of lava here and a similar bed sixty miles across the valley and you can deduce the spot where the eruption occurred. Around a river valley, especially in the West, you can mark the extreme limits of the greenish plant life and you will not be very far off if you say that in man's memory the river has never been known to flood beyond that point. You can watch an industrial plant spewing its poison into a river and measure the number of miles it takes downstream for the poisonous material to spread from bank to bank.

January 28, 1969

(And returning to the subject on November 18, 1969, Bill Rickenbacker wrote:)

I fly because the earth is a beautiful thing to look at, and the United States is a beautiful land. I fly because I meet the nicest names up there—Crazy Woman, Wyoming; Truth or Consequences, New Mexico; Huguenot, New York. One of those is a real town, the other two are names of radio navigation aids. They carry the burden of history, and the pilot who has been reading American history may fly through all the centuries of his native land in an hour or two. The woman was an Indian. The Huguenots settled here. The small airport east of La Junta is called Animas. By the Picketwire River. Why the Spanish word for "souls"? Why Picketwire? Because of Coronado. Four hundred and thirty years ago he and his men trekked two thousand miles through the Southwest in search of the storied treasures of Quivira. No soap. In what is now eastern Colorado some of his men fell to fighting, and there were several deaths and an equivalent number of burials beside the unnamed river— all in the absence of the priests, who had left the expedition before this point. The brawling soldiers were therefore sent to their reward without the benefit of the sacraments and were souls lost in purgatory. The Spanish named the river so: *Río de las ánimas perdidas en el purgatorio. Ánimas!* For convenience the name of the river was soon shortened to Purgatorio. Two centuries later the peripatetic French trappers, working south along the Rockies, came to this river and gave it the proper francophone monicker: Purgatoire. A difficult thing to pronounce, as any drunken cowpoke will tell you, and obviously a foolish French attempt to say the perfectly good English word "picketwire." So it is this day the Picketwire River, the Ánimas, the Río de las Ánimas, the Purgatoire, the Purgatory ... depending on the map you're using, or the plane you're flying.

Oh, I could write a book about flying. But you know something? I'd rather fly.

What Makes a Novelist

John Dos Passos

(Two excerpts from John Dos Passos's lecture to Galileo's Academy of Lynxes upon receiving the coveted Feltrinelli award.)

Part of my service was at the Italian front. We arrived soon after Caporetto. Aside from the excitement of the architecture—glimpses of Palladian buildings driving a Fiat ambulance through Vicenza—a breathtaking sight of Venice across a lagoon sheathed with a thin scrim of ice one winter day—there was the painting. I mention it because I am sure that the great narrative painting of the thirteen and fourteen hundreds profoundly influenced my ideas of how to tell a story in words.

Padua between airraids: when we looked, peeping through the sandbags, at Giotto's frescoes in the Arena Chapel the intensity of their homely narrative was immensely heightened by the feeling that perhaps we were the last men who would ever look on these masterpieces; and the feeling too that perhaps, perhaps, Giotto's Gospel tales might be the last thing we would experience on this earth.

There was, among many of the young people of my generation, a readiness to attempt great things. Giotto and Dante and Orcagna and Piero della Francesca—to mention only a few of the influences we were sopping up like sponges between bouts of driving the poor wounded back from the trenches on Monte Grappa—these men had made eternal their view of the world they lived in. It was up to us to try to describe in colors that would not fade, our America that we loved and hated.

The road had been opened for us. In the United States Crane and Dreiser had already transferred Zola's naturalism to the American scene. James Joyce was knocking established ideas on the novel into a cocked hat with his *Ulysses*. The influence of *Ulysses*, out of snippets printed in the little magazines, was already rampant long before the publication of the book. Artistic styles, like epidemics and popular songs, are borne in the air. They cross the wildest oceans, the most tightly barred frontiers.

From Europe, mostly through the painters of the School of Paris, the artistic ferment of the period between the Paris Exposition of 1900 and the outbreak of war in 1914 was spreading across the world.

After the armistice, during the winter of 1918-1919 while still in the army—the U.S. Army had taken over the old volunteer services the year before—I managed to get myself into what was known as the Sorbonne

Detachment. Servicemen who had either started or finished college were allowed to attend European universities while waiting for their turn to be shipped home. I had become obsessed with the need to write a novel about soldiers. While I went through the motions of attending lectures at the Sorbonne I wrote and wrote in a little room on the Ile St. Louis.

Paris in those years really was the capital of Europe. So-called modern painting—how stale that word modern has become!—really was fresh from the palette in those days: les Fauves, the Cubists, Modigliani, Juan Gris, Picasso. This too, was the Paris of new schools of music. Satie presided over Les Six. There were Poulenc, and Milhaud. Stravinksy was beginning to be heard. The Diaghilev ballet was promoting a synthesis of all the arts.

Paris in 1919. It's hard to reimagine the feelings of savage joy and bitter hatred we felt during that spring. Most of my friends were still in uniform. I was an enlisted man. Never got confirmed even in the rank of sergeant. A doughboy with the rest of them. We still had to salute officers, to sneak into out-of-the-way bistros to talk to our friends who happened to be wearing gold or silver bars. But with the armistice each one of us had been handed his life back on a platter. We knew what dead men looked like and we weren't dead.

The horsechestnuts were in bloom. We knew the world was a lousy pest house of idiocy and corruption, but it was spring. The Peace Conference was going on. We knew that in all the ornate buildings, under the crystal chandeliers, under the brocade hangings, the politicians and diplomats were brewing poison, huddled old men festering like tentcaterpillars in a tangle of red tape and gold braid. What they were doing was too obvious and too clear. The people of the world would wake up. It was spring. The first of May was coming. We'd burn out the tentcaterpillars.

We believed we knew two things about the world. We subscribed to two dogmas which most of us have since had to modify or scrap. We were convinced that life in the militarized industrialized nations had become a chamber of horrors and we believed that plain men, the underdogs we rubbed shoulders with, were not such a bad lot as they might be. They wouldn't go out of their way to harm each other as often as you might expect. They had a passive courage and certain ingrained impulses towards social cohesiveness, towards the common good. Loafing about in little old bars full of the teasing fragrances of history, dodging into alleys to keep out of sight of the military police, seeing the dawn from Montmartre, talking bad French with taxi-drivers, riverbank loafers, working-men, poilus on leave, petite femmes, we young hopefuls eagerly collected intimations of the urge towards the common good.

It seemed so simple to burn out the caterpillars who were ruining the orchard. The first of May was coming.

We felt boisterous and ill-mannered. Too many sergeants had told us to wipe that smile off your face. Too many buglers had gotten us up out of our blankets before we had slept our sleep out. It seemed to us that the only thing of value that survived the war was this automatic social cohesiveness among men that came on whenever they slipped for a moment out from under the spell of the demagogues.

The storied skyscrapers of civilization were tottering. If the old edifice crashed the bosses who lived in the upper stories would go down with it. They had already pretty well shaken the foundations with their pretty war, their brilliant famines. Their diligent allies, typhus, cholera, influenza were working for them still. Now their peace would finish the job.

"All together boys. A couple of heaves and down she'll go. When the dust clears we'll see whether men and women are the besotted brutes the bosses say they are."

This was all fifty years ago.

Now we know that the first of May will never come. Where the workers conquered they allowed themselves to be overwhelmed by regimes even more oppressive than the old regimes they had overthrown. But in these resentful hopes, in these crushing disappointments, these callow enthusiasms lay the roots of satire. By the time I had finished *Three Soldiers*, the book I was working on in Paris, I was beginning to dream of novels that would throw into sharp satiric focus the grandeurs and miseries, the crime and the heroism of the world I knew. I knew damn well the novel was not dead.

The Writer as Hunter

During the last fifty years we have heard endless arguments on this topic. The artist must be *engagé*. The artist must be *degagé*. He must free himself from the propaganda and the demagoguery of his age. The discussion is fruitless. Artistic works to be of lasting value must be both engaged and disengaged. They must have a certain lift, a certain aloofness that separates them from the obsessions of the hour. At the same time they must encompass—in no matter how modest or fragmentary a way—the whole range of the human spirit.

The aim of narrative writing, or poetry or painting or abstract design has been the same since the time of Aristotle and long before. It has been to give the pleasure that all men feel in the expression of skill and through that pleasure in skill, to furnish the catharsis that comes from a heightened understanding, a simplification, a formalization of the unbearable turmoil of life clattering about men's ears. No matter what his method may be it is the narrator's objectivity, sometimes hidden, sometimes apparent, that gives humane value to his narrative. Keats was right when he exclaimed that beauty was truth and truth beauty.

For the novelist, his work is an endless struggle between his passions and prejudices and his need to turn them to good purpose in the objective description of the life around him.

Observing objectivity demands a sort of virginity of the perceptions. Each time he sits down at his desk a man has to clear all preconceived notions out of his head.

The sensitivity of a man's perceptions is in no way increased by the painful squinting of the eyes and the anxious straining of the ears. The state of mind of the dispassionate observer is somewhat analogous to the hunter's. An expert hunter in a duck blind, or walking behind his dogs round the edges of a cornfield, or waiting by a deerpath in the woods, thinks of nothing. He forgets himself. He lets all his senses come awake to respond to the frailest intimations that come to his ears or his eyes of the movement of game. Really good shots, the fellows who really bring down the quail, are people who are able to forget who they are and become for the moment just an eye and an ear and a gun.

To report objectively some scene, some person, the gestures two people make when meeting on the street, the movement of some animal, the shape of some organism under the microscope, the writer has to fall just an instant into the hunter's state of unpreoccupied alertness.

The hunter has to know what to look for. For years he must have been building up a bank of experience. An expert ornithologist can give one glance into a thicket. Where I see only some English sparrows he can pick up a wren sitting on her nest and three different kinds of warblers. As a result of a lifetime of observation a good hunter can tell, from the slight disturbance of twigs and pinetags on a path through the woods whether it was a deer or a raccoon that just passed that way. The trained novelist has to develop this sort of capacity.

He has to conquer his own professional deformations. By the nature of his occupations the man of letters tends to become a man of words and not of deeds. His attention is likely to be on the name of the thing rather than on the thing itself. The literate man tends to believe that when he has named, labeled and pigeonholed some event, some sight, some manifestation of the manifold oddities of life, he has disposed of it. He is likely to apply the label before he has really observed the object. To observe objectively a man has to retain something of childhood's naive and ignorant state of mind. In my experience children and illiterate people often see things more exactly than educated men. The first-rate novelist like the first-rate scientist must be obsessed by his own ignorance. This conviction of ignorance is the first step towards understanding. Astonishment strangely quickens the senses.

To See and to Express

Curiosity is the key. I wonder sometimes if the curiosity which makes a man want to see clearer and clearer isn't related to the hunters' or trackers' alertness which might well have been the quality most needed for survival far back in the history of the race.

The state of mind that makes for objective description, like every state of mind in which you forget who you are, has a sort of primeval happiness about it. You look out at the world with a fresh eye as if it were the morning of the first day of creation.

There is a lucid little paragraph that has given me great pleasure in an English translation of William Harvey's *Circulation of the Blood*. Harvey by the way became a doctor of medicine in Padua at about the time this Academy of the Lynxes was first founded.

Let me read it to you:

> We have a small shrimp in these countries, which is taken in the Thames and in the sea, the whole of whose body is transparent; this creature, placed in a little water, has frequently afforded myself and particular friends an opportunity of observing the motions of the heart with the greatest distinctiveness, the extreme parts of the body presenting no obstacle to our view, but the heart being perceived as though it had been seen through a window.

The aim, the never quite attainable aim of the novelist or historian is to see men's private emotions and their movements in masses as clearly as William Harvey saw the heart of the shrimp and to express what they see as lucidly as Harvey did in the little paragraph I have just read. Undoubtedly this sort of seeing was what Galileo's friends had in mind when they called this academy the Academy of Lynxes.

To see clearly and to express clearly what he sees is still the writer's aim, but with all the narrative skill in the world, how hard it is to attain!

January 16, 1968

The Roots of Honor

Jeffrey Hart

Evelyn Waugh's Crouchback trilogy is a great modern work, a classic of our time. In it Waugh has succeeded in disciplining his energies by means of a complex overall design, and so can establish meanings more ambitious than he had attempted before. As far as its religious themes are concerned, the novel completes the development begun in *Brideshead*, and it will give no comfort to critics who assert, rather hooperishly, that Waugh confuses Catholicism with *Burke's Peerage*. It is also the novel about the Second World War, the one which best assays its actual meaning.

One need read no more than a sentence or two of Waugh to become initiated into his fictional world, for his prose does not merely convey narrative information, but, through its cadences, its diction, and its timing, fully expresses his vision. Take his opening:

> When Guy Crouchback's grandparents, Gervase and Hermione, came to Italy on their honeymoon, French troops manned the defenses of Rome, the sovereign Pontiff drove out in an open carriage and Cardinals took their exercise side-saddle on the Pincian Hill.

Waugh remarks elsewhere that the study of Latin disciplines one's prose. What we find in his own is just such discipline of syntax but, played off against content that may be gently *outré*, as here ("Crouchback," "Gervase," "Hermione," those side-saddle Cardinals) or elsewhere moves into the really odd, the outrageous, or the catastrophic.

Waugh's world is one in which we are delighted to meet "Guy's uncle Peregrine, a bore of international repute whose dreaded presence would empty the room in any center of civilization"—but it is therefore also one in which we are not surprised to meet Brigadier Ritchie-Hook, a "legendary wielder of the entrenching tool" who "once came back from a raid across no-man's land with the dripping head of a German sentry in either hand." And because Waugh's vision can accommodate oddity and outrage it is congruent with actuality: the world is like that—as Waugh demonstrates by making public history part of the structure of his novel. Thus, the "Russian-German alliance shook the politicians and young poets of a dozen capital cities." Or, again, "Churchill's broadcasts had been played on the mess wireless set. Guy had found them painfully boastful and they had, most of them, been immediately followed by the news of some disaster." Thus, England went to war over the German invasion of Poland, and, in a macroscopic pratfall quite in keeping with

Waugh's sense of the absurd, ended up as an ally of Soviet Russia—the country which originally had helped to make the war possible, and which (cream of the jest!) had helped to dismember Poland. The concrete issue in the war, as George Kennan somewhere remarks, was whether Germany or Russia would dominate Eastern Europe. For her pains, England barely survived—to go shabbily broke and socialist.

Two large narrative movements, one ascending and the other descending, order the profusion of events in *Sword of Honour*. It is the story of Crouchback's salvation, and, simultaneously, of the dismemberment of Christendom. There is space here to indicate only the outlines of this design.

Like Charles Ryder of *Brideshead*, Guy Crouchback embarks upon a mistaken pilgrimage, learning in the end that order and meaning are not to be found where he had sought them. Each time he seems to find them, they turn out to be only apparent, not real, and quickly succumb to flux or farce. The Halberdiers and the Commandos, Broome and Bellamy's, the Allied Cause— none escapes. Ivor Claire, aristocrat and horseman,"quintessential England" as Guy thinks, deserts his men on Crete. Ritchie-Hook, a kind of Churchillian alter ego, dies absurdly in Yugoslavia during a phony battle rigged by English Communists to improve Tito's public relations, while Tito himself "runs rings around" Churchill, who has been advised that Tito is something like Garibaldi. England, after declaring war on Finland (!), deserts her Serbian allies.

The developing social tone of the novel reinforces its theme of public disintegration, moving gradually from the traditional atmosphere of the Halberdiers to that of parvenus on the make (Trimmer and Ian Kilbannock), and arriving finally at that of the Soviet alliance and the People's War, with its ersatz relic, the Stalingrad Sword in Westminster Abbey (implicitly, the sword of dishonor), and a cowed and proletarian England, ready to "queue up" for anything. As the novel comes to an end, the sinister Ludovic and an assortment of Communist conspirators dominate the scene.

The theme of disorder, of course, is central to Waugh's other novels, but in none of them does it have the poignancy it has here. One example: Apthorpe with his Thunder-Box (an elaborate Edwardian portable toilet) is an immortal clown; on another level, he represents the solipsism and self-indulgence of pre-war England; but when he dies of fever in Africa we remember Apthorpe the schoolboy at Staplehurst: "Here lay the fields where muddy Apthorpe had kept goal ... the sanctuary where clean Apthorpe in lace collar had lighted the tapers." That Apthorpe was English, too (though even here there are Waughian ironies).

Though Waugh has sometimes been accused of an idolatrous worship of tradition and aristocracy, it is the very point of *Sword of Honour* that these things are only proximate sources of order and meaning, not final ones, and that a genuine eschatology must transcend them. Crouchback pursues a mistaken pilgrimage, but God "with a twitch upon the string" brings him to a recognition that order must be first an inward thing. "Pride," as Yeats said, "must be established in humility." "If a man have not order within him," wrote Pound in the *Cantos*, "he cannot spread order about him." Thus Guy Crouchback, shorn of illusion, and cuckolded by his wife and a parvenu hairdresser, saves his own soul, and redefines honor, by taking the child as his own. Meaning, we understand, does not finally reside in the world of events but in the submission of the will in charity. As Guy's father tells him, in the life of the spirit "quantitative judgments do not apply."

Evelyn Waugh is a great novelist. Do not bet on him to get the Nobel Prize. Still, he most certainly knows where in the hierarchy of values such prizes belong.

February 22, 1966

Evelyn Waugh, R I P

I once encountered a very angry lady in Dallas, Texas, who announced herself head of a vigilance committee to keep dirty books out of the local libraries, and we talked a bit. I forgot just how the conversation moved, but at one point I said that to pull out all the salacious passages from modern literature would require the end of individual reading. All of us would have private readers, like the old eccentric who forced his prisoners to read to him the works of Charles Dickens in the novel by Evelyn Waugh. Who, asked the lady book critic, was Evelyn Waugh? The greatest English novelist of the century, I ventured, but on ascertaining that he was not a dirty writer, she lost all interest, and went off to look for more dirty books to rail against.

I wrote Waugh and told him about the episode. My letter did not include any reference to any business matter, so I knew he would not reply to it; but I knew the little story would appeal to his sense of satire, so strongly developed as to make him, in the judgment of the critic Edmund Wilson, the "only first-rate comic genius the English have produced since George Bernard Shaw." (Waugh's reply, several years later to an interviewer who asked what was *his* opinion of Edmund Wilson: "Is he American?" End comment.) But Waugh was much more than that, though millions of his readers who read only *Handful of Dust*, and *Scoop*, and *The Loved One*, did not know about the other dimensions; did not know that Evelyn Waugh the great satirist was a conservative, a traditionalist, a passionately convinced and convincing Christian, a master stylist routinely acknowledged, during the last decade, as the most finished writer of English prose.

He died at 62 having completed only one volume of a long autobiography. In it he recorded, dispassionately, the impressions of his early years; something of the lives of his ancestors, many of them eccentric; and of the chaos of his undergraduate career at Oxford, from which he was duly expelled, as so many interesting Englishmen are expected to be. He decided, in his mid-twenties, that the thing to do was to commit suicide, and he describes, as he would in a novel, his own venture in this dramatic activity—the verse from Euripides about water washing away the stains of the earth, neatly exposed where it could not be missed by grieving relatives and meticulous coroners; wading out into the ocean, thinking diapasonal thoughts; then running into a school of jellyfish, and racing back to the beach, putting on his clothes, tearing up Euripides, and resuming his career, for which we thank God's little jellyfish.

He was an impossible man, in many respects. At least as far as the public was concerned. Like J. D. Salinger and James Gould Cozzens, he simply refused to join the world of flackery and televised literature. On one occasion when he did consent to grant an interview to a young correspondent from *Paris Review*, because he was related to an old friend, Waugh thoroughly disconcerted the interviewer by arriving at his hotel suite, taking off his clothes, getting into bed, lighting a huge cigar, breaking open a bottle of champagne, and then uttering: "Proceed."

Rather than live a public life, he situated himself in a large old house in the country, surrounding himself with a moat that was proof against all but his closest friends, and the vicar. The piranhas made a specialty of devouring first-class mail asking for interviews, comments, suggestions, whatever. I confess to having successfully swum across the moat, after several fruitless assaults. I discovered that the squire felt an obligation to reply to all letters concerning questions of commerce; so that if you wanted a comment or two on a matter of literature or philosophy or politics, you could hope to get it by dropping into your letter a trivial question relating to business.

But he was a man of charity, personal generosity, and, above all, of understanding. He knew people, he knew his century, and, having come to know it, he had faith only in the will of God, and in individual man's latent capacity to strive towards it. He acknowledged the need to live in this century, because the jellyfish will not have it otherwise; but never, ever, to acclimate yourself to it. Mr. Scott-King, the classics teacher, after his tour through Evelyn Waugh's *Modern Europe*, comes back to school, and there the headmaster suggests that he teach some popular subject, in addition to the classics—economic history, perhaps, for the classics are not popular. "I'm a Greats man myself," the headmaster says. "I deplore it as much as you do. But what can we do? Parents are not interested in producing the 'complete man' anymore. They want to qualify their boys for jobs in the public world. You can hardly blame them, can you?" "Oh yes," Scott-King replies, "I can and do." And, deaf to the headmaster's entreaties, he declares, shyly but firmly, "I think it would be very wicked indeed to do anything to fit a boy for the modern world." Waugh got the best of the modern world, but paid a high price for it: he gave it his genius.

—William F. Buckley Jr.
May 3, 1966

Evelyn Waugh, Supersnob

Sir Arnold Lunn

One of the most amusing afternoons I ever spent with Waugh began in the London Library. He took me around in a taxi to White's, which was only five minutes' walk on foot, and ordered a bottle of champagne in the bar. To the barman, he said, "I'd like you to produce a *really* nourishing sandwich for my friend. He's an author, but not successful like I am, and he looks rather underfed."

We took a specially chartered limousine to Paddington where he missed his train. Back to White's where Waugh ordered another bottle of champagne. He asked me to come down to spend the night with him in the country, but I never accept that kind of invitation after the second bottle of champagne. I did, however, again drive with him to Paddington. "How do you propose," he asked, "to go back to the slum in which you live?" I replied that I'd take the Underground. "No, my friend," said Waugh. "You shall go back in my car. This is a day in fairyland for you."

February 27, 1968

Where Are You, Fr. O'Brien?
Where Are You, Fr. Fitzgerald?

John Brennan

There was a time when all the Catholic clergy in the United States were Irish. Or so it seemed. They came in two sizes, the Pat O'Brien and the Barry Fitzgerald. The Pat O'Briens were men's men and frequently seemed to be seven feet tall. All of them had given up careers in major league baseball to enter the seminary and they packed a wicked right cross with which they sometimes dealt with those sinners who seemed beyond blarney and blandishment. The Pat O'Briens were best at what was then termed "social work." They could talk gunmen down from tenement roofs in the days when no one but Paddy rode in the paddy wagon, front or back.

The Pat O'Briens were especially good at forming basketball teams out of delinquent gangs and at getting final repentance out of quavering criminals when they lay dying in the gutter, 83 bullet holes between the clavicles, in front of the slum parishes where they had once served as altar boys. The O'Brien priest could also brace up a condemned murderer, frequently a childhood friend who had gone wrong, so that he could walk the last mile to the chair like a man. "Steady, lad. It will all be over in a minute and you'll be with the angels."

You could count on the O'Briens in moments of national peril. They recruited shamelessly. "Sonny McKernan, the Hun is sinking our ships and you not in the navy. Let me walk you to the recruiting station." The O'Brien types became chaplains themselves and won untold battles. "Strategy isn't in this old Sky Pilot's line—but if two of you Marines could work your way around that clump of brush we'd have those Japs where we want them."

The Pat O'Brien type is gone. He's throwing duck blood on the Draft Board records.

The Barry Fitzgerald type was a crusty, cantankerous codger whose life revolved around getting money to keep his rundown parochial school operating so that the myriad children of his parish would not be exposed to the numerous perils of a secular education. He thought integration meant going to school with Protestants. The Fitzgerald type was preoccupied with the managerial responsibilities of the priesthood and was very poor at organizing basketball teams. He left that to his curate who usually looked very much like Bing Crosby. Sometime during his pastorhood, however, a basketball would bounce near him and he would kick it back to the boys who were playing and this event would become a parish legend. He refused to recognize the presence of another sex on the planet with the exception of the Blessed Mother and his own dear departed saintly mother. He regarded the sisters who taught in his schools on some days as angelic helpers sent from on High but on most days as trials sent to test his dwindling reserves of patience.

The Barry Fitzgerald type is gone. The Urban Renewers have torn down the old neighborhood and his parishioners have fled to suburbia. He hasn't seen his Crosbyish curate for six months. He eloped with the Mother Superior.

March 11, 1969—Letter from a (Disgruntled) Catholic

Presidential Politics: Campaign '68 The Candidates

George Wallace

James Jackson Kilpatrick

He weighs 155 pounds, soaking wet, and stands a shade under five-feet-seven. Quick hands. Nimble feet. Brown eyes; dark brows; black wavy hair. In full face, chewing a thick cigar, he brings back the image of Edward G. Robinson in the days of Little Caesar. He is a man in constant motion—a go-cart, a catamount, a mockingbird, a bearcat; he is the cue-ball that dominates the table. To Louisiana's Governor John McKeithen, he is a "champion of constitutional liberties." In the view of Barry Goldwater, "he's a conservative and he's a disaster." This bantamweight bull-calf, plunging toward the political china shops of 1968 is George Corley Wallace of Alabama. ... He is built in the Menckenian image of the man who mastered a notable acrobatic art: He can strut sitting down. He's running for President.

The Governor, as he still is universally known [his wife Lurleen was governor at this time] does not converse; he falls into platform speeches—the raised arm, the clenched first, the pointing finger, the pauses for applause. He comes at you in a firehose torrent of arguments, questions, assertions, refutations, digressions. He is full of nervous stage business: standing up, sitting down, the horn-rimmed glasses on, the glasses off, lighting his cigar, licking his cigar, spitting in the wastebasket. There is never a moment of stillness. He is constantly bouncing on the ring ropes and shuffling in the corner, shadow boxing, skipping rope. For 25 years, man and boy, I have been interviewing politicians and I have met some mighty talkers. But George Wallace is the greatest nonstop talker of them all.

April 18, 1967

George Romney

James Jackson Kilpatrick

Romney is distinctive only in his salesman's approach. He sells verities as if he were selling sedans; his "New America" is the '68 model. Go on, he seems to be urging—drive her around the block a few times. He is a hood-thumper, a tire-kicker, a door-slammer. He was born to be number one in the salesmen's annual contest. He is green stamps, Tigerama, door prizes, and the year-end bonus. His performance this Saturday morning (the day he announced his presidential candidacy) was a first-rate performance, fresh from the sales manager's manual, well planned to launch a marketable product in a hotly competitive race. Yet it made no vivid impression on the visiting press. "What's the lead?" asked a man from the Gannett papers. "Fearless Fosdick runs again," said his seatmate. And the reporters trooped off to write their copy...

Whatever the causes, Romney heads into the campaign with a reputation as an argumentative finger-jabber, a lapel-grabber, and a fist-pounder. He is the salesman who *knows* he offers the finest product. He can barely tolerate resistance....

One's impression of Romney today is that he is a man who always is charging the net. When ordinary men are still in restful slumber, he is out running around the golf course. Ordinary men have likes and dislikes in food, and sometimes they take a flier in exotic dishes. Not the governor of Michigan. Ordinary men, slicing off the tee, will let fall a damn or hell. Not George. Doggone, he says. Most men sixty or thereabouts have a bulge around the middle. Not George. Most men tend to get a little rumpled as a day wears on. Not George: he is regularly numbered among the nation's best dressed men. Most men, gazing upon a garden, scarcely know a petunia from a pansy; Romney tends his own garden, and knows every plant by botanical name.

Why did the people of Athens turn upon Aristides? Had he done them injury? "None at all," a voter explained. "I don't even know the man. But I am tired of hearing him everywhere called the Just."

December 12, 1967

Eugene McCarthy

James Jackson Kilpatrick

Eugene McCarthy looked relieved. For the first time, he smiled; he does not smile often, one surmises, except inside. This smile was nothing to compare with Ike's grin or Romney's Pepsodent ramparts; it was a modest smile, the smile of a man reading Thurber in bed by himself; but it was not a politician's smile. The Senator, one observes, is a most impolitic politician.

This became evident as the evening wore along. McCarthy went from the press conference to a room across the hall where 300 guests had gathered for a reception at $50 a head. If any other presidential candidate had been making such an entrance, he would have made an *entrance*. There would have been a band, a greeting committee, a sense of the Very Important Personage arriving. He arrived as inconspicuously as a rowboat docking on a millpond. The hotel's loudspeakers were delivering rock 'n' roll music at full volume. The Senator's first words were: "Could someone turn that noise off?"

Once the noise subsided, and the guests discovered their presidential candidate was in their midst, the reception went quite well. McCarthy seemed at ease. Once he visibly winced when a tweedy arm was thrown across his back, but generally he was on his best behavior. Most of the women were 34 and all the men were a lightly graying 45. A covey of quail in mod stockings, green and white, added a Briarcliff touch. Even at the shrimp bar, the Senator could not escape the war in Vietnam. A bosomy woman in green chiffon pressed him close. "Oh, Senator," she breathed, "let's get out of there *now*." The Senator gave her his Rushmore look, and disengaged his arm.

At seven o'clock, Messrs. Rauh, Kennan, Ireland, Hewlett, assorted committee members, and 1,300 paying guests filed into the banquet hall for the fund-raising dinner. The head table stretched for thirty yards. Above the table, fastened to a great gold curtain, a banner unrolled in red and white: "EUGENE MCCARTHY FOR PRESIDENT." A mammoth portrait of the candidate, bunting bedecked, beamed upon the throng. And where was the candidate himself? He was upstairs, if the truth must be told, with his coat off and his vest unbuttoned, sipping Jack Daniels and eating a congenial steak dinner with the two Washington reporters. ...

McCarthy descended to the ballroom at 8:20. It was precisely as before. A different candidate would have made an entrance through the throng itself, but not McCarthy. The next President of the United States, as alas, he was never introduced, arrived at his largest campaign dinner unannounced. He surfed to the speakers' table on a wave of nice applause, and sat down at once between a crew-cut professor, white-carnationed, and a pneumatic brunette, pink-badged, gold-earringed, who came from New Brunswick. Dessert was being served.

At 8:57 Greg Hewlett opened proceedings with his sad-happy talk. The candidate sat, hand over mouth, apparently thinking of something else entirely.

At 9:16 Joe Rauh took the lectern, his lumberjack face aglow with a fund-raiser's zeal. He asked for $40,000 "to walk with Gene McCarthy in New Hampshire," and the checks came rolling up. Then George Kennan came on, big and leather-crowned and just a tremor in his hands, to make the introduction speech that would steal all the headlines in the morning *New York Times*—a coruscating denunciation of the war. At 9:48.30, he launched into a concluding man-who paragraph. Wearily, rubbing his face, the man-who arose.

Now, if Mark Twain were around to report these affairs, he surely would remark McCarthy's disdain for the rules of such occasions. The rules require that a presidential candidate, on being introduced, shall give forth with a smile exhibiting not fewer than 22 teeth, including the eight bicuspids. McCarthy limited his display to twelve. Arriving at the microphone, a candidate is expected fully to elevate at least one arm, and preferably both; the Senator did not respond in kind. The circumstances dictated a pair of jokes as openers, one at the expense of Joe Rauh, to be followed by a tribute to the beautiful ladies of New Jersey. The Senator ignored this duty altogether.

The statutes make it clear that a candidate may not appeal to the intelligence of the audience before him. He may properly appeal to patriotism, to partisanship, or to pugilistic instincts; he may dwell upon the necessity for preserving the Republic from the depredations of the Administration in power. Other appeals should be reserved for smaller occasions. A candidate is expected to speak not less than 45 minutes and to gesture not fewer than 128 times. Poetry must be limited strictly—two passages from Shakespeare and one from Edgar A. Guest; no other authors are allowed. If a prepared text has been distributed to the press, at least a substantial part of the text should actually be delivered.

McCarthy paid no heed to these rules. "I have a limited measure of courage," he began. Those were his very words. He spoke for barely 23 minutes, and he made no gestures at all. He launched into a high-level discussion of Vietnam and went on to speak movingly of the Negro as a "colonial" in America. He had distributed a text to the press, but he never came within four and one-half miles of that text. He alluded to the poetry of Dylan Thomas and actually quoted from Robert Lowell. He summoned George Orwell to his side; he invoked Toynbee on the history of Rome. The 1,300 guests interrupted twelve times with applause; mostly they sat entranced. When he concluded, they gave him a 1:40-minute standing ovation. It was a good deal short of Barry playing the Cow Palace, but it wasn't bad.

Nor was this the end of the heresy. The rules of fund-raising dinners require absolutely that upon completion of the speeches, the candidate proceed at once to conferences with his local managers.

The gentleman from Minnesota, never having heard of the protocol for presidential candidates, ducked out of the throng as if the devil were at his heels. He took the first elevator to his ninth-floor suite, and retired to his room. The two Washington reporters tagged along. The Senator once again got out of his coat, unbuttoned his vest, surveyed the Jack Daniels, and put his feet on a coffee table. Was he talking high politics till midnight? No, indeed. He was talking mainly of Yeats and Lowell and of Theodore Roethke and Vernon Watkins. And because the reporters lightly pressed him, he talked of the path that had led him to Newark that night.

April 9, 1968

Presidential Politics: Campaign '68
The Conventions

The Nixon Convention

Garry Wills

They arrived [at the Republican convention in Miami] in the order of their chances—the Glamor Boys first, all so bright last January, all suddenly dimmed: Percy everywhere, in the ghetto, in the pool, on the tennis courts; Lindsay, tanned bemused Gregory Peck, trying to insert something in the platform to justify his being Republican; Romney, still electric with the wild unexpellable poisons of his hope renounced. For four years, ever since Gold-

Richard M. Nixon

water's defeat, they had been telling themselves—using their private Western Union, the *New York Times*, to transmit the mes-sage back and forth—that the future of the Republican Party, assuming it to have any fu-ture at all, was wrapped in their shiny tresses. The Right had tried, and failed, and died. The Party would mend its ways now or perish. ...

The real crush came at Nixon's headquarters in the Hilton Plaza, which was henceforth as much the center of the convention as the official headquarters: the Fontainebleau. Traffic was blocked off; a Negro band minstreled away; multi-colored squirts of balloons went bumping up the hotel facade as boys opened large cardboard crates of the gas-inflated toys; the official slogan was everywhere (even one very pregrant woman had a button proclaiming Nixon's the One); a nervous snap in the air, set off in part by toy "grasshoppers" given out so the crowd could "click with Dick."

The clicking would go on all week, in and out of the convention hall, the quiet but omnipresent music of the *fait accompli*. No trumpets. No trombones. Just Clicky Dick.

The deals, the smiles and knives, that followed; the big push to get over on the first ballot. The thing that could not happen, had—a convention sewed up in advance by conservative votes, just like Goldwater's. But done this time, not as a rebellion, by a militant conservative shock force; quietly, rather, by a man also wooing the Left whenever he could get it over in a corner, out of the Hon. Strom's eagle eye (the Hon. Ron had no chance against the Hon. Strom this time out). The Party had not undergone any great internal convulsion. It had simply caved, sifted, and crumbled in upon its center, and the name of the resulting sandpile was Nixon. That the center of the Party turned out to be farther right than people had expected will grow less and less surprising. Apparently the center of the country is farther right now.

August 27, 1968

Convention in the Streets

Garry Wills

T he keynote of the kids' clothing is softness. No edges. Even last year's military jackets have the padding torn out—droopy epaulettes, wilted fronts, frayed bottoms, every sag and hang saying "I ain't marchin' any more." All things tend to be shaggy—soft fringes of adolescent beard, girls' eyes in a shadowy thicket of mascara. The clothes are all of the muffling, involving sort—blankets, capes, serapes, shepherd's coats, hoods, woolly sweaters. Velvet, velour, fur—the favorite hats are Russian astrakhan, soft Indian bead-band, Arab turbans, Foreign Legion veils, swaths; colorful (prophetic) bandages. The shoes are moccasins, soft boots, sandals worn to a velvet pliancy—Paul Krassner takes the thing to its logical term, wearing shoes made of some carpet-stuff that looks like grass. But better even than moccasins are bare feet. The rags are not true cast-offs, though they look worn (mainly because they are slept in and never changed). Girls' bell-bottom pants, for instance, are almost mandatory—worn, preferably, with a light short-sleeve sweater; otherwise, jerseys or T-shirts. No brassières, of course. No edges.

The soft yielding quality extends to the hair, worn in two styles—first, the long divided wavering waterfall; second, the Elsa Lanchester (or electrocuted) style—fizzing out in all directions. Beards are as full as they can be grown—never trimmed. That is why the gentle, supple flow is prized when it comes out naturally. ("Like J. C." one boy nudged another as they saw a male madonna-face go by them under a helmet.) Hair is the sacrament of the real. Some girls affect unshaven armpits. They make a cult of candor, honesty, bluntness, sure that the reality of things is, underneath painted facades, rather dirty, grainy, grubby—the nitty-gritty. They are willing, their carefully chosen symbols say, to face this reality even in themselves; their own sordidness, seediness, their own—well, hair.

September 24, 1968

Gin Fizz

Colm Brogan

(Articles in Time, Esquire, *and the* New York Times *on London lead to certain reflections on London and, en passant, on British mores and customs. Mr. Brogan was at his irreverent best en passant.)*

The subject is London. It is not that I have any strong desire to write about London, but everybody else seems to be doing it and I don't want to be left out of the act.

On the third Sunday in June, intellectual ferment boiled all over the Albert Hall. The occasion was a Full Moon festival of poets, with audience participation cordially invited and a Happening broadly hinted at. The audience participated, all right. The four-letter words that were the main offering of many of the poets were enthusiastically taken up by the crowd, a large proportion of whom were dead drunk. The organized chant, the main piece of the entertainment, was drowned out by a four-letter antiphon shouted from thousands of young throats. Vanessa Redgrave, the actress, appeared dressed as a Cuban freedom fighter, accompanied by Christopher Logue, the poet, who was dressed as Fidel himself. Vanessa's recitation did not go over awfully well. By the time she appeared, a fair number of the audience were unconscious, others were slugging it out, and the rest were making a four-letter noise like thunder everlastingly. The organizer was so disappointed with the performance that he went off to Majorca to write a poem about it.

John Osborne's latest play, staged at the National Theater, created some more ferment, with the author himself handsomely contributing. The play, called *A Bond Honored*, is a freely adapted version of what is an almost certainly corrupt text of a play that is by no means certainly by Lope de Vega. The play is far removed from the conventions of a drawing room comedy. There is murder, castration, sadism, savagery, and one rape among many that has elements of obscurity. The hero rapes his sister, but as he had raped his mother many years before, he is by no means sure that the sister is not really his daughter. I suppose that makes her a kind of half sister. In a program note, Mr. Osborne said that the play has special relevance to our present day. He must lead an exciting life.

* * * *

I hope and believe that beneath the surface froth London remains calmly indifferent to fortune, chance, change or outside opinion. Take the *Times* (the *real Times*). For years Fleet Street has been alive with rumor that the *Times* would at last bow to the *zeitgeist* and put news on the front page. At last the dread day dawned. Not only did the *Times* come out with news on the front page, but it also had a gossip column. This was like Queen Victoria dancing the can-can.

The lead story of the first gossip column concerned that swinging object, of Stop Press immediacy, the Leaning Tower of Pisa. Did you know that the Tower not only leans, but also revolves? It will revolve something like two inches in 900 years. No other paper ever thought of this offbeat approach. Having decided on change, the editor was neither to hold nor to bind. He had an action photograph on a sports page, a cricket photograph. Other papers had weakly conventional pictures of batsmen smiting the ball or of bowlers leaping down the field like kangaroos with malice intent. But not the *Times*. The *Times* had a picture of three English cricketers standing in the middle of the field drinking lemonade. The text below explained that it was rather unusually early in the season for cricketers to want lemonade. Once again, the stimulating offbeat approach. This reminded me of the occasion when Randolph Turpin shattered the entire boxing world by beating Sugar Ray Robinson for the world middleweight title. Next day the *Times* carried a long, erudite, and entertaining leading article on the Ring and its oddities, but nowhere in the whole paper was there any mention of the fight itself, not even the result. My dear friend Gene Fowler was in London at the time. He liked that. He liked it a lot.

It cannot be denied that London has ill-wishers and false friends. For example, there is the man who recently reviewed a book on Boston for the *Times Literary Supplement*. Reviews in the *Times Lit* are always unsigned, but internal evidence strongly suggested that this particular job was done by a man who has academic connections both with Cambridge (Mass.) and Cambridge (Eng.). A man of wide reading, he lacks profundity and perception. He pointed out with unseemly pleasure that the Boston Athenaeum was founded before the London Athenaeum. So, as the saying goes, what? *Gammer Gurton's Needle* was written before *Hamlet*. Need I say more?

The reviewer made another point, not entirely without interest. He said that the classical frieze which decorates the outside of the London Athenaeum compares unfavorably for undesirable flamboyance with the address of the Boston Athenaeum, which is 15 1/2 Beacon St. It must be freely admitted that 15 1/2 is a very good street number indeed for a locally important club. It has a quiet reticence concealing an even quieter conceit that would do credit to an inner London suburb. But the London Athenaeum, *the* Athenaeum, has *no address at all*. Tie that, Boston.

I, myself, belong to the Reform, two doors down the street. This is the club of Dan O'Connell and Lord John Russell, the club which makes acceptance of Catholic Emancipation and the Reform Bill (1832) conditions for all candidates. It is the club where Thackeray let it be known that Dickens was going off with an actress, the club that was the starting point of *Around the World in Eighty Days*, where H.G. Wells, a premature four-letter man, used to tire the air with talk of his fornications, the club from which Churchill and Lloyd George resigned on the same day. (A man they proposed had been black-balled.)

I once entertained an American Jesuit at lunch there. Over coffee, I asked the waiter if he had anything rather special by way of a liqueur. He lowered his voice and said, "We still have a little of Mr. Asquith's brandy left."

Herbert Henry Asquith, KC, MP, Privy Councillor, His Majesty's trusted and well beloved chief secretary of State, Elder Brother of Trinity House, Earl of Oxford and Asquith, defeated candidate for the Chancellorship of Oxford University, Squiff.

A.J.P. Taylor has said that Asquith was the only Prime Minister since Pitt to address the Commons while under the influence of drink. Taylor did not say, perhaps did not know, that Asquith once nearly fell on the flat of his back. However, we may be quite sure that no man ever skidded with greater dignity or more quiet aplomb. His chair is in the Silence Room, labeled and roped off for reverence, like the Tooth of the Buddha. His slightly bottled but imperial bust stands on the mantelpiece of the Morning Room overlooking the table where Burgess and Maclean (son of his successor as Liberal leader) plotted their escape to Moscow.

There is reassurance as well as benignity in that gaze. Outside the walls the sons of Belial may roam unchecked, while awful Englishmen pretending to be Americans are supplanted by appalling Americans pretending to be English, but within the Great Liberal still holds his fallen day about him, and we, the sworn defenders of the Reform Bill, may know that while all is not well, at least all is not yet lost.

We have still a little of Mr. Asquith's brandy left.

July 26, 1966

Jack Kerouac, R I P

S ome of them have settled down in the suburbs now, some of them have gone back to the little towns they came from; some, like Allen Ginsberg, have freaked out way beyond return. And some of them sit in small dark bars in places like Denver and Santa Fe, stranded like bits of driftwood on a beach after flood tide. Men in their forties, gray and used up, and it takes a little more booze each month to work up to anything like a moment or two of that wild old exuberance. "Jack's dead," they'll murmur, and have another one for the road they'll never travel again.

To those of us who did our growing up around Columbia in the Fifties, he was *the* standard, *the* legend. He'd been a high school football hero back in Lowell, and on a good boozy night Scott Fitzgerald just might have traded *The Great Gatsby* for Jack's varsity letter. Then he broke his leg after a long splendid punt return, and that finished football at Columbia. And the stories, apocryphal perhaps, but the stuff of Fifties legend. The wild jags, the fistfight with a professor, the trips with Cassady. And in between, he sat down and wrote a best-seller in 21 days. And so what if it didn't read quite like we expected? To hell with the carping over quality of the prose, the depth of the thought. We didn't give a sweet damn, for he was saying something we all ached to find our own way to say: we loved this country and we wanted to tell it so. And it is precisely this that comes through *On the Road*. A deep, profound love affair with America.

On the day of his death I had a note from him. "Dear Coyne," he wrote, "This brochure reads like a complaint by Al Capone." He referred to a long whining diatribe printed by New Left tax-refusers. He loathed them. They were punks who had made their minds up about the world before they knew anything, and they had expropriated the legend. But their claim was not legitimate. They hadn't earned it, Jack believed, and they never would. For their hatreds were not his, and his love for America will forever lie far outside their experience.

Disreputable, sure. At times perhaps even degenerate. But in a peculiarly American way, the way of Walt Whitman or Hart Crane or maybe even Fitzgerald. And this the neo-Beats will never understand.

And every now and then, against our wills, we'll still make an occasional trip up to the West End Bar, the place that Jack once ruled. We'll drink a glass or two of cheap rotgut wine, and for a little while it will be 1950 and we'll think of the magic names like Denver and Tucson and Santa Fe. And we'll all devoutly hope that Jack's road ended where it should.

— *John S. Coyne, Jr.*
November 4, 1969

Thomas Merton, R I P

There were rumors a few years ago that Father M. Louis, OCSO, had retreated even further into his religious life, and that whereas formerly it was difficult to penetrate the fastness of the Trappist Monastery at Gethsemani in Kentucky to see him briefly—a hooded and very holy figure—it was now impossible. This kind of pious awe amused Thomas Merton immensely, and I once had the fun of listening to this rumor from an academic type who reported it as something of a literary state secret. The fun for me came from the fact that I was able to reply that just the day before Tom Merton had turned up on my porch in Lexington, looking for all the world like Jean Genet in denim jacket and jeans. The rumor had for basis the fact that after 25 years as a monk, Father Louis had decided to become a hermit. And who, as he said slyly, was to say whether a desert father didn't come into town occasionally to catch up on the news and flip through forbidden magazines? *Poetry*, for instance, in which the Abbot had once found an offending phrase, was denied him. Nor did the Trappists subscribe to *The New Yorker*; he found its ads to be a ready index to the world on which he had turned his back. As a hermit he had an enviable cabin deep in the woods about a quarter mile from Gethsemani. A black snake lived in the outhouse; it seemed perfectly natural that a snake should share his saintly life. Here he watched the procession of the seasons, wrote his poems and his books, and received visitors. Theology and poetry made up his library. Visitors were usually instructed to bring beer; he would produce from various frugal cloths a goat cheese, a loaf, and salted peanuts. And afterwards, from under the bed, he would triumphantly bring out a rather far-gone bottle of bourbon, "to keep the cold out of our bones."

What one could not suspect from Tom Merton's writing was the boyish happiness of the man. He seemed to live in that peace which must come after a final subduing of the selfishness which holds us back from God. He had become a Trappist to be himself, for he knew that the self the world had shaped of him was not true. If religion meant anything, it meant that God demanded all, and it meant that God had a purpose in demanding all. That is perhaps why there was nothing of the religious about him, nothing ritually pious. He was disarmingly a simple man. He was no guru, and fled from visitors who came to Gethsemani expecting to find a saint with sincere eyes and forgiving hands to lay on their guilt. His very laughter—a laughter robust, medieval, and utterly innocent—would have dashed their image of him. His hermitry is perhaps unique in the history of the Church. He interpreted his new isolation as freedom from discipline of the monastery and planned wonderful picnics and invited friends to them, specifying women and children as an added luxury.

That he died in Bangkok, of all places, will have been a mystery to the world, as the world did not know that he set out last summer on a pilgrimage to the East. He had studied the religions of the world for years, and he was fascinated by the contemplative religions of India and Japan. He had looked in on our own Indians on the way, and fellow monastics from Kentucky to California. One wonders if the United States, which he had not seen in thirty years, was not as strange to him as the Orient. The week before he died he had been with the Dalai Lama, exiled in India, and they liked each other. It was impossible not to like Thomas Merton. His writings were not quite what the church always wanted, and he appeared to be a saint most certainly, but not any kind of saint one has ever heard of. News of his death reached me not by television or radio or newspaper; these media are too slow, too clogged with the chronicling of frivolity and blather to know about the death of a saint in Bangkok. News has come by telephone, relayed friend by friend around the world.

—Guy Davenport
December 31, 1968

Notes from a Jewish Diary

Nathan Perlmutter

My shaving my long sideburns that night was an act of protest, and the lather of both can be attributed to Lawrence Welk. Had my chair been less deep and less comfortable, I'd have changed the channel. But it wasn't and now, here he was in my living room, "uh-two," by God, a talking cornstalk. I recall thinking a smile, a patronizing one of course, and thinking too, let him be, watch him awhile, you'll better understand those *Reader's Digest* subscribers who voted Nixon.

He played an old Jimmy Dorsey number in the Jimmy Dorsey style. I remembered it; he played it well. Next came Clyde McCoy's "Sugar Blues," trembling trombone, the works; it was good. He recreated the swing and the blues of the Thirties and early Forties, and as warmly and appealingly as a serendipitously found old photograph album. His music wafted me back to my youth. Finally a Tommy Dorsey favorite—three vocalists, two crew-cut All-America types, and a pretty pert-nosed and freckled songstress. That was it! I rose, strode into the bathroom, and in a declaration of comradeship with my own generation and its style, I shaved an inch from my sideburns, thereby saying no! to creeping hippieism.

****

2-C is a clean, three-room railroad flat in a dirty, Brooklyn tenement house. After 42 years of living in it, my mother has moved in with my aunt on Coney Island. Her former neighborhood was once all-Jewish. It is now overwhelmingly Puerto Rican and Negro, and with Mom's departure, the building is all Puerto Rican and Negro. I used to tease her, wanting her to move, that she was the "only Anglo" left in the building. (Compared with my mother's, Molly Goldberg's accent sounds like Julie Andrews'.)

But she wouldn't. As she put it, "the stones know me here." Also, up and down the street, there were her friends, a thinning assortment of elderly Jewish widows. Importantly too, 2-C was the place to which she could always return following stays with us. In a sense, that I understood well, it was her sure refuge from dependency on "the children." It was her turf; it represented her independence.

In the past year, however, the window-barred apartment was broken into twice. Her valuables, consisting of several sheets, pillow cases, and a blanket, were stolen. Also stolen were the contents of her small refrigerator including half empty Coca Cola bottles. Mom, though she minimized it, "it's time already," was frightened. Then my uncle died and my aunt, her sister, was alone too. Now they live together in an apartment house with an elevator on Coney Island.

It's the moving from 2-C, however, that I want to write about.

Forty-two years is a long time. From that apartment my brother and I walked off to kindergarten, to war, to the marriage altar. On the day of moving it was Mom, who had been always waiting, who was at last walking out. In the center of the bare-walled middle room stood several cord-tied grocery and drugstore cardboard boxes containing miscellaneous dishes and pots, pictures, and a motley assortment of broken toys and tattered dolls long discarded and forgotten by her grandchildren.

The fewness and the raggedyness of the cartons seemed to mock the meaning of her life. Was that all it took to wrap up 42 years?

As we left, I tried to etch the scene in my memory, but surreptitiously so as to minimize the occasion. We walked down the stairs, past doors and landings that were familiar, but whose occupants were strangers, and came out onto the street. There, by the stoop, in symbolism any self-respecting fiction editor would reject, lay a dead rat.

I later had a second thought about it. "At least," I thought, "it was dead."

June 30, 1970

Wanted: One 8 x 10 Glossy

William F. Buckley Jr.

Dear Bill: I like the picture of you on the jacket of your book. I wonder if you would object to my ordering a copy of the original from the photographer—and perhaps inscribing it for me? Best, Barbara Robinson

Dear Barbara: I saw your letter of two weeks ago only today and I rushed to write Miss Eastman to tell her to send you anything you want. I'd love the opportunity to inscribe the photograph. Affectionate greetings, Bill

Dear Bill: About that picture, what happened was Miss Eastman didn't have a copy of the one I wanted, the one on the cover. But she happened to have another one on hand that she was sure I would like even more, much more pleasant, etc. I mentioned that you had offered to inscribe it, then she said since the one she had was probably a little larger than what I had in mind, it would be simpler if she sent it over to you first, before sending it on to me. That was all I knew about it.

Bill, Believe me, I didn't ask for or expect anything so elegant. When it arrived I was down with the flu and in a perfectly rotten state of mind anyway. And I don't mind telling you I shed a few tears of embarrassment. Good Lord! I mean it must be ten square yards in size. I decided at first that I'd pack it up and send it back to Miss E. with my thanks, but please could I just have a little old 8 x 10 glossy....But I have now decided that if you didn't approve of my having it, you could have returned it to Miss E. But you didn't, even though you wrote on it that you were not in any way responsible for "the behemoth." So I shall keep it and enjoy it. After all, it does solve the problem of what I would save first if the house were on fire, something I've always puzzled over. Barbara

Dear Barbara: Your description of the receipt of the behemoth is for the ages. Miss Eastman is a lovely woman—very talented, and of a passionate generosity. She has given me a lot of pleasure—not least for having midwifed your letter. Bill

Dear Bill: Since you found my account of the receipt of the behemoth so amusing, perhaps you will enjoy this account of the return of the behemoth. First you must understand that I had no way of knowing Miss Eastman was so renowned, or that accordingly, her prices were extraordinary. When I saw it, I of course realized immediately that it was an expensive picture, but even then I wasn't too concerned. Then I received the bill from Miss Eastman. $900. That, she explained is a considerable discount since it was something she had already made up. The list price is actually $1,500.

Now Bill, it isn't that I don't feel $900 worth of devotion to you. It's just that quite honestly, my mind cannot conceive of any photograph of anyone, by anyone, in terms of $1,500 or even $900. It makes me dizzy. I had already sent it out to a friend to have it framed. I called him immediately (he had just finished it) and asked him to unframe it and for heaven's sake lock it in the safe until I could get by to pick it up. Then my husband took it to the mailing service and had it crated and insured like a Rembrandt and shipped back to Miss Eastman yesterday. Barbara

BARBARA ROBINSON, SAN FRANCISCO. HORRIFIED BY YOUR EXPERIENCE. COULDN'T AGREE WITH YOU MORE. THAT KIND OF DOUGH IS RATHER FOR ORIGINAL REMBRANDTS THAN CONTEMPORARY POLEMICISTS. EASTMAN GAVE ME LARGE PICTURE I TUCKED AWAY SOMEWHERE WHICH I AM SENDING YOU WITHOUT INVOICE.   BILL

WM. F. BUCKLEY JR, NEW YORK. PLEASE DON'T SEND ME ANOTHER PICTURE. I COULDN'T STAND IT.   BARBARA

BARBARA ROBINSON, SAN FRANCISCO. TOO LATE. PIX HAS GONE OFF. PLEASE BURN IT. SEND ME THE BILL.   BILL

WM F. BUCKLEY JR., NEW YORK. RECEIVED YOUR PACKAGE. CONTAINS TWO NOT ONE REPEAT TWO PICTURES. I GUESS THEY MULTIPLY, SHMOO-LIKE. AM OPENING GALLERY.   BARBARA

March 25, 1969—Notes & Asides

Cars, Cars, Cars

C. H. Simonds

A ccording to one of those recent surveys with which the nation so loves to amuse itself, the American male daydreams more about cars than sex. Hush the Freudish gaspings: it's understandable. A woman is only a woman (which is surely enough) but a good car, now that ladies are offering Tiparillos and the saloon is dead, is something entirely else, one of the few remaining masculine preserves. Like a woman, it is something the male creature can latch onto, make a fool of himself over, love and understand. (The number of women who truly love and understand automobiles is tiny: they commit such enormities as refusing to understand the sweet logic of the gearshift, and driving home from the supermarket with stalks of celery and O-Cedar sponge mops protruding from the back seats of Aston-Martins, and saying infuriating things like "Well after all, it's just transportation, isn't it?" or "My car is broken" or—it was said about a birdcage Maserati that I was eyeing lustfully—"Gee, it's sorta *cute!*")

If woman is man's partner, the automobile is his toy; one is fire to the other's frying pan, really, but to live is to dream and delude oneself. The toy function was everywhere in evidence at the International Auto Show, now touring the nation after opening in New York City this spring. Cars of every description were strewn over three floors of the New York Coliseum, like great baubles tossed to greedy children by some benevolence beyond. There were a few sensible stationwagons for the wives, but the emphasis was all on color, style, speed, dash, verve, and whossh; even little Simcas, Renaults, and such were painted gaudy colors and touted as "fun cars," and the Volkswagen display, all practicality and writhing self-deprecation, merely provided the rule by inverting it. (VW offered a modest proposal in the form of its little "Squareback" stationwagon painted Taxicab Yellow and equipped with meter, sliding partition, *et cetera.* Understandably, it drew crowds of admiring New Yorkers; alas, a sign confessed that the thoroughly comfortable vehicle was but a dream because—get this—it was too small to meet size standards for city cabs.)

The show would have maddened car-haters, that strange breed of demi-intellectual (Eric Bently is a car-hater, when he isn't busy fondling the corpse of Bertold Brecht) that reveres Ralph Nader and rails at the tail-fin (which vanished six or seven years ago) as a clear and present symptom of America's ugliness, spiritual emptiness, and moral decay. It displayed the automobile in its infinite variety, and car-haters like to think of the auto industry in terms of three wicked Detroit monoliths that hold the American public in a state of colonial subjugation. In reality, given the cash and the inclination, the car-seeker can have anything from a $1,500 Mini-Moke, a platform holding four tiny wheels, a little Austin engine, a driver's seat, and a surrey top, and designed to take just about anything just about anywhere; a Rolls Royce Silver Shadow for $31,000 (almost a waste, now that the makers have embraced not only dual headlamps but also the Coke-bottle bulge over the rear wheels that Pontiac pioneered back in 1964).

Engines of three, four, six, eight, or twelve cylinders are mounted in front, in the rear, sideways; cars have front-wheel, rear-wheel, and four-wheel drive; there are fat air-conditioned things for bombing down the thruway with Lester Lanin on the stereo tape, snaky sports cars for prowling the back roads of a summer's day, rugged boxy cars for driving right off the road, through a swamp or two and up the nearest mountainside. The man who can't find a car to please him these days must want a Sherman tank.

Almost lost in the array of good things was a prototype battery-powered vehicle from General Motors. Under the hood and in the trunk (for all I know, in the glove compartment and ashtray) were crammed nasty battery cells. This was not, of course, a *car*. Under the hood of a *car* are cast iron and steel, and writhing exhaust ports, and brushed-metal valve covers, and wires wandering all over the place, and when you turn it all on, things roar and spin and move, and or, my ... Oh, well.

July 11, 1967

Naked Emperor

Elspeth Huxley

The crowds, it will be remembered, cheered their heads off as the Emperor in spangled finery, borne aloft by loyal henchmen, glittered by. Only a single non-courtier observed, with some surprise, that the Emperor had no clothes.

At long last some bolder Britons, rubbing stardust from their eyes, are observing that a similar misfortune has overcome their own Caesar. The Empire died but did not die—it rose again as the commonwealth, that noble league of free, loyal, and democratic nations imbued with British principles of justice, order, and fair play, which was Britain's special contribution to the world, and whose 22 other member-states acknowledged, and respected Britain as founder and guide. (All Commonwealth members, it is true, are equal, but Britain is more equal than the rest.) The Empire/Commonwealth had a splendid set of robes.

Nothing that has happened, or not happened, since 1945 will, I suspect, look more astonishing to that overworked body of men, the historians of the future, than the British achievement in keeping this myth alive through thick and thin. Pretty thick, sometimes, too. Nearly all the African members are now military dictatorships or single-party states. Two Asian members (India and Pakistan) waged a cold war which several times flared into a shooting one, and was prevented from breaking out in earnest only by the good offices of the USSR. Well over 100,000 refugees fled from persecution by the rulers of one member-state (Sudan) over the borders of another member-state (Uganda) whose own rulers proceeded bloodily to crush one of their own sub-rulers and his followers. (That sub-ruler, King Freddie, really *did* have no clothes when he escaped into the bush, but survived to have a new set made by his London tailor.)

Another member-state is under the control of Chinese Communists whose takeover was baptized in the blood of at least fifteen thousand inoffensive Arabs (some were crucified) and an unguessable number of others who were driven, with their wives and families, into small boats and told to head across the Indian Ocean for a homeland their ancestors had left several generations earlier. The heads of that regime—quite legal, unlike Mr. Smith's dreadful Rhodesian one—operate forced labor, imprisonment without trial or term, flogging for minor offenses, and other no doubt democratic practices, and lustily denounce the wicked, non-democratic, rebellious practices of Mr. Smith's illegal regime in Salisbury. This, they say, should immediately be put down by force to make way for a more enlightened form of government, presumably more akin to that of what was once, in its unregenerate imperialist days of dhows, ivory elephants, pottering tourists, and exports of cloves, known as Zanzibar.

September 6, 1966—Letter from Africa

Felix von Luckner, R I P

When I heard about the death of my old friend Count Felix von Luckner, the "Sea Devil" of World War One, I thought about a line from the song I had just heard—sung by musical comedy star Pat Moran: "If you make somebody else happy then you will be happy too." In all my years of roaming the world meeting people, I never knew of anyone of whom this was so true. Wherever Count Luckner went, everybody smiled—and how they laughed! By Joe, what a man! I wonder if the world ever again will see anyone to compare with the Sea Devil?

The first time my wife and I saw him was on an airfield, at Leipzig. This huge, hulking man emerged from a fairly small cabin plane, and a slender young blonde then jumped down into his arms. You could hear his voice booming across the field. He spoke to everybody—mechanics, porters, anyone he passed. When we asked about him the reply was: "Why, that's *der See Teufel.*"

You may recall how the New Zealanders captured him. That was after he had run the Allied North Sea blockade with his sailing ship *See Adler*. He had sunk many ships, without taking any lives. Then in the South Seas a tidal wave piled his raider on the reef of a coral atoll, the island of Mopilia, one of the Cook Group.

It was after a Captain Bligh-type journey of several thousand miles in a longboat that he was captured at Fiji. Later he escaped from prison at Auckland, was recaptured, and the New Zealanders nicknamed him "the Sea Devil."

Twenty of us accompanied one of our friends and his bride on their honeymoon aboard von Luckner's postwar four-masted sailing ship, *Mopilia*, named for the coral atoll in the South Seas. One stop on that most unusual honeymoon was at the island of San Salvador where Columbus made his first landfall. The only inhabitant we found was a Dominican priest who was unhappy because he said the people of Chicago had put up a large statue of Columbus, on the wrong side of the island. So, we organized a midnight expedition, and in longboats with chains and crowbars, around we went to rescue Columbus, and please the Dominican priest. I can still hear von Luckner's booming laughter when we discovered that Columbus was too much for us. We couldn't even pull him off his pedestal.

One more memory—at the end of the second war, when I was with General Allen Terry and the Timberwolf Division, we found the von Luckners at Halle, in Saxony, his old home town. The Sea Devil went out alone to meet the advancing American Army, and thanks to Terry Allen he saved the city from destruction. A few days later we put the Count in touch with General George Patton who immediately took a fancy to the Sea Devil and his Swedish lady, and kept the von Luckners from falling into the hands of the Russians. As he said about his host, the American general, "By Joe! What a man!"

Wish I could go on and on about this fabulous World War One hero who raided the seas and never took a life. How in World War Two, Hitler, who had burned his book on America, and even burned his sailing ship, the *Mopilia*, kept von Luckner under guard. But, evidently because of his immense popularity, Hitler was afraid to put him in a concentration camp. American correspondents used to see him with his guards at the bar of the Hotel Aldon in Berlin, where he would drink them under the table and then go home alone. By Joe, what a man!

—Lowell Thomas
May 3, 1966

Arts & Manners

On Breaking Up a Library

Alec Waugh

For the last twenty years though remaining a loyal subject of the British Crown, I have been a resident alien of the United States, limited by currency restrictions to an annual three months' visit to the country of my birth. Now, the home that had housed my library was for sale and there was no practical alternative to the scattering of that library among my children.

It was in a highly nostalgic state of mind that I spent my last hours with it. It was not a large library, barely four thousand books; it was of no great value; I was not a collector. I had bought the books I wanted to read; not those that were likely to "go up in price." I had not specialized in first editions, though, of course, I had quite a number. But it was a very personal library. I knew the provenance of every single volume, whether I had inherited it from my father, bought it myself, or been given it by a friend.

Sadly on my last morning, I walked round the two main rooms that held it, taking my last look along the shelves. What a host of memories! On both sides of the fireplace in the larger, taller room, the shelves ran straight up to the ceiling; along the side wall the shelving was only four feet high. Photographs and ornaments ran along the ledge. On the top low shelf was a row of small books covered in red leather. How well I remember getting them. They were the world's classics. My father, because he had contributed a few prefaces, had been sent the entire series. They arrived all together in a crate, with a couple of small oak cases that they exactly fitted. My father said, "I'll give you these to start your library." I was eight years old. Next morning at school I proudly boasted that I owned a hundred books.

Further along on the same level was the yellow-backed stretch of Wisden's *Cricketer's Almanacks* that I had acquired as a Christmas present, one by one, regularly since 1909. I shall miss them as much as anything. I looked for special treasures. There was the limited collected editions of Max Beerbohm. In 1921 I had drunk beer instead of wine at lunch for a whole month to get my hands on that. That same autumn I had acquired Cabell's *Jurgen*. The book had been suppressed in the U.S.A., but an English publisher had thought that he might "get away with it" if he issued it in an edition limited to three thousand copies, at two guineas each, with illustrations and a preface by Hugh Walpole. The official theory being that the man or woman who could afford two guineas for a dubious book was either too sophisticated to be tempted—or was beyond redemption. How proud I had been to possess that lovely book. How often had I read it? When had I read it last? Since the Second War? I question it. I was tempted to include it in the two hundred or so volumes that I was rescuing from the deluge but I refrained. Better to keep the memory of that long-ago enchantment. I placed my fingers, reverently, on the black-and-gold cloth cover.

West of *Jurgen* was the original ocher-brown Heinemann edition of Turgenev that had stood on the left-hand side of the fireplace in my father's dining room. I had taken it with me to my first London flat in 1924. "You don't mind, do you, if I take them?" I had asked. My father could deny me little. But he looked disconsolate. "If you really want them, my dear boy, of course."

We seek, or at least I do, "in this transitory life" for parallels which provide symbols of survival, and as I waved goodbye to the books that had been the friends I shall never see again, I remembered how often in the days when I traveled by ship and not by plane, I had waved goodbye from the taffrail to the uplifted faces of those who during a six weeks' stay in this or the other island in the tropics, had become dear to me. Never again, never never again. And a mist had come across my eyes.

In just the same spirit on that last morning, I remained silent at my younger son's side as he drove me up to London: then in that same sense of parallel, I remembered how when the group on the dock had scattered and the mountains that flanked the port had grown indistinct, I had gone below and washed my face and when I had come back on deck, with the horizon clear, had thought with a sense of liberation and anticipation, "I wonder what it'll be like in Martinique." In just that way, as the traffic on the Great West Road began to thicken, I found myself saying to myself, "After all it *is* going to be fun, building up a new if very different library in Tangier."

June 3, 1969

The Pittsburgh Organ

William F. Rickenbacker

The pipe organ in Saint Paul's Cathedral in Pittsburgh was installed only five years ago last December and has already passed into legend. It was built by the foremost artisan of organ-building now alive, Rudolph von Beckerath. You will recognize the Beckerath name as one famous in German music circles. The great Beckerath painting of Johannes Brahms at the keyboard, spine tilted back in musical joy, arms crisscrossed in typical Brahms keyboard style, fat cigar stuck in chops—was painted by Rudolph's father. Brahms always stayed at the Beckerath house when he visited Hamburg.

Says Rudolph von Beckerath concerning the organ in Pittsburgh: "*Dies ist mein Meisterstück*"—this is my masterpiece.

What makes this great instrument the center of the organist's world? Two things, certainly. First, the acoustics in Saint Paul's are splendid. During the rehearsal one afternoon (string ensemble plus organ, the brilliant Karel Paukert in command), I moved throughout the cathedral and discovered the volume and balance and timbre of the sound were almost constant from wall to wall and from narthex to transept. At a guess I would say that 80 percent of the cathedral got full value from that noble instrument.

Second, of course, the loving attention of the master craftsman, von Beckerath. Paul Koch, organist and musical director at St. Paul's, tells a revealing story. Some years ago, when Beckerath first came to Pittsburgh to visit the cathedral and began to solidify his ideas about the organ he would build for it, he walked around downstairs while Koch played various tones from the former organ. At one point Koch mentioned that the acoustics were such that a certain tone reverberates for four seconds and one-half. Beckerath went back to Hamburg with an intimate knowledge of the acoustics of that cathedral. He had a book of average temperature and humidity readings in Pittsburgh over the years. He purchased certain kinds of wood and treated them over the years to bring them to the point where they would settle down comfortably in the Pittsburgh climate. Years passed. The time came to install the organ. Beckerath went to Pittsburgh and stayed there for seven weeks, installing each pipe himself, voicing it, tuning it, supervising the balance of the instrument.

Balance: here is the soul of organ building. Paul Koch showed me something of it one morning in the short interval between a funeral and a nuptial mass. He depressed a deep pedal on a 32-foot stop and I remonstrated that it made very little sound. True, he said. He offered a quiet modulation on the swell and remarked that the modest tone of the pedal was well wedded to the registration of the manual. Then he threw in a bank of stops and played a similar passage on the manual without altering the registration of the pedal— and lo! I could hear the same small voice speaking under this new storm of sound. Those pedal pipes were balanced: Balanced exquisitely between the inner and outer limits of the pipes which they would be asked to harmonize. The instrument is absolutely incapable of uttering an unlovely sound.

How did this great instrument come into existence? In Pittsburgh they will tell you that Paul Koch bullied it through. And Paul Koch may very well have done such a thing. After all, Pittsburgh has the oldest continuous series of public concerts in America, and this series (the Sunday organ recital in

Carnegie Hall) was maintained for fifty years by Paul's father Caspar. Paul took over his father's position as City Organist about ten years ago. Everyone in Pittsburgh knows about Caspar Koch and Paul Koch and now little Carol Koch, Paul's daughter. Carol is a gifted musician—like her mother Kay, her father Paul, her brothers Paul and Damien, her grandfather Caspar (and like the Koch who, in 1685, was one of the three godfathers of Johann Sebastian Bach). You see it is quite possible for Paul Koch to insist that Pittsburgh have the finest in organ music.

What is the finest? American organists are beginning to know. They are tired of the noise and claptrap, showmanship and razzle dazzle, of the average organ maestro. They go to Pittsburgh and humbly beg permission to touch the keys of this infinitely subtle, generous, rounded, reposed, straightspeaking *Meisterstück*.

April 9, 1968

Part Four

1971 to 1975

The Week
Selected Editorial Paragraphs

December 17, 1971

Mrs. Indira Gandhi has come up with a surefire solution to the current India-Pakistan border war. She suggests that Pakistan evacuate Pakistan.

October 27, 1972

The key to the election is the crossover vote, politickers are saying. Right. If Republicans cross party lines to vote for Nixon and Democrats cross over to vote for McGovern, look for more of more or less more of the same and less of the same. If, however, the voters are too cross with both candidates to go to the polls, the pols will have to run for private office and there's no telling where it would end. Courage.

December 8, 1972

The ACLU calls on the Supreme Court to decide whether the Pentagon is guilty of sex discrimination in its policy of discharging, automatically, pregnant servicewomen. The ACLU, reports the *Washington Post*, wishes to know "why women are singled out for anti-pregnancy regulation." We can't think of it for the moment, but we're sure there is a *perfectly* reasonable explanation.

March 30, 1973

And who do you think the federal marshals found when they arrived at Wounded Knee, sitting on the ground by the embers of the dying fire, crossed-legged, his long wild hair flowing around his shoulders, but the famous warrior Big Chief William Buttinsky Kunstler Himself, summoned by smoke signal to bring his scalping knife and have another go at the Great White Father in Washington? How!—about that.

April 27, 1973

The boycotters struggling to make meats end obviously do not understand that the problem is the falling price of the dollar, not the rising price of the meat. Insofar as the boycott is successful, it will discourage beef production and thus increase beef prices two years from now. The ladies would do better boycotting Federal Reserve notes.

June 8, 1973

Having banned one of the few useful weapons in the battle of the bulging, sodium cyclamate, the Food and Drug Administration is now preparing to ban the other artificial sweetener, saccharine, because rodents fed massive overdoses of the stuff— in research sponsored by the sugar industry—occasionally develop bladder cancer. That's no big deal. We get bladder trouble just thinking about bureaucrats being fed massive overdoses of tax dollars.

July 6, 1973

A federal judge has ruled that the Illinois Department of Public Aid cannot deny welfare money to unborn babies (payable, presumably, to mothers of unborn babies). For your midterm exam, sort out, as among judge, welfare mothers, and taxpayers, who's doing the screwing, who's getting screwed, and who's got a screw loose.

October 12, 1973

One scenario: Nixon resigns. Spiro Agnew is duly sworn in as Pres. He names Nixon as his Vice President. Agnew is then impeached. Nixon succeeds to the Presidency. This allows him not only to make a fresh start but, since a period as Vice President has intervened, to elude the constitutional prohibition against running for a third term. Nixon runs in 1976 and carries all fifty states. He runs again in 1980 and wins. By 1984 the statute of limitations has run out on all crimes committed in 1972. Nixon retires majestically to San Clemente, the mortgage for which turns out to have been underwritten by Chou En-lai.

November 9, 1973

This may be looking too far ahead, but there now seems the possibility of President Ford being shot at the Lincoln Center.

November 9, 1973

Sigh. No more fat Japs. No impudent corps of effete snobs. No radic-libs. No nattering nabobs of negativism. Sob. Gerry Ford wristwatches. Groan.

December 21, 1973

THAT'S THE WAY TO GO, COMRADE. The death of Pablo Neruda, as recounted by Philip Bonosky in the Communist *Daily World*: "As he lay dying the greatest poet of our age rose from his bed of pain and delivered a curse on the betrayers of his country that will yet scar their corrupted bones. 'Voracious hyenas,' 'hellish predators,' 'rodents gnawing,' 'satraps who have sold out a thousand times.' Then he cursed them. And he named them: Nixon. Frei [former Chilean president]. Pinochet [junta chief]. He pronounced anathema on them. He indicted them: 'Prostituted vendors of the North American way of life,' 'pimps of the whorish bosses.' He hurled his contempt for them with his last breath."

January 17, 1975
The Irish government has reworded its form to "request" payment of taxes instead of "demanding" payment. Very civilized. Persons refusing to pay will be asked politely to go to jail.

March 28, 1975
The total federal, state, and local tax bite now exceeds half a trillion dollars a year, and is moving briskly to the point where it will take one-half of our national product. Then every worker will spend half his life in servitude to Uncle Sam, and we'll find out whether the nation can long endure half slave and half free.

September 26, 1975
First the good news. I. F. Stone has just received the Eleanor Roosevelt Peace Award for 1975, given by the Committee for a Sane Nuclear Policy.

Solzhenitsyn: Two Editorials

Man of the Year

With the publication in Paris of *The Gulag Archipelago*, Aleksandr Solzhenitsyn's struggle with the Soviet system reaches a climax of almost unbearable intensity. On the one side is this great writer, armed with his genius, a kind of colleague of Tolstoy, and also with his religious faith, his integrity, and his astounding courage. Arrayed against him is the entire Soviet totalitarian-imperial system, from Mr. Brezhnev on down: the secret police, the bureaucrats, the Party organization and the Writers' Union, the censors, jailers, and torturers, the admirals, generals, and border guards, Smersh, the Soviet delegates to the Committee on Human Rights, the editors of *Pravda* and *Izvestia*. The remarkable thing is that against these odds Solzhenitsyn is not only holding his own, surviving, being heard, but perhaps winning. *The Gulag Archipelago* is a stunning political act. It will not bring down the totalitarian structure, but it does damage it, and the damage is of a sort that cannot easily be repaired.

The book consists, in its brilliant foreground at least, of a detailed and devastating account of Soviet police terror and the bestiality of the prison camp system during the period 1918-1956, including an account of Solzhenitsyn's experiences during his own 11-year sentence to the camps. The "archipelago" of the title refers to the police system, a state within the larger state, islands of concentrated terror, yet, and this is Solzhenitsyn's point, reflecting the true essence of the larger state itself. Here is life within the archipelago:

> Sukhanovka was the most terrible prison the MGB had. They used it to terrify prisoners; and interrogators hissed out its name ominously. Those who had been there weren't subject to further interrogations: they were either insane and talking only disconnected nonsense, or else they were dead.

But here is life "outside" the archipelago:

> As Tanya Khodekevich wrote: "You can pray freely/But just so only God can hear." And for these verses she received a sentence of ten years.

Or:

> You are arrested by a religious pilgrim who has stayed "for the sake of
> Christ" with you overnight. You are arrested by a meterman who has come
> to read your electric meter. You are arrested by a bicyclist who has run into
> you on the street, by a railway conductor, a taxi driver, a savings bank
> employee, a cinema theater administrator. Any one of them can arrest you,
> and you notice the concealed maroon-colored identification only when it is
> too late.

The archipelago is a state within a state, yes, but also a totalitarian prison
inside a larger totalitarian prison.

Ever since the supposed end of the cold war, it has been fashionable to
pooh-pooh the concept of totalitarianism as developed earlier by Hannah
Arendt and others. Solzhenitsyn returns us to it with a vengeance. Here before
our eyes is the thing itself. As Arendt wrote: "The concentration and
extermination camps of totalitarian regimes serve as the laboratories in which
the fundamental belief of totalitarianism that everything is possible is verified
... the means of total domination are not only more drastic but ... totalitarianism
differs essentially from other forms of political oppression known to us such as
despotism, tyranny, and dictatorship. Wherever it rose to power, it developed
entirely new political institutions and destroyed all social, legal, and political
traditions of the country." Solzhenitsyn's book, however, is a political
bombshell because it is not only, or even centrally, about the *past*, about
"Stalinism" as distinguished from "Brezhnevism" or some other later mutant.
Solzhenitsyn's voice sounds from inside the whale. His point is that the police
system remains the central institution of the Soviet state, that the system of
repression is structurally inseparable from the Soviet system itself.

The publication of the book constitutes an act dramatizing that truth. The
manuscript was completed some years ago. Last August, the police arrested a
woman who had a secret copy and subjected her to a lengthy and brutal
interrogation. When she was released, she hanged herself. Solzhenitsyn
reasoned that since the police had a copy anyway, he might as well publish the
book—in Paris. Some thaw.

It is part of the supreme drama of these circumstances that the entire
tyrannical system cannot now defeat him. It can arrest him, and by so doing
prove his point. It can put him in a "sanatorium." It can torture him and even
kill him. But any option it chooses can only further dramatize its true nature.
Solzhenitsyn has struck a blow that the totalitarians cannot really parry.

One further quotation from *The Gulag Archipelago* cannot be omitted
here: "In their own countries Roosevelt and Churchill are honored as examples
of statesmanlike wisdom. To us, in Russian prison discussions, their systematic

shortsightedness and stupidity stood out as astonishingly obvious. How could they, in their descent from 1941 to 1945, fail to secure any guarantees whatsoever of the independence of Eastern Europe? How could they, for the laughable toy of a four-zone Berlin, their own future Achilles' heel, give away broad regions of Saxony and Thuringia? And what military or political sense was there in the surrender by them, to death at Stalin's hands, of several hundreds of thousands of armed Soviet citizens determined not to surrender?"

Again, the analytical double focus. That is about 1945, but also about 1974. Solzhenitsyn is the man of the year, the man of any year.

—Jeffrey Hart
January 18, 1974

Solzhenitsyn

(On February 12, 1974, two weeks after the appearance of the editorial "Solzhenytsin: Man of the Year," Soviet authorities expelled Solzhenitzyn, and stripped him of his citizenship.)

Solzhenitsyn had warned Soviet authorities what sort of behavior they could expect at his trial: "I shall not go there on my own legs. I shall be taken there with my hands bound, in a police van. At such a tribunal, I shall reply to none of its questions. Condemned to incarceration, I shall not submit to the verdict unless manacled. Once incarcerated ... I shall not work even for one half hour for my oppressors." And so, because they could not leave him as he was, holding the world's enthralled attention in his witness against the regime, they arrested him and sent him off not to prison or camp on the soil from which he drew his strength, but to forced exile in West Germany. A brilliant strategic move.

Solzhenitsyn, the exile, living in comparative luxury in the West, even though his wife and children remain as pawns in the Soviet Union, is a martyr deprived of his stake, of his garrote. Speaking from an alien land, he is no longer one with the suffering peoples of the Soviet Union. "All my life I have trod my country's soil," he wrote in refusing to go to Stockholm to receive his Nobel Prize, for fear that what has happened to him now would happen to him then. No matter what the brilliance of his pen, he now becomes a writer among writers—wise, sensitive, impassioned, but somehow, because he does not write in defiant scorn of prison, torture, or death, diminished in the popular mind. The great crusade for personal freedom in the Soviet Union—freedom as we know it—that he and Sakharov and the Medvedevs, Grigorenko, Sinyavsky, and all the others threatened to touch off among free men everywhere has been derailed by the cold technicians of terror in the Kremlin who, carefully pondering the alternatives, chose the one that leaves Solzhenitsyn free of their shackles, yet shackled.

The apostles of detente may hail Solzhenitsyn's exile as a triumph for their policies. See, they will say, how gently the authorities handled the premier dissident in their midst. They let him go; why they even gave him his fare out. But it is very precisely the point that the Soviets, in this as in all else, see detente as a one-way affair: they are to be allowed to do what they want and as they want to do it within their empire as it suits them. It suited them to handle the Solzhenitsyn crisis as they did because there are things they wanted more— hardnosed things like credits, and trade, and Western technology—than to murder him. But detente means to them also that they consider themselves free to "deepen the international class struggle" howsoever and wheresoever they choose, by whatever weapons they choose: by infiltration, by subversion, by terror, by wars of liberation, by force of arms.

And yet, and yet, as Solzhenitsyn wrote upon receiving his Nobel Prize: "Woe betide the nation whose literature is interrupted by force. This is not merely a violation of freedom of the press, it is the incarceration of the nation's heart, the amputation of the nation's memory."

—Priscilla L. Buckley
March 1, 1974

Christmas Greetings
...*from the Dismal Science*

William F. Rickenbacker

A lady from the Midwest has asked me why economics is call the dismal science. (Why must it always be a *lady* from the Midwest? Are there no *gentlemen* in the Midwest? Are we in some obscure way holding the ladies up to public ridicule? Who, after all, married Aunt Jane from Dubuque if it wasn't a gentleman from the Midwest? What strange sort of birds are they out there, anyway? *Has the Audubon Society been notified?*)

Why, she asked, is economics called the dismal science? (The "she" in this case may be taken generically, or with a pinch of salt, whichever feels best on the tailfeathers.) Economics is called the dismal science because it was invented by a Protestant clergyman. Fair enough, sweetie?

A gentleman from a small hamlet on the edge of the Great Dismal Swamp—a retirement community of impoverished real-estate promoters—just south of Norfolk, Virginia (where the mortal remains of General Douglas MacArthur rest, as Churchill said of the same portions of John Duke of Marlborough and his frenzied wife, "in victorious peace"—this is becoming rather complex so let's begin again. A gentleman from Virginia, who describes himself as a resident of the Great Dismal Swamp, writes in to ask whether economics has been named after his local geographical feature. The answer to that is definitely no. The answer, sir, is no. The Dismal Swamp was named after the Dismal Science, since both were discovered by Protestant clergymen.

A psychiatrist who says he has no economic problems writes in to inquire whether there is any psychological connection between economics and a general human predisposition to be unhappy. The answer to this is easy. But first I would like to know more about this psychiatrist who says he has no economic problems. Did he have a happy childhood, I fondly wonder. How about SEX? Does he have recurring dreams? Does he have recurring periods of consciousness? Does he have an obsessive desire to wash his monopoly? Does he have a tax attorney? How about SEX? If he saw a pigeon engaging in shameless promiscuity during the hours of business (thereafter by appointment only, unless the answering service provides servicing answers), would he, of his own volition, contrive to notify the Audubon Society? Next week (for $40) we shall discuss this further. I'm afraid we can't come to any definite conclusions at this time, doctor. Clearly you have suffered, in your life; but these are things we can learn to deal with. Next week, then?

We are lacking a close-parenthesis in the third paragraph, above. Here it is:). And now back to our show:

[Hah! Chris Simonds! Priscilla! Betcha I gotcha on that one!]

A professor of economics at Harvard has had a literate friend of his write to me to inquire whether sunspots are (is?) part of the economic. To which we reply, yes, and no. Sunspots is part of the economic *pari passu* they create natural conditiouns (Middle English—from time before beginning of Protestant clergy), isn't part of it but how so far they can be traded, tendered to government in payment of imposts outrageous and confiscatory, or treated in catallactic way.

My mother has written to me to ask me to stop doing this. It is not dignified, I know, nor educational, nor does it have redeeming social value, but I cannot help myself.

Same Harvard professor as before has called me on telephone, very much out of breath, to inquire: What is (are?) catallactics? I reply: Catallactics be science of exchanges. Once upon a time, in a kingdom over the sea, there lived a man who believed in his heart of hearts that 1) the blonde up the street had her eye on him, and 2) economics is the science of exchanges. I forget her name, and his; but here's how the story worked out. He was wrong about 1) and 2), and lived happily ever after, having exchanged 1) for the nifty brunette who lived under the bridge at Avignon (I have discussed, elsewhere, the common misconception concerning the spatial relations in the French nursery tune), and 2) for ignominy.

Junior editor of NATIONAL REVIEW sends telegram to inquire why I mentioned the great General Douglas MacArthur, above, third paragraph, in connection with real-estate promoters. This is a simple question. Military business is real-estate business sans the willingness of the exchanges effected. All war is conducted in order to trade real estate. Rickenbacker's Nineteenth Corollary (derived from Third Corollary Thrombosis) proclaims: Real Estate Is The Cause of War. Peace that passeth understanding is just around the korner, kids, if we can just abolish real estate. Get *US* out of real estate! Junior editor: hang head in shame. Haven't they told you stories about the old days down there? Haven't you got the word? *Never* ask Rickenbacker *anything*!

President of United States has written to ask: What is Keynesian? I reply unprintable.

January 5, 1973

Arnold Lunn, R I P

A rnold Lunn died in London on June 2, but at 86 was absolutely undaunted, though the flesh had become very weak. He was at work for the next issue of *Ski Survey* on his contribution to the Olympic Committee's history of the Games. Also on a book—this time on Lakes Thün and Brienz; on several articles, including one for this journal; and he was expecting, in America, the reissue of his book *Spanish Rehearsal*, about the civil war. His most recent article had appeared in *The Tablet* only the day before, and his son Peter, and his wife Phyllis, read it aloud to him in the hospital. I can imagine his chuckling over his words, which greatly amused him as they did everybody else, save possibly their victims who, come to think of it, probably constituted a majority of readers. He took an unrestrained, unaffected pleasure in his work, which was amiably sarcastic, in the maieutic British tradition, wonderfully well turned, unrelenting but good natured. He was a most serious man, who saw the humor of every situation.

His career had begun only months after graduating from Harrow, a few years after Winston Churchill. He wrote *The Harrovians*, an exposé of sorts of public school life, tame stuff by the standards of *The Fourth of June* by David Benedictus, which came along fifty years later about life in Eton; but enough to launch him as a radical young writer. His interest in sports and mountaineering dominated him in those days; and one summer before he was 22 he fell while on a solo climbing expedition. For several hours he was without help, then they found him, took him to the hospital, and he blessed himself that a) the anesthetist was incompetent and b) he understood German, because he was awake when he should have been unconscious, enough so to hear the doctors making preparations to amputate his leg. This, from his strapped-down position on the operating table, he forthwith forbade, summoning all the authority he could in his youthful voice. The result was a leg deformed, slightly shorter than the companion leg. Athletes and mountaineers of the world wondered what the competition would have been from Lunn if he had had normal legs. Because he scaled everything in Switzerland there was to scale, and raced with the early British ski teams, and was made president of the Ski Club of Great Britain over fifty years ago, and founded the prestigious Kandahar Club in Mürren. It was in those days that he conceived the idea of the slalom, which he introduced into Olympic competition where it's been a fixture ever since. As the years went on, he found skiing more and more difficult, but he persevered, and I skied with him once when he was 75 years old.

He lived in Mürren during the winter, a ski eyrie that faces, across the Lauterbrunnen valley, the Jungfrau and the dread Eiger. At Mürren he was visited by princes and paupers in his little suite at the Jungfrau Lodge, made available to him by the hotel's owner who recognized that Arnold Lunn had done more for mountaineering and skiing than any Swiss—indeed he was knighted in 1952 by King George in acknowledgement of those achievements—and that he was broke. To reach him, one rose by funicular, or took the new awesome lift, developed just in time to be exploited in one of the James Bond movies. In Mürren, where there are about three hundred residents, he was the most illustrious of them all, and the most beloved and most indulged. When he was 85, Lady Lunn left to visit very briefly her aged mother and gave Arnold his detailed instructions on how he was to behave during her absence. He listened with great attentiveness and apparent docility, and the moment she was off on the funicular, he picked up the telephone and ordered the concierge to produce his skis. The concierge told him 45 minutes later that he had looked for them in vain, that they must have been lost, after ten years of neglect. But a few minutes after that, very nearly in tears, he confessed that he had hidden them at the express instructions of Lady Lunn who suspected her husband might be just mad enough to try them on.

Sir Arnold used to say that all of mankind is divided inflexibly in two classes. There are the "helpers" and the "helpees." He had discovered early in life that he was a member of the latter class, that no marriage was successful that united two members from the same class. His first wife, Lady Mabel Northcote, was a helper; and when she died, a dozen years ago, he wed Phyllis Holt-Needham who, in addition to all her other qualities, was a born helper: so he knew he was licked. Disconsolately he set out, using the two walking sticks on which he now depended, across the snowy path toward the Jungfrau's dining room when, suddenly remembering his wife's several admonitions, he found his hand slipping down his front to verify that he had remembered to button his fly. But experiencing nothing there at all, he concluded he had his pants on backward. It was all he could do to survive the three days of her absence, and she was never absent again, and was with him when in the early afternoon, failing to rally, he died at the Catholic Hospital of St. John and St. Elizabeth near London.

He must have found it an inconvenient time to die. Two days later he was to have spoken at a golden jubilee dinner of the Kandahar Ski Club, of which he had been the central figure since its founding. "Phyllis has told me not to be controversial in my speech," he had written me. "I must be amusing. I thought after the president had proposed my health as founder of the club to begin my speech saying, 'Phyllis tells me I must not be controversial. So I will begin by expressing cordial agreement with all the very nice things the president has said about me.' " He'd have laughed greatly, telling his friends this. I think he must have spent half his life laughing. During the other half, in addition to the usual things, he wrote 54 books, discovered Christianity, and for his friends, reminded us more than any man I have ever known, what is meant when one talks about the irrepressibility of the human spirit.

—*William F. Buckley Jr.*
July 5, 1974

The Blue Train

William A. Rusher

W hen I was a boy, trains—and above all, on trips overnight or longer, Pullman sleeping cars—were indisputably the way to travel. My earliest memories of lengthy journeys with my parents are redolent of the sights and sounds, even the smells, of the great trains. The huge, hissing engine; the steps too tall for a little boy; the narrow, car-length corridor; the stiff dark green upholstery of the compartment; the musical clank and clatter of the wheels along the tracks; the authoritative note of the train's whistle; the telephone poles, the cornfields, the crossings, the villages whizzing by. I can still see the heavy white napery in the dining car, and feel that thick, baroque silverware. The Great Age of Train Travel lasted barely a century, but I am glad I shared at least part of it.

The idea of traveling really long distances by train, in circumstances of true luxury, is fast becoming one with Nineveh and Tyre. Which brings me to the Blue Train, God bless it.

From Johannesburg to Cape Town is about 800 miles as a South African crow (if there were such a thing) would fly, or just under 1,000 by the narrow-gauge track of the South African Railways. The 727s of South African Airways cover the distance in about the time it takes to fly from New York to Chicago—say, one and a half or two hours, This past September, being in no special hurry, I decided to take the famous train.

I was waiting on the platform of Johannesburg's great central station when the 16-coach train, painted royal blue, glided in. My car and room number had been posted on the platform bulletin board, and a nattily uniformed attendant welcomed me aboard. Promptly at 11:30, with the noiseless grace of an ocean liner, the Blue Train pulled out of Johannesburg.

I looked around my spacious room. The train, drawn by a powerful electric locomotive, was almost silkily silent; the vibration and noise I had always associated with train travel were nearly gone. The upholstery was blue; the fixtures, a golden color. The window—wide and spotlessly clean—was almost imperceptibly tinted with a microscopic layer of gold, to deflect heat and glare. A venetian blind rose, fell, and tilted as I controlled a knob. Another knob regulated the air-conditioning; still others, the four radio entertainment channels and their volume. My private bath boasted a shower; but here I was conscious of sitting below the salt, as it were: if I had been traveling with a wife, we could have had a suite composed of a sitting room, a bedroom with twin beds, and a private bath *with tub*! We bachelors have to rough it.

If such gloomy reflections depress you (and, to tell the truth, they never even occurred to me at the time), you can buzz for the car attendant. He has a phone in his office, and will gladly use it to ask the dining car or the bar to send along refreshments to your room. My guess, though, is that you will want to drop back to the lounge car and have your cocktail there before proceeding to the dining car for lunch.

There are dining cars and dining cars. This one, however—in keeping with the general principle of the Blue Train—is the last word. Fresh flowers, for instance, on every table. Two sittings to choose from at lunch and dinner—and your seat, once chosen, thereafter reserved for you. First-rate food, and above all those truly splendid South African wines. (The Nederburg Selected Cabernet, for example, belongs well along toward the top of any international ranking.)

Outside the gold-layered windows, the veld is gliding by—flat, tawny, limitless, under that vast African sky. And "gliding"—not rushing. This is no "flier," trying to beat the Japanese for some railroad equivalent of the Blue Ribbon of the Atlantic. The train's top speed is a very respectable 110 kilometers per hour (equal to about 70 mph), but this is reached only during the night hours. For the rest, speeds of 60, 50, and even 40 mph are quite common, and thoroughly in keeping with the train's general atmosphere. If you can afford to ride the Blue Train, it seems to be suggesting, you are not a person who needs to hurry; your affairs in Cape Town will wait patiently for you.

Back in your room at last, after a final South African brandy with some new friends in the lounge car (remember to specify "KWV Ten Year Old"), you will find your bed prepared, as you had instructed. Now for a comfortable night's sleep, rocked gently by the motion of the train.

There were three stops (including Kimberley, the diamond center) before bedtime, and three more while I slept. When I awoke about 7:45 A.M., we had just left Touwsriver (right on schedule), and the scenery had changed dramatically. The highveld was now hundreds of miles behind us—and far above us, for we had descended nearly 4,000 feet since leaving Johannesburg, and would descend another 2,000 before reaching Cape Town. All around us now were the mountains that make Cape Province one of the loveliest parts of Africa. Over breakfast in the dining car I watched as the Blue Train curved and recurved through the beautiful Hex River valley—yellow with mimosa in the quickening September of the southern hemisphere's spring. On every side, the vines in their geometric rows awaited the sweet burden of the grapes.

Now at last the towns were growing larger and closer together. And over there, through that haze to the southwest, was that?—yes, there was Table Mountain, with a white fringe of "tablecloth" clinging to its top. The Blue Train curved around its base, picked its way deliberately, almost daintily, through the maze of rail lines in the outer yards, and drew to a final stop in

Cape Town Station. You could have set your watch by that action: precisely 11:30 AM.

Civility, in its sense of sheer *consideration*, is not so common in the world anymore that we can afford to take it for granted; and I think it is the civility of the Blue Train that I like, even more than its indisputable luxury. Somebody has so obviously taken care to attend to every detail.

February 15, 1974—Arts & Manners

Mirror of Language: Fitzgerald's Homer

Hugh Kenner

Chinese dogs bark "wang wang," Greek dogs bark "bou bou," English dogs bark "bow wow." So much for the notion that language says things as they are. Languages register simply the observation that dogs say something abrupt, and say it twice. Only human beings really say "bow wow," and English-speaking human beings at that, and what they say resembles what a dog says only to an ear that experience has filled with the rest of the English language.

A local stress in the language field, that's a "meaning."

And no word of Homer's is an isolated event, "meaning" something all by itself. It is a point of stress in the fabric of his dialect, the whole of which responds when the word is uttered. From which it follows that no one can translate Homer (or anything else) "correctly." Look up *polyphloisbos* in the lexicon, and what you find is "loud-roaring." Look up its most famous Homeric occurrence in Alexander Pope's *Iliad* (1715), and for the line in which the priest Chryses, after being rebuffed by Achilles, fares silently home along the shore of the sounding sea, you will find only

The trembling priest along the shore return'd:

from which you may be tempted to conclude that Mr. Pope left something out. (George Chapman—1958—wrote "the sea-beate shore.")

But Mr. Pope was not so naive. He supplies a note on the reticence of Homer, "eloquent in his very silence." The priest says not a word, but walks pensively along the shore, "and the melancholy Flowing of the Verse admirably expresses the condition of the mournful and deserted Father." And Pope then quotes the Greek line: ... *para thina polyphloisboio thalasses.*

"The melancholy flowing of the verse"! Despite lexicons, Pope knew better than to interject something loud-roaring just at that instant. He was listening to the sound of the whole line, and observing that *polyphloisboio*, despite being a big word, doesn't make a big noise. On the principle of eloquent silence, he omitted it.

Robert Fitzgerald [in his translation of the *Illiad*, Doubleday/Anchor] also listens to the sounds the whole passage makes, and his various dealings with this famous work are elucidative.

So harsh he was, the old man feared and obeyed him,
in silence trailing away
by the shore of the tumbling clamorous whispering sea ...

Fourteen years ago, in his *Odyssey*, he dealt with its two occurrences in that poem in two wholly different ways, responding to different local effects. Once, quickening Homer's narrative, he has only "foaming": the Phaeacian ship bore Odysseus back to Ithaca,

> *her bow wave riding after, and her wake on the purple night-sea foaming.*

The other time, when Odysseus walks despairing by the sea as Chryses had walked by the sea near Troy, and Homer employs the identical phrase he had used in the *Iliad*, Fitzgerald writes

> *And then he wept, despairing, for his own land,*
> > *trudging down*
> *beside the endless wash of the wide, wide sea*
> *weary and desolate as the sea.*

The endless wash, the wideness, the desolation, these do not answer to separate Greek words, they are all extrapolated from that polysemous *polyphloisboio*.

Such multifariousness tends to bewilder scholars, who prefer the Lincoln-log verse of Richmond Lattimore, sturdy, opaque, its members trundled to the site and pegged together. But it is Fitzgerald, unafraid of being thought "rather free," who has accomplished our time's penetration into the enduring mysteries of Homeric rhetoric. He can manage the famous similes as deftly as the captains by Skamander managed their troops:

> *And as migrating birds, nation by nation,*
> *wild geese and arrow-throated cranes and swans,*
> *over Asia's meadowland and marshes*
> *around the streams of Kaystrios, with giant*
> *flight and glorying wings keep beating down*
> *in tumult on that verdant land*
> *that echoes to their pinions, even so,*
> *nation by nation, from the ships and huts.*
> *the host debouched upon Skamander plain.*
> *With noise like thunder pent in earth*
> *under their trampling, under the horses' hooves,*
> *they filled the flowering land beside Skamander,*
> *as countless as the leaves and blades of spring. ...*

One needs a good deal of context to gauge the local excellences.

What Homer said of the cranes and swans was "long-necked," a bit of lore worth fixing with language in a time of no zoos nor picture-books, but pointless today. "Arrow-throated" is Fitzgerald's admirably martial invention, and a mark of his concern that nothing shall seem pointless. Then Homer built his first long sentence around eight syllables that resound like anvils, *klangedon prokathizonton*, "uttering their cries the birds keep settling ever forwards." English has no equivalent for that verb, and no strident word with the authority of *klangedon*. Fitzgerald's

> *with giant flight and glorying wings keep beating down*
> *in tumult*

gets its effect not by word-for-word substitution but by disrupting with enjambment and splendor of diction ("glorying") the progress of his equable measure. And

> *With noise like thunder pent in earth*

—two syllables short, that line tramps like a host.[1]

Fitzgerald's secret—so far as we can disentangle it from his immense resourcefulness—is a straight-running unobtrusive idiom and a straightforward ten-syllable line in which the slightest deviations become expressive. (Shine polarized light through clear Lucite: every strain makes a rainbow pattern.) It yielded him in the Fifties a magnificent *Odyssey*, arguably *the* Homeric version of our century. If his *Iliad* is a little less successful, that tells us something both about our time's idiom and about the *Iliad*, which will capitulate less often to a technique of iridescences.

The speeches of the Gods are often obdurate. Homer's long line can roll cliché about with Olympian authority, and Chapman's can echo it:

> *He spake, and all the Gods gave*
> *eare: 'Heare how I stand inclind—*
> *That God nor Goddesse may attempt t'infringe my soveraigne*
> *mind ...*

—which is what the Thunder might say, thunder not being renowned for subtlety of thought. Pope's gavel-like rhyme has a like authority:

> *Celestial States, Immortal Gods! give ear,*
> *Hear our Decree, and rev'rence what ye hear.*

---

[1] Chapman: "The din/Was dreadful that the feete of men and horse beate out of earth."

This time Mr. Fitzgerald's

> *Listen to me,*
> *immortals, every one,*
> *and let me make my mood and purpose clear*

smacks rather of a Balkan cabinet meeting.

And it is a wintry sobriety, expecting no pain to be mitigated, that sustains the *Iliad*'s endless giving and receiving of wounds: a spear between Skamandrios' shoulder blades, a spear through Phereklos' bladder, a spear through Pedaios' nape (upward through the root of his tongue and against his teeth: "So Pedaios fell in the dust, and bit the cold bronze"): all this unrolls with a slow-motion implacability for which Mr. Fitzgerald's line is paced a little rapidly, forcing forward the brilliant details as though Homer were trying to be picturesque.

In the *Odyssey*, a tricky shimmering poem by comparison, the rhetoric of the picturesque is seldom out of place. If the *Iliad* gives Fitzgerald few opportunities to do what he can do best, he meets the opportunities when they come. The great similes from nature have never been so sinuously rich in English, nor the Mediterranean warmth of details neither martial nor Olympian: such details as the infant frightened by his father's helmet plume.

His father is Hektor, repeatedly "gleaming-helmed," an emblematic epithet which Mr. Fitzgerald, avid for effects of light as is no other translator, at least once renders "glimmering." And Hektor has spoken farewell to the boy's mother; they both know that they will perhaps not meet again.

> *As he said this, Hektor held out his arms*
> *to take his baby. But the child squirmed round*
> *on the nurse's bosom and began to wail*
> *terrified by his father's great war helm—*
> *the flashing bronze, the crest with horsehair plume*
> *tossed like a living thing at every nod.*
> *His father began laughing, and his mother*
> *laughed as well. Then from his handsome head*
> *Hektor lifted off his helm and bent*
> *to place it, bright with sunlight, on the ground. ...*

Just that domestic plainness of idiom—"the child squirmed round": "the father began laughing"—is what can retrieve this from grand opera, as Hektor's recurrent emblematic epithet, "gleaming-helmed," comes to life and assaults the child with all that a child can perceive of the lethal strangeness of war. The crest tossing "like a living thing" is an infant's vision and Mr.

Fitzgerald's contribution. Sensing how things look to children is part of our time's sensibility.

What an age can read in Homer, what its translators can manage to say in his presence, is one gauge of its morale, one index to its system of exultations and reticences. The supple, the iridescent, the ironic, these modes are among our strengths, and among Mr. Fitzgerald's. Our best habits of response to life and fortune have no more convincing mirror than his two versions.

April 25, 1975

Death of a Colleague

Frank S. Meyer, R I P

William F. Buckley Jr.

I called him from Peking (which I knew would give him a kick) and he told me that the cause of the pains that had begun seriously to hamper him in December was not yet diagnosed, that the culture sent out a few weeks earlier to discern whether he was suffering from tuberculosis had not yet matured, that meanwhile he had no appetite, but was getting on with his work as usual. "I never guessed I would sit here hoping I had tuberculosis," he said, and quickly got on to the subject of Nixon's mission in Peking, which he had been following closely, very closely, even as he had been observing the international chess tournament, his son Gene's progress as a freshman at Yale, his other son's preoccupation with his law paper, the awful behavior of the *New York Times*, the erratic habits of one of the book reviewers for NATIONAL REVIEW, the absolute inability of the young to spell even the simplest words, the developing congressional sentiment against the Family Assistance Plan, and who should review Garry Wills' new book about modern

Frank Meyer

Catholicism? By Frank Meyer's standards, it wasn't a long conversation, but I caught a quiver in his voice which when I spoke to him next, from Switzerland, had acquired amplitude, and then the day after returning to New York, on Monday, the news came in. Cancer. Inoperable. He would return from the hospital to his house on Wednesday, to die there, in a month or two (he believed); within two weeks (his wife Elsie confided to Brent Bozell). On Thursday morning he spoke over the telephone for the first time in ten days—there was not such a stillness since quiet came to the Western Front. He asked Priscilla if the book section was all right, and she told me, moistly, after he hung up, she doubted he would last for two weeks.

I arrived the afternoon of Good Friday, tense with the pain of knowing that never before had I visited with someone when the lifesaving dissimulations ("The doctor says you'll be fine in just a couple of weeks") were simply out of the question, but his instinctive consideration saved me. Otherwise he was wonderfully querulous, shouting at the top of what was left of his lungs for Elsie (*El*sie! Elll*sie*!!) every two minutes, wanting his leg moved or that pillow lowered or the oxygen cap refitted—mostly what he wanted was for her to sit there holding his hand, as she had done hour after hour day after day, since the plunge of March 11. But then he asked her to leave the room, and also his son, and the nurse, and he said to me did I know that "Gene" (The Very Reverend Monsignor Eugene V. Clark, young, learned, buoyant, and devoted unofficial chaplain to New York conservatives, secretary to Cardinals Spellman and Cooke) had been there the afternoon before? Yes, I said. Well, said Frank, he wanted to join the Church, but he had declined yesterday to be baptized because he did not believe that the Church's position on suicide was convincing. Frank was not going to give up arguing merely to expedite death. I said Frank, do you mean it isn't convincing, or do you mean that you do not propose to observe the Church's prohibition? His mind wandered a bit, and he told me that "Gene" had said he would return on the next day, and I said that I was no scholar on the subject but that it was my impression that the self-knowledge that one will transgress in the future and even that one will seek to justify one's transgression, is not sacramentally disqualifying, and he nodded. Did I know, he asked, that his son John quite coincidentally was thinking of joining the Church? No I didn't, I said, recalling, years ago when I knew him only over the telephone, back when he was writing the book reviews for the *American Mercury*, his telling me that he believed, and that if only he could figure out a way of taking the collectivism out of the Church (the emphasis of Vatican II on collegiality set Frank back ten years), he would come into it, though there was the problem—"I'm a Jew," he said, "and it's always harder, especially if there's persecution going on. Maybe I'd better hurry up, because usually there's persecution but right this second [this was 1954] there isn't much that I can think of."

He was small, grey-white crew-cut hair, baggy clothes, smoke-stained teeth, that cigarette in hand, whisky voice, solemn mien, a pacer, an athletic gait, though I doubt that in his lifetime he exerted a muscle more vigorously than necessary to move a pawn on the chessboard. I thought, my arm on his bed, which he let his own arm fall upon when he took a second's doze, that now he didn't have the strength to do even that, lying on his bed in his study. Looking past his emaciated features I could see three volumes immediately behind him. *The History of Ancient Sicily. The History of Medieval Sicily. The History of Modern Sicily.* Three of the twenty thousand books that came to the little house on Ohayo Mountain during the last fifteen years which he didn't send out to review, didn't give away, which he "skimmed," storing something in his mind from them. Elsie called, and told me the nurse would give him now, for the first time, a shot of Demerol, that the doctors had delayed beginning it because he'd need a lot of it toward the end. El-*sie*!!—she went in with the nurse, and he submitted, they turned him over, and I left. The next day he was worse, much worse. That afternoon he saw Father Clark, and made the great submission, and a few hours later I was called to the telephone. It was his son, Gene. I told him the truth, that his father was a great man, and hung up.

The Editor

Hugh Kenner

His book review section was in constant tension between his generosity and his vigilance. Generosity had the best of it, usually. That was why it was comfortable to review for *NR*. He trusted his reviewers, and passed for publication all manner of statements his principles urged him to worry at like a pup. Being the most deductive of libertarians, he deduced the need to give writers liberty, though what they did with it was in frequent collision with all his other deductions. His was a nineteenth-century virtue, once called Liberalism before the liberals made off with that word, and he'd probably like it if I called him a Victorian sage. Many doughty debaters have awaited his coming in heaven. The next time you see sheet lightning, you can fancy it's Frank Meyer taking on Carlyle.

Teacher

Peter T. Witonski

Now that his voice is stilled, it is fair to ask, what was his importance for the conservative movement? The answer is simple. He was our greatest teacher. He was the first conservative theorist thoroughly to comprehend the uniqueness of American conserevatism, and to explain this uniqueness to the conservative rank and file. Whenever conservatism might stray from the course of common sense, it was always Frank Meyer, standing athwart history, who called us back to our senses. Socrates said that virtue can be taught, but, he added, there are no teachers of virtue. In Frank Meyer, the conservative movement found a teacher of virtue. He is gone, but we shall continue to hear his voice.

Mentor

Priscilla L. Buckley

I ask the young man on my left how long he has known Frank, how well, and how did he meet him in the first place. Not long, he answers, very well, he says and—sadly—that he never did get to meet him. But the way he got to know him was this. He had noticed that a friend was writing an occasional brief book review for NATIONAL REVIEW. If that particular friend was good enough to write for *NR*, said Young Man,* certainly I was. So he wrote Frank a note, suggesting a review. A few nights later, a phone call. Two, three minutes on the question of the review—and suddenly they were discussing Ruskin. Why Ruskin, he couldn't for the life of him remember. But he got the assignment and he and Frank talked "regularly" after that—and became friends. And so the young man on my left and others from cities all over the land had come to Woodstock, to attend the Mass, listen to Taps, watch Elsie accept the flag, to form their own honor guard around the flag-draped coffin, on this cold spring day. There were dozens of them. Funerals are for old people. The young—when possible—find excuses not to attend. But Frank's funeral was a young people's funeral. You couldn't have kept them away.

* Future Reagan speechwriter Aram Bakshian.

Host

Christopher H. Simonds

Hundreds of people must remember that comfortable old coat of a room, the cobblestone fireplace faced by the couch and flanked by the two chairs, Frank's and the one that after five minutes was one's own forever (coming again, a month or a year later, one sank back down and the conversation resumed), the books from floor to ceiling on every wall—the house was insulated not with rock wool or Fiberglass but with the wisdom of the West. That first night one rediscovered the pleasure of sheer, undistracted conversation. About everything—politics, baseball, philosophy, aerial dogfights in the world of professional chess, being Communists together ("Frank was terrible—he was always telling me I was subjective." "Well you *were*, dammit!"), Tolkien, Henty, gardening (Elsie's was beautiful, even viewed by flashlight), and always civilization and the barbarians.

The Quest

Garry Wills

Frank was an anti-Communist who had been a Communist. Not a radical or leftist or sympathizer or fellow traveler or pro-Communist; not a worker who joins the Party because he has been led to believe it is fighting to improve the literate judgments of Guy Davenport, Hugh Kenner, Theodore Sturgeon, Arlene Croce or Francis Russell. And Frank knew the review-page advantages of an Anglophile long before the *New York Review of Books* was born.

Though we all live inevitably toward our death, Frank had also moved very consciously all his life toward a faith that would account for man's weird vitality of spirit to challenge that death. In one brief half-a-day last week, those two journeys converged for him. Lucid in the afternoon, as he prayed aloud through cancer-ravaged lungs, he was baptized—and then the tensest of vibrant men relaxed. Six hours later he was dead; and three hours after, it was Easter.

Friend

Guy Davenport

"Who would have thought," he once said at my house, "that we would become journalists?" We had been talking about Oxford (he was at Balliol), and we were both, I think, looking back wistfully at the green idealism of our college days. Frank had just spoken ("Was I too shrill?") in Philadelphia, and we had settled in to one of those all-night conversations which he considered perfectly normal. He was an old-fashioned arguer, leaping on any difference of opinion as an opportunity to broaden the discussion. A different idea was an adventure. I can remember arguments that lasted over the years: comparisons of Spengler and Toynbee, of Lord Randolph and Sir Winston Churchill, of Victorian and modern poetry. There was the great debate over the phone as to whether Vladimir Nabokov's father was or was not a member of Kerensky's cabinet. He was suspicious of the arts after certain dates, and I would thus find myself defending the craftsmanship of Picasso, William Carlos Williams, and Charles Ives. Whether there has been a civilization in Africa other than the Egyptian was another subject calculated to enrich the coffers of Bell Telephone.

Lord, how I shall miss those conversations!

April 28, 1972

Living and Dying in Boston

Francis Russell

At half past nine of an early September evening the young woman in the flowered dress walks along Blue Hill Avenue down the slope from Franklin Park. Most of the small stores she passes on the Avenue are empty, boarded up since the riots of six years ago, their fronts pasted over with now tattered and faded Black Power posters and smeared with crude slogans. Only the liquor stores, those hardiest of weeds, have managed to survive here, their windows bricked down to slits and protected by layers of steel mesh.

The young woman is pretty in a casual way. Her errand is obvious. She is carrying a red two-gallon can of gasoline from a Grove Hall filling station to a car stranded somewhere in the no-man's-land of streets between Dorchester and Roxbury. As she nears a dilapidated corner house, six young Negroes step out of the darkness into the blue-white range of the arc lamps. Shouting obscenities they encircle her, shove her from one to the other like a rag doll, force her down the narrow alley between the corner house and an apartment block. There in the litter of a vacant rear lot they order her to pour the gasoline on herself. She refuses. They beat and kick her until finally she gives in. When she has drenched herself to their satisfaction, one of the gang flicks a lighted match at her. She takes fire like a torch, and they run off laughing and jeering.

After vainly rolling on the ground to put out the flames, she staggers down the alley, her clothes and hair ablaze, and screams her way past half a dozen closed shops to the open liquor store. Customers and clerks pull off her burning clothing. A police car that happens to be cruising by takes her to the City Hospital. She has second and third degree burns over all her body. Four hours later she is dead.

She was Evelyn Wagler, a 26-year-old German-born Swiss, married but separated from her husband, the mother of a six-year-old boy. A drifter, she had lived in communes, with Women's Liberation friends, on Chicago's tough South Side, worked as a carpenter, a waitress, a truck driver. Five days earlier she had arrived in Boston after hitchhiking from Chicago and taking odd jobs along the way. She moved in with four girls she had known previously—three black and one white—who lived in the upper floor of a two-family house on the edge of Dorchester. She was looking for a job when her borrowed car ran out of gas. Before she died she managed to tell the police that she had been confronted on the Avenue the day before by three of the same gang. They had warned her: "Whitey, get out of this part of town!" It was just more of the same sort of street "jive," she told her roommates, she used to hear in Chicago. After her death her estranged husband explained to reporters that she had been killed "by the system, a system that creates ghettos and racial hatred." Her body remained in the morgue unclaimed.

A week later no one had been arrested, and Evelyn Wagler's name had disappeared from the newspapers.

The tale would have been one to which I should have reacted in transitory horror and then inevitably have pushed aside as new tales intervened. But Dorchester, where Evelyn Wagler died, happens to be the section of Boston where I grew up, the place of my first memories, the only part of the earth that has come to seem instinctively home to me. So I felt her death as something personal, as if we were somehow related. Blue Hill Avenue was for me *the* Avenue before I knew there were other avenues, a Via Appia running die-straight from the Blue Hills to the provincial city on the horizon.

We lived a mile or so the other side of Franklin Park on Walk Hill, bordering on Blue Hill Avenue, a segment of Dorchester that still kept the Indian name of Mattapan, Place-of-the-Ford. For me it was the hub of the universe. From the row of pignut trees on the Hill's crest one could look north to the hazy tentacular city four and a half miles away and sometimes on bright afternoons catch the glitter of the gilt State House dome. On grey days the sky itself seemed held up by the granite obelisk of the Custom House tower. East lay the harbor islands, beyond the yellow bulk of the Dorchester High School.

Until the Boston Elevated Street Railway Company extended its line from Grove Hall to Mattapan in 1908, the Hill was a supernumerary bit of property owned by Wellington Holbrook, a feckless *Mayflower* descendant who lived on the bits and pieces of his diminished inheritance. Thanks to the Boston El, Mattapan became a streetcar suburb and Holbrook was able to develop his empty drumlin into a settlement of one- and two-family houses, run up as cheaply as possible on postage-stamp-size lots. With passing vanity he changed the Hill's old name to Wellington Hill. It became a bourgeois community of those who considered themselves simply Americans but would later be labeled WASPs—clerks, salesmen, petty officials, minor professional men, and the occasional teacher.

With the advent of World War I, shops with kosher signs began to spread down Blue Hill Avenue, each year creeping closer to Walk Hill. District after Dorchester district became solidly Jewish. As soon as a few Jews bought into a street, the other families would become restive, FOR SALE signs would appear in their windows, and in a few seasons they would have moved away. Dorchester was becoming, not ghetto, but a *kahal*, an expanding Jewish community, soon to be the most densely populated area of greater Boston.

Most of the Jews who moved to the Hill were foreign-born, and in the rush before the more restrictive immigration laws they were willing to spend their last dollar to bring in their assorted relatives. We stayed on for six years after the first invasion, and I became used to the sight of full-bearded old men—like the Rabbi Sheshevsky who bought a two-family house not far from us—in long black coats and wide black hats. On summer evenings they sat on their front porches with *yarmulkes* on their heads, and the old women wore wigs that sometimes peeped askew from beneath their shawls.

The Dorchester *kahal* became the center of Boston Jewry. In those years before the New Deal, the Jews voted Republican in opposition to the Irish Democrats. By the late Thirties the more prosperous Jews were leaving Mattapan and Dorchester. The children and grandchildren of Chelsea peddlers and ragmen, of Blue Hill Avenue tailors and fishmongers and delicatessen proprietors, had through their relentless pursuit of education become lawyers, doctors, teachers, professors, financiers, members of all the professions. From the three-deckers and two-family houses of Dorchester they had moved to spacious single homes in Brookline and Newton. There were Jewish sections of those towns but the *kahal* itself had vanished.

After the Second World War Dorchester and the Hill remained undividedly Jewish, but the population was thinning. Those who stayed behind were those who had not made it, the has-beens, the failures, the elderly. Dorchester remained a slightly obnoxious memory. The proud marble bulk of Temple Mishkan Tefila loomed up across from Franklin Park an empty shell, its name and substance having been translated to Newton Center.

Sometimes on a summer evening in the early Fifties when I happened to be driving in to Boston from Wellesley, I would park my car near Walk Hill Street's Martha Baker School, where I had attended the first five grades, then like a revenant walk up the Hill and along the streets with the uneasy familiarity of a dream, past the house I once knew, the gabled house where I once lived. The Hill's line of pignut trees had been replaced by the brick solidity of the Solomon Lewenberg Junior High School. Who he was I had no idea, but then I had never known who Martha Baker or Edmund P. Tileston were. But I did know that the Lewenberg School had the highest scholastic standing of any junior high school in the city. On such a lingering summer evening the Hill people sat on their porches, in their minute yards, even on their front steps, calling back and forth in a lighthearted neighborliness that I, the revenant, found myself wishing I might share, that someone might nod to me as I passed.

After World War II Boston's Negro population suddenly expanded, bursting its static boundaries, flowing to Dudley Street and then across Roxbury to Dorchester. A number of old Yankee families had persisted in the large and solid Victorian mansions of the Roxbury Highlands, and the Jewish invasion had flowed round rather than through them. The black tide of the Fifties and

Sixties drove out the Yankee lingerers when they were faced with what they had never encountered with the Jews—violence.

On casual trips to Boston in the Sixties I would sometimes drive up Blue Hill Avenue to watch the progress of the black tide. It was easy to spot. For some reason lower class Jewish families never had window curtains but merely shades or Venetian blinds. Where on lower Blue Hill Avenue the windows in the drab brick apartment buildings had been neat though bare, they suddenly became smeared, the blinds twisted askew, the shades torn and stained. Blacks had arrived. One could trace the tide by the condition of the windows. It seemed to move at about half a mile a year. By the time it had covered the down slope from Franklin Park to Franklin Field, though there was still a mile to go, I knew the Hill was about to "change" again.

In the Roxbury-Dorchester riots that followed Martin Luther King's murder, most of the shop windows along Blue Hill Avenue were smashed as far as Franklin Field and even beyond. The boarded-up fronts remain. A few proprietors did reopen because their little shops were all they had. But their customers dwindled away and they found themselves threatened and challenged by young blacks, robbed in their shops, mugged on the street. These tough teen-age gangs soon made the Avenue a street of peril. No longer did the pushing gossipy crowds throng the sidewalks on a Saturday night, no longer did flaring lights welcome the customers into the shop interiors. Old men still huddled in the G&G, drinking tea and reading Yiddish papers, but each time I dropped in there were fewer of them. The Jewish wave that I had seen crest and break so long ago had receded, leaving only a few pebbles behind.

I did not come back to Blue Hill Avenue until the week after Evelyn Wagler's death. Nor did I linger on Walk Hill, for the Lewenberg School was letting out shortly and that was dangerous ground then. The school was all black now, tumultuous, its proud standards obliterated. Now, when school let out, the remaining shops on the Avenue closed for an hour. I was not going to risk having my car rocked over with myself in it, as had almost happened to me one earlier afternoon. Yet in my brief Hill transit what had struck me was the aura of fear. Many of the better-kept houses now had protective grillwork on the windows and doors. Others were surrounded by chain-link fences. No longer was it Jewish fear of the Negro, but blacks fearing blacks, men fearing other men.

Beyond Franklin park I stopped for a moment opposite the spot where Evelyn Wagler had been cattleprodded down the alley to her death. The alley was only a few feet wide, fenced in but with a gap wide enough to squeeze through. The back area was open to a side street that ran off the Avenue beside the dilapidated green corner house. Someone in that house or the apartment next to it must have seen. But no one ever came forward to say so. I drove round the block in the now semi-darkness. There was the same conjunction I found on the Hill and all over Dorchester: ramshackle houses, empty houses, ruined houses, the yards overgrown with pig and ragweed and ankle deep in debris; and, in between, houses as well-groomed, with yards as green and tidy, as the most proper "executive" suburb. Except for a few children skipping rope, the only figures I saw were those of young black males anywhere from 16 to thirty, standing or leaning against doorways or store fronts, eyeing the world, and me in particular, and challenging hostile glances. I drove round the block twice, and the second time these young men in their slouch hats watched me more narrowly, stabbed out their cigarettes with contempt as I passed, and I could sense their latent threat like a declaration of war. Unemployed, unemployable, they were as scornful of liberal panaceas as they were of me. These or such as these, could have set Evelyn Wagler afire. What did they want from life? Unformed, consumed by an anger as vicious as it was undefined, I don't suppose they knew themselves. Their satisfaction was that they brought fear with them.

For the last time I drove back along the Avenue, down the long slope from Franklin Park. Great Blue Hill lay directly ahead on the horizon, the nipple of the weather observatory on its summit outlined against the grey sky. Just as I used to notice from the streetcar in my schooldays, Blue Hill seemed to recede into a kind of infinity as one moved downhill toward it. Blue Hill Avenue itself was empty, a scarecrow boulevard, like an artery drained of blood. I could see a planet over the dark hulk of the Lewenberg School, Venus or Jupiter I wasn't sure which. I knew then that, when everyone else had forgotten her, I should not forget Evelyn Wagler. I knew that I should not come that way again.

November 23, 1973

The Man Who Went to Dinner

Colm Brogan

When the diaries of a well-known man are due for publication, people who knew him are interested and even anxious. Am I mentioned favorably? Or unfavorably? Perhaps, and most depressingly, I am not mentioned at all.

My mind was untroubled by surmise when the *Observer* announced the serialization of extracts from the diary of Evelyn Waugh. I had unbounded admiration for Waugh as a writer and I knew him fairly well, but not well enough to make it likely that he would waste any words on me. I was wrong. In, I think, the fifth installment Waugh talks of going to a public dinner with Graham Greene and wrote these words which I would like to have carved in marble or cast in bronze or loudly proclaimed with an accompanying flourish from the Queen's trumpeters: "Colm Brogan joined us."

If this noncommittal sentence doesn't seem much to you, obviously you haven't read the extracts. After reading it I walked so tall I felt I was on stilts, and when I breathed I swallowed all the oxygen in the room. Nor was my pride ill-judged. Friends spoke to me with a new respect as if I had joined an extremely small and select company, something like the Order of Merit, only more choosy. After all, the members of the Order of Merit could not be counted on the fingers of both hands, but the number of those who appear in the diary with such a neutral remark as "Colm Brogan joined us" if counted on the fingers would leave enough fingers over to play a guitar.

The key for the series is set by the first installment [on Waugh's Oxford years], but as Waugh grew older his comments extended far beyond moral character. His judgment on people's manners, pretensions, and abilities are sprayed over the pages like asperges of vitriol. Even his praise is subtly qualified. For example, Father D'Arcy, who received him into the Church, has "a fine, slippery mind." Nobody, least of all a Jesuit, would appreciate his fine mind being called "slippery." Far better the nobly austere statement "Colm Brogan joined us."

The dinner where "Colm Brogan joined us," was given in honor of Archbishop Griffin, later Cardinal, who had just come to Westminster. It was a dinner of the Catholic literary gents of Britain, and the guests were mostly distinguished enough, even though Waugh dismissed them as Rotarians. By the way, he described the Archbishop as "common," which he seemed to regard as being much more seriously sinful than being a sodomite.

It was Comptom Mackenzie who made the speech of the evening, toasting the deplorably common Archbishop. It was not a well-judged speech. He called on the Archbishop to give them a lead and tell them what to say, but added that the writers would not necessarily follow his lead or pay attention to what he told them. This put the Archbishop in some difficulty and his own speech was not much more convincing.

Still the evening was pleasant enough. I was sitting between Waugh and Graham Greene. Waugh surprisingly told Greene that he should write a novel about me. Greene replied firmly, "Brogan's no good to me. He'll never end in seedy decay." Little did he know. If he could see me now, hobbling in a walking frame and boasting feebly of my mention in the diary, just like a Graham Greene character, I am sure he would agree that I am ripe for the treatment.

By shaking the Rotarian dust from his feet too early, Waugh missed what I thought was the best part of the evening. I came across Comptom Mackenzie affably laying down the law. He was saying that Stalin was the greatest man of the age; an historical giant and, of course, a mighty force for the higher righteousness. As they say in my native Glasgow, I got tore into him. I asked him if he had joined the undertakers. This called for an explanation which I promptly provided. In 1939 after the fall of Poland, Mackenzie gave an eloquent broadcast address attacking the Allies for basely allowing Poland to be conquered and partitioned once again. His final flourish was to ask if the nation of shopkeepers had become a nation of undertakers.

MacKenzie said he remembered the broadcast, but history had since forced him to admit that he had completely misjudged the Russian leader. This was more than flesh and blood, or at any rate I, could stand. I let him have it good and hard. I noticed that people were drawing in their chairs to enjoy the fun. But the thought of a fellow Scot letting the side down so calamitously made me reckless and my language went from the intemperate to the profane and touched dangerously close to the obscene. I knew that someone had drawn his chair up right behind me, but I paid no attention until I caught a glimpse of red. I turned round, and there was the Archbishop, all ears as the saying goes. Anxiously recalling the language I had used I started to stammer an apology, but the Archbishop whispered, "Go on, go on. *I* can't say it."

It may have been the memory of this evening that prompted him to take the chair at a meeting I addressed in Battersea Town Hall. Afterward he told one of the committee that he thought I would make an excellent Labour MP. That was too much. Seedy decay, if that was God's will. But a Labour MP—some things are not to be borne.

September 28, 1973

Redeemed from Fire by Fire

Russell Kirk

In 1978, Piety Hill would have been a century old: vast antiquity for our part of Michigan. It was loved by everyone in our village, and our firemen fought like angels to save it—all in vain. Once the tongues of flame touched those resinous pine timbers and boards, six fire engines could do nothing. And now, in Eliot's lines in "Little Gidding":

Ash on an old man's sleeve
Is all the ash the burnt roses leave.
Dust in the air suspended
Marks the place where a story ended.
Dust inbreathed was a house—
The wall, the wainscot and the mouse.
The death of hope and despair,
  This is the death of air.

Piety Hill was a dear old friend of many. The neighbors come with tender condolences; kind people I never met before invite us to dinner; the telephone in the library rings all day with sympathy calls from friends throughout these United States. We are too busy to weep.

Innocent Smith, in Chesterson's story *Manalive*, says that he would not be very surprised to find in Heaven the lamp post and the green gate of his own dear house. Heaven is a state, says Father Martin D'Arcy, in which all the good things of our earthly lives are eternally present to us, whenever we desire them. If that be true, and I pray that it is, then Annette and I and our three little daughters shall have Piety Hill always.

There were signs and portents before Ash Wednesday. For one, our friend Archie, who cuts wood for us, came not long ago to tell us how his big stone farmhouse burnt this winter. "Take a lesson from me," he said, "and make a list of everything in this house." Now we know that his house and ours burnt from the same cause: the collapse of the old sand-bricks that formed part of the chimney. We had rebuilt the base and the top of the chimney in recent years, but in the attic remained a section of the original sand-bricks: every house has its Achilles heel.

The house was haunted, and not by memories only. Some of our many guests were affrighted, from year to year, but I never felt dread. Why should shades of my great-grandfather and great-grandmother and their son and daughters linger quietly about Piety Hill? Why, out of love. Perfect love casts out fear.

I was away at Olivet College, that midnight when the chimney collapsed; they telephoned me at half-past two in the morning, to say that the Old House was lost altogether, but that the New House, the tall brick wing we built four years ago, might be saved, and that all of our household were safe. I went down on my knees to pray. "The Lord giveth and the Lord taketh away: blessed be the name of the Lord."

We shall build a new dining room and a new kitchen at the back of the New House—and other rooms too, if the times permit. The cheerful scholars of the Intercollegiate Studies Institute will gather with us once more, as they did last Christmastide and the Christmas and New Year's before. The Europeans and the South Americans and the Asiatics will come to stay with us as they have done these many years. If the specters will shift through the fire door, they will be doubly welcome.

"To be redeemed from fire by fire," Eliot wrote during the Second World War, is our hope or our despair. He meant that only Purgatory fire purges us of the fires of will and appetite. The burning of Piety Hill was a purgatory for us, and the common ordeal has deepened our love of one another, and of those who preceded us in time. We have our hope and our work. Above the stone doorway we plan for the new facade of the New House we will set an old stone long ago inscribed with a line from Vergil: "With the help of God, labor prospers."

Guests used to sleep very late in the haunted bedrooms of the Old House: I would tell them that they had come to the land of the lotos eaters, and that I had cast a spell upon Piety Hill, so that it lay outside time. So it does now. The old portraits are ash, and the old books, and the old clock, and the very toys of yesteryear. Knowing that we cannot step in the same river twice, we do not hope to turn again, back beyond last Ash Wednesday. Yet at that still point where time and the timeless intersect, we shall see always the tall windows and the hanging lamps of Piety Hill.

March 28, 1975—From the Academy

Bill Rusher as Cult Hero: A Frolic

D ear Mr. Buckley:
"...if there's gotta be a right-wing cult hero, why don't you make it Bill Rusher? If you could get everybody hooked up on Bill Rusher, get all the impressionists to do Bill Rusher routines, and get him to ride a motorcycle and go to Truman Capote's parties and everything maybe then when you come around people will listen to what you say and wait for him to come raise his eyebrows at them? I think he could pull it off. ... And then if your brother Jim decided to try for the White House, he wouldn't have everybody saying, "Look, it's Bill Buckley's brother ..." Oh God, I'm getting *that* wrong. Now it sounds as if they don't take *him* seriously.

Forget it. Anyway, I like what you've been up to, as much of it as I understand, and I'm gonna subscribe again as soon as I get another job. If I said anything bad here, I didn't mean to.

— Stanley Michael Matis
Jefferson, Mass.

December 7, 1973
MEMO TO: Bill Buckley
FROM: Bill Rusher
RE: Progress report on turning me into a cult hero.
           [Nov. 23]

It's a mixed bag. Frankly, I'm getting discouraged.

1. The eyebrow bit. For various obscure physiological reasons, my eyebrows simply won't go *up* high enough. I can wiggle my ears, especially my right ear (pure coincidence—no symbolism intended), but I doubt the gesture would be visible on television at a distance of more than six inches.
2. The Bill Rusher sweatshirt. I have located a manufacturer who would be willing to turn out a gross of these at a ridiculously high price, but then who would wear them? One of my godsons—a likely purchaser—has told his father that the kids on his block have threatened to beat him up if he wears a Bill Rusher sweatshirt.
3. Truman Capote simply refuses to return my phone calls.
4. On the other hand, I am getting so I can twiddle a red pen almost as well as you can. It's rather like baton twirling, right?
5. I have set myself to learn one new big word a day. This week so far, for example, I have learned *prevenient*, *susurrant*, and *dichotomous*.
6. I flatly refuse to ride a Honda. For one thing, they're dangerous in this Manhattan traffic. For another, I live only three and a half blocks from the office, so it isn't necessary. If you really think some unique mode of

transportation is essential to the image, I can rent a Shetland pony from a stable up in Westchester, but you'll have to keep it here at the office.

Really, instead of trying to turn me into the new cult hero so people will take you seriously, it might be better if we reversed our strategy and tried to sell me as an *anti*-hero: i.e., a guy so irredeemably square that he becomes famous for it. I am sure I could do it; I think people might buy it; and it would be a hell of a lot easier on me.

November 23, 1973—Notes and Asides

Pablo Casals, R I P

S omewhere along the line Whittaker Chambers remarked that one must forgive birds of paradise political naiveté. Surely this is true if one is dealing with men of captivating personal sincerity: Casals and Picasso were both geniuses and both gave their name and prestige to the Left. Picasso was devious. But Casals was never in search of the Communist state, but rather of Brook Farm, and the distorted attention he gave to the repressions of General Franco in a world of Stalin were the mark of the perfectionist, not of the man of guile. Let us remember, then, only his genius. As there are notes on the scale so highly pitched that only dogs are said to hear them, there is art so sublime that it all but escapes human comprehension. Such was Casals' art. It is said that perhaps his mastery of the cello exceeded the mastery of anyone, ever, over any single instrument. His devotion to his work, his personal philanthropy, the nobility of his relations with his instrument, with his music, and with his musicians, made him probably the most popular, as well as the most respected, musician of his age.

William F. Buckley Jr.—The Week
November 9, 1973

The Inside Out BLACK WHITES and
The Inside Out WHITE BLACKS

John Keefauver

Once upon a time there was a dedicated inventor who, after reasoning that everybody must be white on the inside, or at least not black, and that within this theory lay the answer to solving the world's racial problem once and for all, set about to invent a pill that would make blacks white by turning them inside out.

After years of toil, the inventor, who was a black, one evening popped a pill into his mouth, and the next morning, sure enough, he woke up with the black outside of him in and the white inside of him out. Ecstatic, he at once started making more pills and knocking on doors in his black neighborhood, announcing excitedly in his new inhaled voice that if the black would swallow the pill he would wake up with his white insides out.

Some blacks took the pill, although dubiously, and overnight became inside out black whites, but many of them refused, especially those who had known the inventor in his pre-inside out days and whom they now branded as being nothing more than an Uncle Inside Out Tom. On the other hand, some of the blacks who had never known the inventor refused to take the miracle pill *because* they didn't know that he was an inside out black white, and they weren't about to take anything from such a crazy white man.

Regardless of what was thought of him, the dedicated inventor went around the world offering his pill to any black who would take it, and gradually many blacks became inside out black whites and, of course, lost their natural rhythm. Some of them, in fact, became whiter than whites, which caused the whites who had never liked blacks when they were black to dislike them even more when they were white. "They're trying to be whiter than we are!" they bellowed when they found out what was going on.

In fact, some whites in time became so prejudiced against inside out black whites, especially the inside out black whites who were whiter than regular whites that they, stealing the magic pill, began taking it themselves, their reasoning being that if blacks could turn even whiter than whites by taking it, they, the whites, could be whitest of all by swallowing the miracle pill.

Alas, their reasoning was faulty. Or perhaps it was the fault of the pill, the inventor admitted glumly. For when the whites swallowed it, instead of becoming whiter they became blacker than regular blacks and discovered they had natural rhythm. "They're trying to be blacker than we are!" the regular blacks bawled when they found out what was going on.

It wasn't long, then, before nobody knew if whites were regular whites or inside out black whites or if blacks were regular blacks or inside out white blacks—and, as the poor inventor soon found out, it was very important for both whites and blacks to *know* for they soon demanded that the inventor do something so that they could figure out who in the hell was who.

The unhappy inventor, throwing up his hands, decided the only thing to do was to invent a second pill, one that would turn inside outers back into outside outers, no matter what color they had been originally.

After years of inventing, he finally swallowed a pill one evening that, by the next morning, put his inside black skin outside and his white outside back in.

So once again he set off around the world. He soon learned, though, that the inside out black whites, no matter what they had said before, preferred to remain what they were even if they were being called Uncle Inside Out Toms by the regular blacks (who called themselves, incidentally, inside out dropouts, or simply outside outs), particularly since many inside out black whites were not only now whiter than regular whites but getting even whiter by the day. With their new inside out insight, or outsight, they refused to take the second pill. In fact, the inside out black whites who were not turning white enough to suit themselves wanted another one of the first pill, the black-to-white kind.

Additionally, there was the problem of the whites who had turned black. When these inside out white blacks, who had taken the first pill in order, they thought, to become whiter than the blacks who, after taking the first pill had become whiter than whites, remembered how mistaken they had been for the first time, they refused to swallow the second pill even though the inventor swore it would change their color back to what it had been in the first place.

By this time the poor inventor, who had an eye defect anyway and hardly knew what color he was himself, was so confused that he got the pills mixed up and, additionally, got regular whites mixed up with inside out black whites and regular blacks mixed up with inside out white blacks. The result of all this was that he gave both kinds of pills to all kinds of people, so that he made some regular whites into inside out white blacks, some regular blacks into inside out black whites, some inside out white blacks whiter, some inside out white blacks blacker, until nobody knew what color he had been in the first place.

Which was how the racial problem was finally solved once and for all.

October 11, 1974

J. R. R. Tolkien, R I P

John Ronald Reuel Tolkien, who died a fortnight ago in his 81st year, was as much a writer of his time as the archetypal modern from whom he seemed to differ so radically and so sharply. All the arts of our century have been revivals of forms long abandoned. Joyce was our Homer, Pound our Dante. Tolkien dared to resuscitate romance, a form requiring the genius of a Rabelais or Spenser, a form which was shattered after its brilliant flowering in the hands of Boiardo and Ariosto by the publication of *Don Quixote*. Thereafter the demon realism ruled the roost.

Tolkien dared the improbable and perhaps the impossible in writing *The Lord of the Rings*, a three-volume romance of such magnificent design and charm of narration that it has been for almost twenty years now a magic book among the young. For many, it was their sole example of literature, and they took to it with the cultist enthusiasm of young Elizabethans reading *Orlando Furioso*. Most of its readers had little awareness that they were reading a Christian parable. The book is apparently beyond scholarship and criticism; nothing written about it seems to be about the same book that people begin again as soon as they reach the end, or read for days without sleep, or can allude to like a Puritan quoting Scripture. Who can say why the Orcs have Hittite names? Who has noticed that Gandalf is Sherlock Holmes in a wizard's hat?

Some years ago, I was talking with Allen Barnett, of Shelbyville, Kentucky. It turned out that he was a classmate of Tolkien's at Oxford and may have been his only friend to have survived the First World War. Tolkien, he said, loved to hear about the Kentuckians, their contempt for shoes, their fields of tobacco, their countrified ancient English names like Proudfoot and Baggins. It was the rule of Tolkien's art that he invented nothing cynical. He transmuted into the loveliest vision the world as he knew it. If the Shire is flavored with touches of Kentucky, we need but know that Tolkien was born in South Africa to see what he was remembering in the lacy golden trees of Lothlórien. Not since Spenser has an English writer had so gorgeous an imagination.

Like his own Hobbits, Tolkien was an all but invisible man. He was orphaned at 18, became a philologist after serving in the Lancashire Fusiliers, and spent his life as a university professor. He also spent it as an artist of incomparable power. *The Hobbit*, published in 1938, was written, like so many splendid books, to read to his children. *The Lord of the Rings* set out that way; one son remembers receiving chapters of the great book when he was an RAF pilot. Publishers were not interested in the work, and it lay around until 1955.

Of *The Lord of the Rings* we can say easily that it is the best book of the century though the greatest is *Ulysses*, and Lewis' *The Human Age* is the book we deserve most to be remembered for. Its vision of harmony and simplicity, of honor and heroism, is an articulate symbol of our inarticulate yearning. The dread Orcs, who look like the Chinese army, the Nazis, and our highways and streets, are what humanity looks like when deference has been replaced by power and civilization by efficiency.

Tolkien himself said the one fault of *The Lord of the Rings* is that it ought to have been longer. Would that it were.

—Guy Davenport
September 28, 1973

Burials

D. Keith Mano

“This, Mr. Mano, is beautiful Fern Valley.”

My God, beautiful? A filing cabinet has more aesthetic voltage. Stacked one atop another, four squares high—a block-long granite ice-cube tray on its side. The dead, pigeonholed. Mausolea bulk like a low-income housing development over the abused, suburban countryside. All it needs: a couple washlines, some TV antennae, your old grandma leaning out a window on her elbows. Man, heights scare me to death. It’s the apartment dweller’s nightmare necropolis: A Big Condominium in the Sky.

Several thousand under construction: A burly crane sets the modular bureau drawers into place. Containerization’s the word today. But Fern Valley is a mere nothing. Down in Nashville, the salesman tells me, they had this twenty-story office building that bombed in the rental market. Now it’s a high-rise cemetery. He swears, honest: You grab an up elevator, somber Muzak playing, to hang a wreath on the Loved One. Take that, Khufu: twenty stories. You’ll want a new liturgy: “We commit this body into mid-air ... through Our Lord Jesus Christ at whose coming the earth and the sea and the 15th floor shall give up their dead.” Amen. Bong, going down.

Here’s a swift kick in the Cheops for you. Talk about peer-group pressure. I read this full half-page enormity in the *New York Post*: “Through the ages mausoleum interment above the ground has been the choice of spiritual leaders of the bible [lower case sic], of royalty, and of the wealthy.” Moses says: Buy a slot, folks, not a plot. “The shrines of the world leaders and statesmen, the Pyramids, Taj Mahal, and Westminster Abbey are examples of man’s desire to avoid the harsh elements of the earth.”

The gall of it. Dead, you thought you were through keeping up with—or above—the indefatigable Joneses. I quote again, “Until now mausoleum burial was available only to the privileged few. Now it is available to *all* at low cost with easy payments—ACT NOW FOR 30 PER CENT SAVING DURING CONSTRUCTION!” While they’re putting up your A-frame in the Poconos, we can be squaring off your crypt in Westchester County. And, having secured an unsolicitable testimonial from the Pharaohs, they give you miracles of modern science. “Technology and new construction methods make it possible. And since mausoleum purchase is a one-time, all-inclusive investment you are forever free of gardening and perpetual-care bills.” It’s the only way to be free of perpetual-care bills—forever. Once a month they run you over with a dust cloth and some Johnson’s Pledge. Beats Johnny Carson’s $50 interment: where they bury you, one hand sticking up and out, with your American Express card in it.

"It seems," I shrug, "a little too, well ... cold. Sort of like a bunch of mailboxes in some apartment-house lobby."

"Mr. Mano. I don't want to say this, but there are other cemeteries ... they shall be nameless. They stack them up ten high. And indoors. The place smells of death. Ten high. Just try to visualize. I know people with loved ones—when they go to visit Aunt Julia ... well, they have to use field glasses." He takes my elbow. "Come inside. We'll talk down payments and interest."

It *is* reasonable. Two grand if I buy now. Ten per cent down, forty a month in easy installments: only $500 interest. Serious now: social concern on his face. "Are you interested in ecology, Mr. Mano?" I nod. "Think of the land we'll save. This will allow us to set aside an area for picnic tables and recreation at Fern Valley." Lord, weenie-roast smoke on my buffed granite surface.

I resent it. The modulated intimidations; the shameless advertising gimmicks and their vicious snob appeal. I resent the terrible neat anonymity of cubbyhole death. And I resent most the last implication: that my atoms will somehow not refurbish the earth.

August 17, 1973—The Gimlet Eye

On the Way to the Moon Shot

John Dos Passos

There are dates when history turns a corner. December 24, 1968, was such a date. Ever since the discovery of atomic power men had been tortured by the fear that science had unleashed forces beyond human power to control. The success of the Apollo series of flights is proving that the achievements of scientific technology can be directed with undreamed of precision. Man is reaching for mastery over matter. On December 24, 1968, three men, cool at the controls, detached enough to make humorous cracks as they went along, proved they could command the intricate energies technology had placed at their disposal. Our thinking about the universe, about life on earth can never be the same since that moment when the astronauts of Apollo 8 orbiting the moon paused from their routine at the keyboards of the spaceship to look back tenderly over two hundred and forty thousand miles of emptiness at the tiny blue earth which was their home: "the only touch of color in the universe."

John Dos Passos

Their voices instantaneously reaching the earth, as clear as if heard from an adjoining room, shattered all preconceived notions of space and time. Mankind was on the threshold of a new beginning. The words they chose to express their emotion came from the beginnings of the civilization which had nurtured the minds that made the journey possible. Before blastoff Frank Borman had typed out the first chapter of Genesis on fireproof paper. Genesis means beginning. It is not often that a great moment in history finds the right words to express it. This time it did.

As they looked down on the steep craters and the brutal ranges and erratic zigzagging canyons on the moon's colorless face passing below them, there had come a moment of real apprehension.

They were out of communication and behind the moon. Would the control systems set off the rockets at the right time that were to snap them out of the moon's orbit into their path toward the earth? No one had ever tried this before. They were confident but not quite sure. Would all systems go? They did. Just after midnight on Christmas morning, James Lovell's voice came into the

Houston control center loud and clear: "Please be informed there is a Santa Claus."

The homespun phrase, echo of generations of innocent American childhoods, expressed the relief, the exultation, but also the humbleness of victory. The paramount problem of space travel: how to come back, was solved. A man landing on the earth was assured.

"What good will it do?" people ask. "Couldn't the money be better spent on earth? Is it worth all that expenditure and effort to coop a man up in a spacesuit so that he can take a few steps in that desert?"

The answer is not fame or fortune. The answer is not that men are impelled to the moon, like the first man to climb to the top of Everest, "Just because it is there." The answer is not: "We do this for national glory," or to prove that some system of political economic organization worked better than some other system. The answer is that by his very nature, man has to know.

In our century we have seen everything that is hideous in man come to the fore: obsessed leaders butchering helpless populations, the cowardice of the led, the shoddy self-interest, the easy hatreds that any buffoon can arouse who bellows out the slogans, public derision of everything mankind has learned through the centuries to consider decent and true; but now, all at once, like the blue and white stippled bright earth the astronauts saw rise above the rim of the moon's grisly skeleton, there emerges a fresh assertion of man's spirit.

Throughout history the human spirit has advanced unevenly. The best brains and the most ardent imaginations tend to face one challenge at a time, leaving other sectors to stagnation and degeneracy on the eternal battlefield where man struggles to dominate the evil within him and the impartial pressures of his material environment. The landing on the moon in the summer of 1969 may well inaugurate a period when the most fruitful human effort converges on space exploration. Already the technology developed for the accomplishment of the Apollo program can be seen as a permanent achievement available for the solution of a hundred different problems.

The most ignorant layman bused through the installation at Cape Kennedy can't help but be stirred by the feeling that knowledge is being expanded dizzily fast all around him. After this the world, the universe will look different to him. Some astonished awareness of the great implications must account for the emotion people show on the packed viewing stands as they follow the countdown on each lunar flight. The families on the beaches, the groups with field glasses and telescopes along the shores of the Indian River wait tense with excitement as the minutes tick away. "This is like pioneering in the old days," fathers tell their children. "You are going to see something no man has ever seen before."

With each successive launching the tension has risen. Apollo 11 is the climax. All the rest were practice heats. Through the long apprehension of the countdown a myriad anxious eyes watch the gleaming white pencil wrapped in its dainty plume of steam on the launching pad miles away.

"Two minutes, thirty-six seconds and counting ... all systems go." Ears throb in anticipation, hearts beat a tattoo. Suppose something went wrong. "Thirty seconds and counting." Now the fire. Red and yellow flames. The great white pencil lifts itself slowly out of its billow of brown smoke. That enormous rumbling roar fills the sky. Faster, higher. The flaming rocket curves into the clouds. Frantic throats answer the jet engines' roar only to be hushed when the quiet workday voices of the spaceship's crew take over the radio. Worldwide, uncounted millions of television viewers join in a prayer for the men in that golden bullet. In every one of them the need to know, the smothering spirit of adventure, buried deep down under the routine of every day, flares for a moment like the rocket engine into soaring flame.

February 9, 1971

Jacques Maritain, R I P

Jacques Maritain looked a frail man. As far back as 1950, still in his sixties, it seemed the very next corridor draft would snatch him away. Shawl on shoulder, stooped, pasty-faced, great-aged at the eyes, leonine mane of hair whited through, he came to class in mid-afternoon once a week and somehow made it through the next three hours of lecture and seminar, wise, benign, we thought a very late autumn leaf, the small, accented voice feeding on exiguous material reserves. Somehow, too, he made it through to a ninth decade of terrestrial life, somehow he wrote fifty books, twenty of them in actual old age, somehow he touched every base of possible human concern and scholarly endeavor, and ah! that "touch" was a hand-spread over a full octave at the grand piano of being.

Truth alone, he said, keeps things permanently in place. And it, the hold on it, the hunt for it, kept *him* in place, indefatigably at his writing desk, in his frail body, close to Raissa, his mystic-wife, Aquinas short-leashed to his wrist, in his massively energetic assault on it and, indeed, on God's Own life. "Maritain is not lazy," Gilson, hardly the laconic man, would say of his old warrior-pal. "Whenever I go out on call," said the Princeton physician, housed across the night street, "his study lamp is always lit ... Maritain is always at his work."

Some people have to do it—sinking the drill into the stubborn hardpan of being, cutting deep to the very heart of Existence Itself, to keep our human lamps supplied, dimmed now after six centuries of the manufacture of lampblack and nasty street vandalism by The Enlightenment, Inc. Maritain, the mercy of God never failing us, lately recovered from a near fatal brush with Rationalism, rose up among us, and looking around with compassion (perhaps—he was human—with fear and apprehension), bent his slender shoulders to the heavy tackle. We are immeasurably healthier, holier, happier for his work. The Augean Stables are cleaner now, stained with his very sweat, worked as they were through half a century with unremitting toil, a toil, it should be said which barely kept the wolf of poverty from his own door. Well done, M. Maritain. Keeping faith with Truth was your thing. I think it now, verily, your sweet portion forever.

John Kiley—The Week
May 25, 1973

Here It Comes!

William F. Rickenbacker

This is the thirteenth consecutive edition of *NR*'s famous forecasts of Things to Come, a happy haruspical handsel unmatched for accuracy and felicity, and couched in nouns and verbs of genuine distinction. But hark! The oracle speaks.

In January the President—any January, any President—will, for the thirteenth consecutive year, present an almost balanced budget to the Congress. The next 12 months of budgetary planning will be spent explaining the unforeseen—unforeseen by *them*—rises in the estimated budget deficits. Toward the end, when it is time for the President to offer his next almost balanced budget to the Congress, the "final explanation" will have been announced from the Explanations Secretary: the deficit was planned, after all, to offset the recession.

In February the President will present to Congress, as he has for the last ten years or so, his Annual Economic Message, which will declare that we have not been in a recession, and that thanks to his clever policies the recession is ended. It was a slumpflation following an unprecedented stagboom, and the concomitant boomcession augured an inevitable reboomslump, as had been predicted earlier.

That pesky drought that set in the summer after the Bolshevik Revolution of 1917 will, surprisingly, bring about the 58th consecutive annual crop failure in the Communist bloc. [Ed. note: this forecast has been nominated for the Pulitzer Award for Economic Forecasting.] [Auth. note: the award has been blocked by a self-serving coterie of sore losers in the Kremlin.] [Ed. note: get outta here; these brackets are mine.]

In mid-January the editor of *NR* will be issued a new set of brackets, with distinctive design and appropriate weight and fineness. Counterfeit bracketing will become more difficult, and consequently more rare, and accordingly more valuable. It would be pointless to follow this line of reasoning further. It is eating its tail. *Après vous.*

Mr. Ehrlichman will testify, through tears, that he never discussed amnesty with the Argentine Firecracker of recent memory, or with John Mitchell also of memory. Mr. Haldeman, his eyes red and puffy, his cheeks wet and gleaming, will testify that he never saw Mr. Ehrlichman crying at all, in the White House or elsewhere. The Argentine Firecracker, sobbing, will testify that she is a professionally trained dancer and would never think for one moment of going that awful hangout road. Mr. Nixon, weeping, will depose that he never saw any member of his Administration purposefully crying while on official duty. Gerald Ford, bawling, will testify that he pardoned Mr. Nixon on the advice of the Salinity Secretary, who had warned that the levels in the White House had approached the point of questionable toxicity. Judge Sirica, if there is one, whining and whimpering, will defend his conduct of the trial.

The Congress of the United States, in a sudden switch, will be turned into a pillar of salt.

The following people will disappear: Diane von Furstenberg, Nelson Rockefeller, Robert Redford, Arthur Goldberg, the Secretary General of the United Nations (you know his name), President Smith of the Ford Motor Company, that smartass cop at the Tidal Basin, and the entire faculty of Harvard University, not necessarily in this order.

Best flick: *The Trial of Billy Jack*. Most sensitive directing: *The Mistrial of Billy Jack*. Most wanted actor: *Billy Jackass*. Best juvenile performance: Marlon Brando in *The Ass of Billy Jack*. Best legal documentary: *The Pons Asinorum of Billy Jack*. Best flick on dietary laws: *The Roast Suckling Pig of Billy Jack*.

The following countries will collapse: England, Chile, Ceylon, Arabia Deserta, Borneo, Abyssinia, the western section of the newly discovered Terra Incognita, virtually all of the Weimar Republic, sections of downtown Freud, the middle countries of Weltschmerz, and so on and so forth—the same ones, in general, that collapsed last year.

Exactly 47 city dwellers will write books or newsletters telling you how to survive the onrushing disaster. How to build a log cabin. How to skin a squirrel. How to plant beans. How to pop your gold coins in a woodchuck hole. How to make gunpowder and bullets. How to apply a tourniquet, saw off a leg, arrange a decent burial and other such frontier lore. As soon as all the Smart Money has moved into woodchuck holes in the northern forests, stragglers in the open country will notice that the Mississippi River is still flowing. A report from the field will mention the early evidence of sap in the trees. Investors who haven't traded in their thermometers for gold bullion will observe a warming trend in the daily readings. Very old persons will recall how it used to be—when the warm weather came, when the birds came, when the crops rose up in the fields.

Yea, this very year shall have its harvest. All daisies and lilies.

January 17, 1975

Part Five

1975 to 1980

The Week
Selected Editorial Paragraphs

April 2, 1976
Correcting an oversight, Sweden may soon abolish its repressive incest laws. A government committee has filed a report recommending repeal and now it's up to Parliament. If you think most Swedes look alike now, wait a generation.

August 20, 1976
Now that the Supreme Court has restored capital punishment it seems just a matter of—but soft! Hark! It sounds like ... yes! ... it's Tom Wicker! "If the first person to be put to death is a black, as is statistically likely ... repercussions in the Third World will be extreme, if in some cases hypocritical." So what's the problem Tom? We'll just start with a honky.

November 12, 1976
The strangest political issue in modern times has popped up on the front page of the strangest newspaper of all times, the *New York Times*, to wit: "Washington Unable to Spend Funds as Rapidly as It Planned." The "experts" are apparently disturbed at inexplicable federal lethargy that has left some $8 thousand million unslushed. That amounts to a whole week's worth of social problems unsolved, favors unbought, doggles unbooned. Holy Keynes! If the bureaucrats can't waste on schedule, where will it end?

January 7, 1977
A Newark city maintenance inspector making a "routine check for zoning violations" nabbed a would-be counterfeiter with $100,000 in phony bills. Counterfeiting is illegal unless you are zoned for Federal Reserve activity.

April 1, 1977
After his election to the Rhode Island legislature, it transpired that William Bailey was a wanted man in Michigan: in fact, he had criminal records in three states. He still hasn't been sworn in, and is fighting both exclusion from the Rhode Island House and inclusion within the Michigan Big House. Maybe he could serve concurrent terms?

May 13, 1977
In the House of Representatives, a recess is called a "district work period." In the Senate, a recess is called a "nonlegislative period." Among the taxpayers, a congressional recess is called blessed.

September 16, 1977
The General Service Administration, in an effort to save gas, has instructed federal drivers not to idle cars for more than one minute. Thanks, but we'd rather keep the politicians idling: look what it costs to put them in gear.

November 11, 1977
In the interest of austerity, the Department of Energy is moving to new quarters. Secretary Schlesinger will not have a private dining room, and Deputy Secretary O'Leary will not have a shower. The move will cost $17 million.

February 3, 1978
Our last President told us that Poland isn't Soviet-dominated. This one tells us that Poland shares our devotion to human rights. Poles are asking each other how many American Presidents it takes to change a light bulb.

September 29, 1978
In the Soviet Union, the conviction of Yuri Kropotkin has been overturned. The police neglected to inform him that he has no rights.

October 27, 1978
Edgar Bergen, R I P: Wanted: Straight man with warm lap, by professional comedian, age 50, ligneous, disconsolate.   —C. McC.

November 24, 1978
Q. What's the difference between "voluntary" and "mandatory" wage-price controls?
A. About three months.

March 30, 1979
Presidential candidate George Bush tells this one. Seems President Carter was trying to reassure an audience of apprehensive businessmen about the state of the economy, and told them, "If I weren't President, I'd be investing right now." To which a canny businessman replied, "If you weren't President, *I'd* be investing right now."

July 6, 1979
The FDA has released, as expected, its new list of suspected cancer-causing agents, including Mom, apple pie, the flag, strawberries, Chevrolets, senior proms, family reunions, Western movies, square dancing, hot dogs, baseball, holding hands, and the light of the silvery moon.

August 17, 1979
There is little truth to the rumor that the new federal policy of forcing you to work in 78° heat is the result of lobbying by the deodorant people. They just get the windfall profits.

June 13, 1980
I'm sorry I made an ash of myself. Lava, come back to me. Love, Helen

November 28, 1980 (First and last paragraphs in first issue after Reagan's election.)
Ain't it fun?

With the election of Ronald Reagan, NATIONAL REVIEW assumes a new importance in American life. We become, as it were, an establishment organ; and we feel it only appropriate to alter our demeanor accordingly. This is therefore the last issue in which we shall indulge in levity. Connoisseurs of humor will have to get their yuks elsewhere. We have a nation to run.

December 12, 1980
Our congratulations to Mr. Carter for managing to rise from Jimmy *Who*? to Jimmy *Who*? in four short, make that interminable, years.

December 31, 1980
Heading for retirement, George McGovern says he looks forward to having "time to think." Better late than never.

The America's Cup

Nicholas King

N*ewport, R.I.*—The America's Cup is the most aristocratic and fetish-ridden of yachting events, and the fact that it is held off Newport redoubles its glamour. There are the ocean, the green-gold landscape, the magnificent sailing craft—mysterious in their action, cloud-like in their beauty. There is the city too, historical and worldly. The city and the Cup race co-exist in harmonious imperturbability, for the event is fleeting, yet it recurs with the predictability of the tides.

The America's Cup activity has been more strenuous this summer than in the last races three years ago, because this year there were four challengers from three countries, whereas previously there had been two at most. Since this is a one-to-one match—with only one challenger and one defender—the French, the Swedish, and the two Australian boats have had to fight it out in trials and elimination all summer long in Block Island Sound. Indeed the multitude of trial runs, statements, protests, crew changes, and tantrums have been too much for people to follow, and the growing cloud of boredom was not dissipated by the widely held expectation that the American defender, *Courageous*—she of the green decks and the green spinnakers, skippered by the crafty anti-hero Ted Turner—would have little trouble beating *Australia*, which has been "campaigned" by the Alan Bond syndicate. (Turner is the man described by a Newport hostess as "a rough diamond—he's only had his money for one generation.")

The Swedes were the popular foreigners this time. They conquered Newport with their looks, their manners, and their style, not to mention a tourist campaign that extended as far as New York and brought with it an influx of blue-and-yellow yachting gear in the shops. Moreover, the King of Sweden was said to have promised to fly to the U.S. in the event *Sverige* won the trials, a thing that Newport understood thoroughly. The French never had a look-in in any department after their incredibly bad luck in building a new boat specially for the races only to discover that their old boat, left over from 1974, was distinctly the better of the two.

Furthermore, if the cup has to be lost, it is infinitely preferable to have to go to Stockholm to get it back than to some antipodean yacht club in the suburbs of an Australian city. As it was, the Swedes ensconced themselves on both sides of the narrows entering Newport harbor, and, as if claiming a colony, hauled up two giant blue flags with yellow crosses, one at the dock of Hammersmith Farm (once the home of Jackie Onassis), the other across the way at their private shipyard, for these boats have to be hauled out of the water nearly every day for cleaning and tinkering.

It requires a terrible push to get to see the races at all. There are no more great yachts from whose decks on might watch them in comfort, or, if there are, they are not owned by one's friends. One is obliged to take tickets by the day—not cheaply either—on some tubby ferry recruited from its regular run to Cuttyhunk. Nor are the Twelve-Meters, which are not very big, clearly visible to the naked eye even in the best of weather, since such great distances must be kept from them. In fact, one can easily go out and sit in a dense fog, so common at this time of year, for eight hours.

Such matters, of course, are of very little concern to the yachtsmen themselves, who pursue their activities with a fierce and often self-conscious fever. There seems to be no sport at all (if the word "sport" does not pop its backstays under the strain), not even equestrianism, which breeds such contempt for the layman, or more vainglory among the initiates. The yachtsmen involved in the America's Cup—that is, the skippers and navigators and sailmakers and designers and managers, even plain ordinary "winch beef"—give the impression of being not sailors but supernal businessmen who loose their demonic energies, like a series of white squalls, over the water. It is as if Captain Kidd took leave of his duties as the head of the Harvard Business School every so often, stuck a knife between his teeth, and embarked upon a little prestige searoving.

Indeed, the awe-inspiring precision that is necessary to the winning of races; the intensity of hull design and sail cutting; the arcane pains taken to make the boats go as fast as possible, including, they say, the application of contact-lens fluid to their sleek flanks; the nervous horror of instantly fatal mistakes—all serve to define a world of strain and effort into which no outsider can enter, and from which a forbidding ill-humor seems to keep all but the staunchest.

It is true that the New York Yacht Club boards and committees which reign as Olympian stewards over the Cup and its competitions still manage to exude the gentlemanly relaxation of old, what with their ribboned straw hats and their red trousers. But their briefcases and their conference-room preoccupation belie their outward ease of manner. They certainly are not to be stopped for an answer to any question, especially a question posed by one of the chumps in the spectator fleet.

And it is quite a fleet: Newport Harbor has never been so full of floating objects. In many cases, only a few feet of water separates one boat from another, for this is the marine fashion show of the year. Along the piers and wharves lie some of the bigger craft, power yachts mostly: great floating bars-and-grills adazzle with varnish and chrome and furnished according to nautical fantasies that run from ultra-suede pillows to Duncan Phyfe dining rooms.

These sea-going limousines, designed for inordinate comfort and cut along ungainly if not downright hideous lines, cost hundreds of thousands of dollars to buy and hundreds of thousands more, every year, to stock and keep up. No wonder so many of them are registered in Delaware, that haven of corporation home-porting.

They have awful names too: some are those painful combinations of male and female—*Jan-Ed*, say, or *Mar-Bara*; others are thunderingly arch, like *Teachers Pet IV*, or *Hatterascal*. The sailing ships, somehow, perhaps innately, are generally called by something more imaginative or dignified, so that one can actually imagine their owners repeating them. But the sailing ships have also degenerated. They so often have a lumpy or oafish look, heavy with cabin structures and machinery, their metal spars and stays rattling like tin cans, their sails, when set, gleaming with synthetics or reduced to obvious stabilizers. No wonder the sight of an old, diminutive Herreschoff Fifteen catches the eye, its gaff mainsail filling with all the beauty sun can bestow on canvas, reminding one that a sailing ship is still the most animate thing ever made by man.

The press, naturally, is here in numbers: the yachting press first and foremost, supported by that press which is not strictly yachting and which yaws about in the wake of the experts picking up the crumbs of expertness. There are correspondents from France and Sweden and Australia, as well as the regulars of the American yachting publications and the more august of the daily sports pages. They have their headquarters in a closely secured granite armory on the waterfront, with rows of telephones and typewriters and a blackboard for announcements, and an area with semi-circles of chairs set aside for briefings; it could as easily have been arranged for the coverage of a diplomatic conference or a murder trial.

Whatever the character of Newport's interest in all this, the place has done its part and the list of credits would be long. Boat people complain about the high cost of dockage and general ship servicing, and lodging is scarce, expensive, and not very comfortable; but surely such things are calculated everywhere in the world at a cost the traffic will bear. There are too many automobiles and it is hard to get about the narrow streets of this most authentic and graceful of colonial seaports. Meanwhile, the yachtsmen are welcomed everywhere they wish to go, and a spectacular America's Cup ball is given in their honor at Rosecliff on Bellevue Avenue, Stanford White's white marble version of the Grand Trianon. But if people move on from discussing the America's Cup to the fact that there are two Duchesses of Argyll in Newport at the same time and how does one tell which is which, no one can blame them for fickleness. Interest in either subject is perfectly natural.

October 14, 1977

Seeing Shelley Plain

Guy Davenport

Wordsworth pushing a wheelbarrow containing Coleridge with blistered heels; the grave infant Milton watching lean Will Shakespeare and fat Ben Jonson staggering home from the Mermaid; Rousseau hiding all day in his own attic because he'd had the servant say to Boswell that he was out and the intrepid Scot shoved his way in to sit stubbornly until the philosopher showed; Joyce and Proust in a taxi, the one lowering the windows because of his claustrophobia, the other raising them because of his asthma, up and down, down and up, all the way to Maxim's; Eliot and Pound lifting their feet to accommodate the imaginary vacuum cleaner of a lunatic while they conversed in a cell in St. Elizabeths' Hospital—the literary anecdote, as Donald Hall observes in the introduction to his *Remembering Poets* (Harper), is a genre all to itself "at the edges of literature."

Hazlitt was a master of the form; what would the English Romantics look like without his account of them? It was gossipy Henry Crabb Robinson who gave us our images of the Blakes reading *Paradise Lost* in their back garden, naked, pink, and chubby. And what else was Boswell doing but compiling an epic portrait of Johnson out of anecdotes?

Now that literature itself has become paperborne, the literary anecdote may be the last survivor of the oral tradition. It would, I think, be awkward for a poet nowadays to offer a recitation of his verses at a dinner party (something you went to dinner parties *for*, once upon a time, when a duke's wink from deep inside a ruff of squirrel fur activated a page, who brought a candle to the shoulder of Maister Chaucer, who unfolded a sheaf of parchment and began to speak in octosyllables), but if he has spent a drunken evening with Cal Lowell, or sat at the colossal knees of Robert Kelly, or played billiards with Sam Beckett, he has an audience all ears.

Gossip is a social art form, it is intimate, and it is a tradition as old as eating in company. It does not go easily into print (one of Professor Hall's triumphs as a writer is that his style keeps the feel of *telling*). If it's literary gossip, it has few occasions for native expression; you can't tell an anecdote about an obscure poet, and you must also have the sense that you are satisfying curiosity. I would venture a grander role for the anecdote than Donald Hall modestly claims; it is the folklore that plays around a high seriousness, the saints' legends of a religion, and usually has the truth of myth rather than of fact.

Hall omits the anecdote of Dylan Thomas' question to Harry Levin, who he had just learned was a professor of Comparative Literature: "What," Thomas asked in his best Welsh White-Trash voice, "do you compare it to?" The deliciousness of this cannot be explained to the uninitiate (but it isn't a snob's anecdote; snobs can't tell literary anecdotes worth a damn). Harry Levin is a gracious and civilized soul with a poise that one cannot imagine being discomfited, and yet his immense usefulness to the world is explaining literature, and here he is, in Cambridge congeniality, being cheeked by a poet. The *Urgestalt* of the anecdote is Diogenes asking Alexander the Great to get out of his light.

Donald Hall, poet, short-story writer, critic, teacher, and *raconteur*, tells us what it is like to have known Eliot, Thomas, Frost, and Pound, not for any length of time—know a great man too well and you can't write about him at all—but in intense intermittences: a hair-raising day of pub-crawling in London with Thomas, and an overnight stay with his pitiful family in Wales; visits to Eliot's lair at Faber and Faber; sessions with Frost at writing conferences; Fellini-like visits to the ancient Ezra Pound in his decade of ghostly silence. And with all, business. Hall is no lion-hunter (they can't tell anecdotes, either); he is, as best one can make out from his book, a literary diplomat. To him we must pay our gratitude for the very last fragments of *The Cantos*.

Professor Hall was a student of his poets' writings; underneath his very human curiosity about them as men with children to feed and mortgages to pay off was his concern for seeing into the work with the leverage of the person. Talk about pitching mercury with a fork!

In meeting great men a wholly unexpected and peculiar chemistry transforms the psyche, provided, of course, that one has the hero worship, the awe, the plangently romantic giddiness of anticipation and fulfillment. I wonder that some psychological boffin has not anatomized for science this longing of admirers to see distinguished men; somewhere deep in the phenomenon is a clue to faith, loyalty, and all the gaudier kinds of enthusiasm.

July 7, 1978

Presidential Politics: Campaigns '76 and '80

The Democratic Convention, 1976

James Jackson Kilpatrick

Madison Square Garden—In the popular verdict, the Democratic Convention was a bore. The popular verdict miscarried. This Convention was not a bore. All week long we witnessed a splendid spectacle: one by one the party sachems publicly buried their hatchets; and each of them, we noted, carefully marked the spot, the better to dig up the hatchet again some day. We watched the reunion of North and South, Minnesota and Georgia linked inseparably in chains of Kelly green crepe paper. We had moments of poignancy, as old warriors hung up their shields. Only the unobservant fellows—the same fellows who regard a pitcher's two-hit shutout as a bore—could have failed to find excitement at the Garden.

And the press. By one reasonably reliable estimate, there were 10,000 of us there, including the TV technicians, the foreign correspondents, and half a dozen freckled Little Leaguers, all of them fugitives from second base. The working press had a desperate time. Over a span of six days, there was one piece of hard news: the naming of a vice-presidential nominee. Otherwise we drowned in journalistic tapioca; we paddled in a sea of hominy grits. Saul Pett of the AP had the week's best lead in a piece for the Tuesday A.M.'s: "Tension is not mounting today at the Democratic National Convention."

The Convention got under way, in a manner of speaking, only 15 minutes late on Monday evening. Chairman Bob Strauss ordered the aisles cleared, and the reverend invoker, whose name escaped me in the babble, prayed for miracles and for stamina. Mr. Strauss spoke of "unity," a word we would hear 4,287 times before the final gavel.

After a half-dozen short subjects, Mr. Strauss then launched into the first, and arguably the worst, major oration of the entire consistory. The party chairman began with a reference to a time a few "short years" ago, and continued with a polemic upon the eight "long years" of Messrs. Kissinger, Simon, Moron, and Butz. This had been calculated to whip the delegates into a chanting frenzy, but the delegates were not about to be whipped. When the orator at last concluded, two union stagehands came forward to haul away the very large egg that had just been laid.

The stagehands had to be summoned again a half-hour later to perform the same charitable mission for the Honorable John Glenn, the former astronaut and incumbent Junior Senator from Ohio. He was a keynoter who missed the key and could not sing a note. He earned his merit badge for effort, but looking into his scoutmaster's honest face we wanted to ask, what's a nice fellow like you doing in a place like this? He subsided at 10:43:02 by a press gallery watch, and the applause died down at 10:43:18. It was a record for keynoter coolth not likely to be soon surpassed.

They brought on Barbara Jordan, Representative for the 18th District of Texas, at precisely 11 o'clock that Monday evening. It was no accident, of course, that her very presence evoked all the dramatic memories of the House impeachment hearings two years ago. This was the principal purpose. The gentlewoman provided even more—a lesson in elocution that every public speaker could profitably attend. God gave Miss Jordan a full voice, and with it she gave cry to empty platitudes. Hers is the remarkable gift to declare that "we cannot flee from the future" and bring a hall to its feet.

So much for Monday.

August 20, 1976

John Anderson, Doonesbury's Candidate

Richard S. Brookhiser

John Anderson has been called the most eloquent orator in the House. What his admirers mean to say is that he is just about the only orator there, or anywhere. Connally gives the stump speech, half auctioneer's patter, half cheerleading. Reagan draws a bath of emotion, in which anecdotes, one-liners, and ideas bob and float. Kennedy speaks the language of the New Frontier, which is modeled ultimately on the symmetries of Cole Porter ("I say 'tomato,' you say 'tomahto' "; "Ask not what your country can do for you [etc.]"). Anderson—orates. He pads his sentences with the upholstery of sermons, commencement addresses, and old-fashioned summations; they suggest wing chairs, athenaeums, 11th Editions of the *Encyclopedia Britannica*. When speaking, he stands stiffly, but all his gestures fall in the right places.

The defense rests, time for questions. ... *Have you ever given your support to Democrats?* This is a popular question just now, and George Will has written a column on it. In a fund-raising letter for the National Abortion Rights Action League, Anderson has warned against "a reactionary coalition of right-wing groups" which was planning to destroy the political careers of some of the nation's most progressive leaders ... George McGovern, John Culver, Bob Packwood [the lone Republican in the list], Birch Bayh, Patrick Leahy ... Unless you and I act immediately," Anderson went on, "the right-wing extremists are likely to succeed." He says now that the charge is "totally false," the letter "was not an endorsement," all those Democrats were just names in the body of the text. The accusation "comes with ill grace from Mr. Reagan," he continues, who was "riding his palomino" when Ford needed votes in the 1976 election. And anyway, six conservative Republicans recently signed an invitation to a fund-raising party for Democrat Larry McDonald. No one calls the bluff, and Anderson takes the pot with two lies and an irrelevancy.

April 18, 1980

The Last Kennedy

Richard S. Brookhiser

Queens has Greeks—thousands of them, concentrated in Astoria, on the very northwest tip of Long Island. Kennedy has voted with the Greek-American lobby all his senatorial career, and he is here now to cash in some of those chips.

Kennedy is late coming in from LaGuardia Airport and the crowd inside has been waiting over an hour. The band (electrified bouzoukis) must be rated according to taste. "Led's and gentlemen," the MC says at last, "may I have your 'tention please—" The crowd stands and Jackie Onassis enters the room. The cameramen cloud around her like gulls following a tramp steamer. Yet they only reflect, in an exaggerated form, the reaction of the crowd. "Please take your seats," the MC admonishes, "she's com' round to every table." But still no Kennedy. The band takes up its regular repertoire again in good earnest, only to cut it short when Kennedy suddenly appears. Miss Cyprus 1979 offers him a bouquet "on behalf of all the 200,000 refugees in Cyprus": four girls and a boy in blue, red, and white Greek costumes sit on the front of the podium; the head of the national Greek Americans for Kennedy Committee makes an introduction. He opens simply enough, chanting Ken-ne-dy ("Senator Budge," wrote Chesterton, "emphasized his points by throwing his false teeth up into the air and catching them in his mouth"), but builds to a climax of fine grammatical density—"a friend of Americans, the poor, the hard workers, a friend of Astoria, a friend of the Greeks...Edward Kennedy."

The crowd cheers lustily, standing of course, some standing on their chairs. The years may mug him some day (we have not, in this generation, seen an old Kennedy), but that day won't come soon. His jowels have thickened, and he has more grey hairs than Ronald Reagan. But his smile shines and charms. He wears a blue suit and a bright striped tie.

"I had my birthday the other day, and I was given three wishes ..." You may have read accounts of Kennedy's oratory; he is said to have a tendency, when reaching for emphasis, to slip into a tone the papers call "booming." Booming hardly does it justice. He shouts, his laughs explode into cackles, his voice cracks. He sounds ludicrous, grotesque, like a carney barker—like a Mel Brooks impersonation of a carney barker. And the strangest thing is that he can speak perfectly normally; maybe he thinks the sound is bad (it couldn't be *that* bad). The crowd, be it noted, does not mind a bit.

And what did he wish for on his birthday? One—"success in New Hampshire." Two—"to be successful here in New York ... And three—that the Turkish troops withdraw from Cyprus!" Cheers and applause.

Kennedy quickly gets back to the matter at hand. He recalls the first piece of legislation he ever pushed through Congress, the Immigration Act of 1965—"introduced by President Kennedy, supported by Attorney General Kennedy, and floor-managed by myself." Because of the Act, Greek "sons and daughters, brothers and sisters" were reunited. (He pounds the lectern, causing small electronic booms.) But what about the Greeks in Cyprus? There, since the Turkish invasion, Greeks have been "separated from their families, separated from their land, separated from their churches, separated from their graveyards, separated from the remains of their ancestors." Other nations, some almost as undemocratic as Turkey, have heeded Kennedy's advice in such matters: "I have gone to the Soviet Union, and I have spoken to the members of the Kremlin. I have seen families reunited." Same in Peking. But Ankara? "The answer from Turkey, year after year, year after year, has been no!" President Carter has squeezed military aid to Turkey out of Congress with promises of cooperation. "Well, you tell *me*—whether there has been any progress in Cyprus!" He rephrases it as a question, but the crowd is already roaring.

March 21, 1980

George Bush

Richard S. Brookhiser

S lowly, Bush's labors bore fruit. On November 2, Howard Baker flew up to Portland, Maine, with the national press corps to record a Baker triumph in a local straw poll. Bush won instead. Two weeks later, he did well in another straw poll, in Florida. Connally was squandering money and staff, Baker was trying to build a house from the roof down, Reagan was as visible as the Man in the Iron Mask—and suddenly, the week of Iowa, there was George Possum, jogging across the cover of *Newsweek*.

The subsequent month appears, in retrospect, to have been one long tactical blunder. Reporters scrambled onto the Bush plane; Bush spent as much time telling them how he was going to win, as what he intended to do once he did. He debated Reagan twice in New Hampshire. The voters were not impressed. Bush lost again in Vermont, and scraped a narrow win in Massachusetts.

The tactical errors reflected a strategic problem. Bush lacked the temperament to hit Reagan hard personally. At the same time, he lacked the desire or the opportunity to hit him ideologically. Bush couldn't run as a liberal thoroughbred, because he isn't; and there was nothing to be gained from Liberal Republicanism in any case: Anderson can collect Tom Wicker columns till Doomsday; all they're good for, in the Republican Party, is lining the bottom of bird cages.

Yet the efforts Bush could and did make to distinguish himself have been enough to incur the disapproval of much of the party's conservative wing. Part of the conservative suspicion of Bush was outraged loyalty: Reagan had labored in the vineyard, fought the good fight; how *dare* anyone oppose him? Reagan supporters reinforced their protectiveness by spying defects in Bush himself: abortion, ERA, an economics that seems prone to fits of timidity.

But there were subtler forces at work. Some opposed Bush as a matter of class. No patrician, the self-styled populists argued, could communicate with the masses. To which the answer is: It depends on the patrician. One blue-blood from Hyde Park managed to be elected to the White House four times. The anti-patrician talk asserts that which is to be proved.

April 4, 1980

Mohammed Reza Pahlevi, R I P

One day in his early teens Mohammed Reza Pahlevi was walking with his father through the manicured gardens of the Palace in Teheran. The old Shah tried to draw out the reticent lad, to learn what interested him. When the Prince spoke of history and social science, the fierce one-time stable sergeant of a Cossack company, now King of Kings, smote his son on the back, propelling him into a lily pond. "Donkey! Social science! Hah! You will rule this land. Now watch, and learn how to be King of the Persians."

Apocryphal? Perhaps, but real, nonetheless. It's hard to be the heir to a ruthless warrior-king. But if being cowed by a tyrant-father was his dialectical thesis, then consider the traumatic antithesis—the old man dethroned in 1941 and packed off by the Russians and British to exile in Mauritius, death in South Africa, and a grave in Egypt. Synthesis? A callow, 21-year-old Prince torn between the recollection of ruthless paternal power and the reality of paternal humiliation, cast up into the powerful Peacock Throne but, in reality, more like a ball of yarn buffeted back and forth by covetous Persian cats, not to mention a few first-class tigers called Stalin, Churchill, and Roosevelt. This was not synthesis. This was the matrix of breakdown.

It nearly happened, too—in 1953. The Shah's writ would not run past the Palace gate and was scorned by the weeping Mossadegh, the embittered clergy (predecessors of Khomeini's new Savanarolas), and the Communist Tudeh. But it didn't quite happen. Thanks to fate, to the mistakes of his enemies, and to the marginal support of a friend, the United States, he got what history rarely grants a failed leader—a second chance.

And he made full use of that second chance, combining his father's authoritarianism with the progressive ideas he had absorbed from the West, the past with the future. To regain control of Azerbaijan he turned to his father's old Cossack comrade, Marshal Shahbakhti, ramrod straight and tough. But when the Shah received us (the American, French, and Turkish Consuls in Azerbaijan) privately, he spoke softly and meditatively, like a scholarly historian, of Iran's narrow escape, of the need to eradicate ancient social evils, and, pointedly, of correcting the "mistakes all of us have made—*at all stations.*"

Well, he did correct some of them—but not others. In less than three decades more economic, social, and educational progress was made than in the previous two or three centuries. And the country was made strong, a major power in the Middle East and Indian Ocean. For 25 years the Shah forced the pace with an instrument forged of two elements a) adopted Western progressivism—which generated energies needing release; and b) inherited

Persian authoritarianism—which provided no escape valve. For 25 years he held the fulcrum of past and future in Iran, but finally, when a tiny gap appeared, it widened rapidly, reaching to the spirit of the Shah himself—and he lost the present.

The Shah is in a grave in a strange but friendly land where his father once lay—until the son brought the father home. He was alone, as the great of the world turned their backs, but was comforted by what must have been one of the most steadfast friendships since Damon and Pythias. We knew Sadat as a daring statesman, but this episode has illuminated him as one of the extraordinary souls of our time. That this one man should stand firm gives reason to hope that the Shah's contributions to his country will be recognized, and that he may some day be returned to rest in his homeland next to his father.

—*Norman B. Hannah*
August 22, 1980

André Malraux, R I P

A ndré Malraux was born in 1901. His life thus covered the greater part of the twentieth century from its beginning, and Malraux has usually been seen as an archetypal twentieth-century man—the exemplar of the century's storms and stresses, its wars and revolutions in art and idea as well as armed combat, its extremes. This perception is surely justified in externals. In his early manhood, Malraux was writing like a surrealist and getting entangled in Asia's embryonic anti-colonial revolutions. By the Thirties, he had swung toward Communism, plunged into the Chinese revolution, and written, out of his China experiences, what is probably his best and certainly his best-known book, *La Condition Humaine* (translated as *Man's Fate* in the American edition). Allied with the Communists, he joined passionately in "the struggle against war and fascism"; in the Spanish Civil War he helped organize, and flew in, the Republicans' primitive air squadron. In 1939 he joined the French army (as a private in the tank corps), was captured as France was overrun, escaped, joined the Resistance in 1944 (using as *nom de guerre* the name—Colonel Berger—of the hero of his book *The Walnut Trees of Altenburg*), was captured by the Gestapo, was freed by Resistance forces as the Germans collapsed, and finished in command of the Alsace-Lorraine Brigade that liberated Strasbourg.

In the course of the war he had swung from the Communists to de Gaulle, and from then on his political activities were linked with the fate of de Gaulle. When de Gaulle returned to power, Malraux joined him as his sole personal confidant as well as his Minister of Culture, in which latter capacity he washed the face of Paris, to the astonishment of all Parisians and all visitors to that soot-covered queen of cities. As Minister and after, he visited China and conversed for unprecedented hours with Mao, whom, alone, he ranked with de Gaulle in our time. In his last years, following de Gaulle's retirement and death, he continued writing—personal reminiscences of de Gaulle and semi-autobiographical "*antimémoires*"—and tried to join the fight of the people of Bangladesh against Pakistan.

The history of these 75 years could be embroidered around Malraux' life, deeds, writings. But, though his scene was the twentieth century, his essence sprung out of the nineteenth. Like D'Annunzio, T.E. Lawrence, or Antoine de St.-Exupéry, with all of whom he recognized kinship, Malraux' person—or, more accurately perhaps, persona—was nineteenth century: of the nineteenth-century's Romantic genius-type defined by Otto Rank, out of Fichte, Schiller, and the other German Romantic philosophers, Byron and the poet-liberators, Kierkegaard, Dostoyevsky, and very clearly out of Nietzsche.

Whatever outward form the action took, the essence of the challenge, for Malraux, was always death. Death was always near him in his personal as in his public life ("I have been much shot at," he once remarked). His father committed suicide. His mistress and both his half-brothers were killed. His two young sons were killed in an auto accident in 1961 (they were the same age as my own two, and as I read the cold dispatch I automatically remembered the evening a decade before when we had talked enthusiastically about exchanging our pairs for a year or two as part of their twentieth-century schooling). "Man," he wrote in *Antimémoires*, is the only animal that knows he is going to die." He kept death's blackness close: his hair was black; he wore black clothes, and drove in a black Citroën with a driver in a black uniform. His eyes, too, seemed so dark as to be black—though deep in their blackness you could see mesmerizing fire that held you immobile as he talked—his eternal cigarette drooping, his dark face twisting in its strange nervous tics.

—James Burnham
December 24, 1976

Fifty Years from Le Bourget

John Chamberlain

It was the age of Bobby Jones and Babe Ruth, F. Scott Fitzgerald and Ernest Hemingway, Thomas Edison and Henry Ford. But the greatest of them all was the man who flew the Spirit of St. Louis *to Le Bourget.*

On the fiftieth anniversary of Lindbergh's pioneer flight from New York to Paris, we will surely hear more of an old story. Frederick Lewis Allen popularized it in his *Only Yesterday*. It is the story of how a daring young man, who had been a stunt flier and a mail pilot, had, by making the first continent-to-continent trans-Atlantic flight (there had been island-hopping flights before), rescued the American people from the fetid swamps of the Twenties and provided them with an authentic hero to worship.

John Chamberlain

There are bits of the Allen thesis that one doesn't quarrel with. The Twenties had been a cynical era, at least in part. It had been a time of debunking, to use the word invented by W. E. Woodward, and there was a hunger for clean and chivalrous deeds in those years when daring had seemingly been patented by the bootleggers on Rum Row. It was the age of the F. Scott Fitzgerald look, with the flappers more in evidence than the philosophers. But the picture of the boyish Charles A. Lindbergh as counterpoint to an epoch is not quite as I remember it. The real truth is that Lindbergh was very much of the Twenties himself, a hero in an age that worshipped heroes with the sole proviso that they should be non-political.

The Twenties loved a record breaker. It could be any record—home runs, airplane flights, swimming the English Channel, or even flagpole-sitting. It was the golden age of the sports hero, Bobby Jones in golf, Big Bill Tilden and Little Bill Johnston in tennis, Jack Dempsey in the prize ring, Babe Ruth and the rest of Murderer's Row at Yankee Stadium, and Red Grange of Illinois, who was once carried two miles on the backs of students for his exploits in football. Our heroes had to be men of action: Doug Fairbanks, who married America's sweetheart, Mary Pickford, owed his great screen popularity to an athleticism that was as remarkable in its way as anything exhibited by the Four Horsemen of the Apocalypse who rode down the gridiron opposition for Notre Dame.

The worship of athletes was not a matter of mere dumb-jock appeal; it was part of a wider admiration for skills. The Twenties had this admiration as no decade has had it since. The writers who dominated the latter part of the decade—Fitzgerald, Hemingway, Glenway Wescott, Elizabeth Madox Roberts, e.e. cummings—were more skillful craftsmen than any of their successors. The more admiring of the prose-poem biographies that dot John Dos Passos' *U.S.A.* trilogy are men of great skill, such as Edison, the "electrical wizard," Luther Burbank, the plant breeder; and Charles Steinmetz of General Electric: these men fare much better than any politician who engages Dos Passos' attention. The Twenties brought the intricacies of mass production to their perfection, as Henry Ford, Boss Kettering, and Bill Knudsen built on the scientific management skills provided by Frederick W. Taylor, the time-motion genius who thought the value of a tool

Charles A. Lindbergh

was best measured by the exact cutting speed at which it is completely ruined at the end of twenty minutes.

The true importance of Charles Lindbergh was that he combined the qualifications of skill and daring to become the most exalted—and appealing—hero of the Twenties. He was the man of action *in excelsis*, willing to back his own nerve and judgment in the trans-Atlantic gamble. But he never thought of himself as a gambler. He hated the song "Lucky Lindy, the Flying Fool." Long before the phrase "calculated risk" came into vogue, he was the prime exponent of it. And, as Murray Godwin pointed out in one of the really perceptive early analyses of Lindbergh's accomplishment, it was not that he managed to hit the continent of Europe, it was that he had the skill to hit Le Bourget airfield outside of Paris squarely on the nose. Clarence Chamberlin, who came after him, was forced down in Germany, and Commander Byrd was lucky to wade ashore after ditching his ship in the sea off the French coast. Chamberlin and Byrd were the "flying fools," and the men of "luck," not Lindbergh, who worked out his problems in advance to micrometer perfection.

May 27, 1977

Flossenburg

Joseph A. Rehyansky

uschwitz, Dachau, Bergen-Belsen, Treblinka ... Flossenburg. In most countries its infamy would live forever, as Andersonville's has in the United States. But Germany ranks high in the all-time mass extermination sweepstakes, and Flossenburg is little noted. Flossenburg accounted for a mere seventy thousand lives, less than 2 per cent of the total, and most of them were non-Jews such as political prisoners, prisoners-of-war, and other undesirable ethnic types. Shirer gives the camps eight pages of his monumental work. Flossenburg is not mentioned therein, but gets part of one sentence a hundred pages farther on, and then only because two of the 4,980 persons executed for their alleged part in the July 20, 1944, plot to kill Hitler met their end there: Admiral Canaris and General Oster were dragged naked from their cells and hanged on the camp grounds less than a month before the German collapse. And even they were spared the agony of many of the other accused plotters who were also hanged—but with piano wire strung from meat hooks affixed to a dungeon wall.

So Flossenburg is a jerkwater on the genocide circuit, a footnote in the tour guide to hell. From Nuremberg you drive east on the E12 autobahn until it ends near Amberg. Then it's north and east through the crystal center of Weiden, and into the fantasy-land beauty of the *Oberpfälzer Wald*. The city, and the camp on its outskirts, are less than three miles from the Iron Curtain.

The sign that welcomes you to this pleasant, prosperous looking little town of perhaps five thousand souls also informs you that you are entering a *Ferienort*, a vacation spot. As we drive up the main street of the town we see a large yellow and black sign that points the way to "KZ"—*Konzentrationszentrum*.

There is ample free parking and a booklet, in German, relating the history of the camp, which opened in May 1938 and continued to operate until the last days of April 1945. It was not, primarily, an extermination center, but a working camp. Prisoners labored in nearby granite quarries and died mainly of hunger, disease, and neglect. Political prisoners and those too weak to carry on were usually dispatched by casual shooting, occasionally by hanging. There were never more than three thousand persons confined here at any one time, meaning that the camp had a 100 per cent population turnover 23 times in seven years.

The most striking structure on the grounds of the former camp is an exquisite stone chapel, built from materials left over when the guard towers were torn down in 1946. The homelands of the various victims have contributed stained-glass windows depicting scenes of suffering with patriotic messages. Small plaques on the walls memorialize the dead of 18 nations, including Germany. It is good to think of the Eucharist being celebrated here, the Host distributed in a house of God built from the rubble of hell.

Once outside the chapel, you descend a circular stone staircase that leads to a rectangular courtyard. It is a scene of impersonal beauty. A high mound of human ashes, twenty feet square, has been planted with grass and surrounded by decorative stones. The walkways leading up to the crematorium are of natural wood and rough-hewn granite, and flowers are everywhere. Lining the courtyard are identical plaques bearing the flags of the nations whose citizens died here, with neatly carved numerals: Russia, with 26,430 souls, sustained the greatest losses. We try, in vain, to imagine the separate sufferings of 26,430 Russians, 17,546 Poles, nine Englishmen, and "two unknown American pilots" who were shot down near Flossenburg and misdirected to this inferno. We cannot, among the flowers, the fragrant trees, the clear air, call forth these ghosts with emaciated, unwashed bodies and filthy clothing. Their teeth, their bones, their hollow rinds of shoes are neatly displayed in glass urns in the chapel and in the crematorium—dusty, disinfected by time. The German guidebook mentions dysentery, smallpox, typhus, the nouns capitalized and crackling with consonants; nothing suggests the reality of blood, suppuration, the moist misery of infection in bodies too weakened to resist disease.

Beyond the pyramid is a wall of rough stone, about four feet high and ten feet long, with an inscription in three languages: "Prisoners were shot in mass here." I have been a target, have clawed the vibrating earth while rockets detonated around me, have believed firmly in the imminence of my own death. But these experiences are no help in dealing with a few square feet of dirt and bricks used for casual, wholesale slaughter.

A few dozen steps from the wall is the crematorium, a grey stone building some thirty feet square. *Desinfektion* is printed in blood-red letters over the door, but its chilling effect is blunted by the plastic No Smoking sign immediately below it, in four languages. Inside, the oven itself is disarming. It looks much like the furnace that heated the two-family house I grew up in. Only its long, narrow interior and the stretcher hanging near the door indicate its grisly purpose. The oven and the walls are hung with flowers and memorial plaques, many from individual families whose close relatives were traced here, their intimate inscriptions plaintive in the solitude of this cold little building: "To René: We will never forget you. We will always love you." "To our father, Paul, whose memory will live in our hearts forever." In the back of the room hangs a memorial to Admiral Canaris, erected in 1965 by his comrades in the Abwehr.

A German walks in with his wife and two sons, about eight and ten years old. They are an attractive family, neatly dressed. The father sizes us up quickly, my jeans and London Fog raincoat immediately giving us away as Americans. Few Americans understand German, so they proceed as if we weren't there. He examines the glass urns, filled with bone fragments, ashes, charred teeth, and comments to his wife, "Not very careful about emptying ash trays, are they?"

They laugh together. He picks up the younger boy, holds him under one arm, head pointed toward the open door of the oven. "You'd make quite a loaf of bread, wouldn't you?" he asks.

"*Nein, nein!*" yells the boy, laughing. His father puts him down and they all leave. Still facing the plastic flowers from René's parents and the engraved marble tablet placed there by the children of Paul, we feel a protective anger.

We walk toward the camp gate, through the unpretentious mass graves on either side of the path. Five thousand lie here under a hundred or so representative headstones. An occasional marker bears a name and a date, usually indicating that the victim died at the very end of April 1945. Some of them even managed to outlive Hitler, but could not escape his madness. As the Allies advanced, the pace of the murders quickened.

The lives and sufferings of men are bounded by time, and thirty years have passed over Flossenburg. Germany is once again a member of the community of free nations, proof that descent into unimaginable depravity need not be irrevocable. And that fact offers hope for the future to millions of oppressed victims from Mecklenburg and Slovenia to Uelen and Con Son. In reflecting on the past, the French, as usual, say it best. The monument in the courtyard to their 4,771 dead reads:

> *The sufferings of these martyrs are ended. They have vanquished their executioners. Above life, there is honor.*

June 25, 1976

Eyes on the White House Lawn

S. L. Varnado

For the first time in about a hundred years we have a President who speaks with a Southern accent (give or take a few phonemes), and the nation seems to be enjoying the fact. Everybody is making jokes with "y'all" and shucks" in the punch lines, talking knowingly about "good ole boys," and casually using expressions like "madder than a long-tailed pig in a revolving door." This Era of Good Feeling is bound to end, however. Southerners and Northerners think they speak the same language, but in actual fact they do not; and I would bet my last chitterling that it won't be long before the hostilities break out. Here are some examples of the confusion I foresee.

1. Misunderstandings caused by the pronunciation of the long *i* sound. Northerners pronounce the long *i* sharply in words like *rice* and *ice*. Southerners, on the other hand, drag the thing out as if they were really enjoying it. Instead of *rice*, a Southerner says *rise*; instead of *ice*, he says *eyes*. This could cause some problems for President Carter. Returning to the White House on a cold winter day, he phones up the head of the maintenance staff: "Good afternoon, this is President Carter. I just wanted to report that I noticed a lot of eyes on the White House lawns and sidewalks."

The maintenance man puzzles over this for a moment. "Eyes on the sidewalks, Mr. President? You saw eyes on the sidewalks?"

"Yes. Lots of eyes. And some broken limbs too."

"Eyes and broken limbs! Shall I call an ambulance?"

"Ambulance? What for, man? There's been no accident yet; but there will be if we don't get the eyes cleared away. How about sprinkling it with salt?"

"Sprinkling the eyes with salt?"

"Yes. That's what we do in Georgia when the eyes gets heavy. 'Course it doesn't happen often."

"No. No, I wouldn't suppose it does."

"Can you take care of it?"

"Can I —? Yes, of course. Eyes and broken limbs around the White House. Yes, I've seen that often. Quite common. Now here's what I want you to do, Mr. President. Stay right where you are, and in a few minutes there will be some nice men who will come over to help you. They won't hurt you. Everything is going to be all right."

2. Confusions involving the short *o* sound. Southerners tend to flatten the short *o* so that it sounds like a short *u*. The most bizarre example of this is the word *bomb*, which a Southerner invariably pronounces as *bum*.

"Hello, this is President Carter. May I speak to the Russian Ambassador?"

"Spicking, Mr. President."

"Mr. Ambassador, I think we need to sit down and have a nice quiet talk about the number of bums in your country and mine."

"The number of bums? I do not theenk I understand."

"Simple enough, Mr. Ambassador. I feel that both your country and my country have got too many bums around. We must get rid of some of the..."

"Correction pliss, Mr. President. In Russia we haf no bums. Also, it is none of your business."

"Do you take me for a fool Mr. Ambassador? Why, you have as many bums as we have. Maybe more."

"Excuse pliss. That iss capitalist lie. We haf employed our bums."

"Oh, you have employed your bums, have you? Well, then, maybe we will have to employ our bums, Mr. Ambassador. Think that one over."

April 29, 1977

Flannery O'Connor: The Village Theist

J. O. Tate

In part, Flannery O'Connor's posthumous literary life has been so vigorous because of continuing publication: since her death, Farrar has released the second short-story collection, *Everything that Rises Must Converge* (1965); the occasional prose, collected in *Mystery and Manners* (1969); the compendious *Complete Stories* (1971); and now—a new and privileged look into her world—Sally Fitzgerald's edition of Flannery O'Connor's letters (Farrar). Beginning in 1948, while the young Flannery O'Connor was struggling with *Wise Blood*, and ending in the summer of 1964, just six days before her death, these letters are charming and disarming when they are not chastening and instructive.

But this book is more than epistolary autobiography of a great American writer. It is also a "good read," and then some. Like everything O'Connor wrote, no matter how serious, it is very funny. The book intertwines the developing stories of her career, her many friendships, the progress of her omnivorous education, and her ordeal by disseminated lupus erythematosus, which ended her life at the age of 39. These various stories are united in the sensibility of the woman who lived them, and reveal qualities of resolution, professionalism, honesty, warmth, reason, universality, humor, courage, and acceptance. O'Connor wrote that "vocation implies limitation," a fine thought; she also proved this truth in the trial of experience.

Flannery O'Connor was a master of paradox, as in her famous story "Good Country People." There we watch the collision between an existentialist philosopher and an illiterate Bible salesman. The nihilistic thinker, a PhD with a wooden leg, finds that her smug plan to seduce and "liberate" the naïve salesman does not quite work out, as the situations are devastatingly reversed. In her letters, O'Connor testifies over and over about such delectable items as Tube Rose Snuff commercials, religious aberrations, absurdities from the newspapers, etc., while at the same time commenting on her progress through Proust or her reading in theology. The catholicity of O'Connor's tastes and interests is staggering. But she can focus the whole of her mind in a single aperçu: "[Henry] James is a master of vulgarity. A good part of all his books and the whole of many of his stories are studies in vulgarity." The truth of this observation should not obscure its source: The same author who read James and Conrad with care was also familiar with Fireball Roberts and Tiny Lunn, the stock-car drivers. Any lingering canards about O'Connor's isolation, which never were true, must henceforth be gone or be damned.

The power Flannery O'Connor displayed in her greatest works—the authority she achieved—was based on knowledge of the world, and a completely developed technique for conveying that knowledge. Her whiz-bang catalogue of American humor features used-car salesmen, traveling salesmen, various con men, the farmer's daughter, street preachers, absent-minded professors, narcissistic writers, frustrated liberals, and "innerleckshuls." These denizens of a real world are also good citizens floating on the mainstream of American literature, folklore, history, and culture. Ichabod Crane and Brom Bones, the Confidence Man and his victims, and the Duke and the Dauphin would have felt right at home in the world limned by Flannery O'Connor. That world is a meretricious catalogue, "a shelf of false hands, imitation buck teeth, boxes of simulated dog dung to put on the rug, wooden plaques with cynical mottoes burnt on them ..." (*The Violent Bear It Away*). O'Connor was never over-refined.

The other side of the paradox is O'Connor's serious pursuit of art and learning. For her, this was finally and necessarily congruent with the theological underpinnings of her devout Roman Catholicism. Perhaps the most impressive strands in the letters are her accounts of her reading, sensitive literary advice to aspiring writers, and eloquent addresses on her faith composed for friends and correspondents. "The only thing that kept me from being a social-scientist," she writes, "was the grace of God and the fact that I couldn't remember the stuff but a few days after reading it."

This fusion of literary loftiness with low laughter focused O'Connor's penetrating powers. Although she was forced to make concessions to her debilitating illness, in no way did she "adjust" to anything else. She was always an acute observer, a keen intelligence cutting through to the heart of things. She beheld and judged the Zeitgeist with the same zest with which she enumerated the banalities of mass culture. Indeed for her these were much the same thing. She wrote to John Hawkes, "I don't think you should write something so long as a novel around anything that is not of the greatest concern to you and everybody else, and for me this is always the conflict between our attraction for the Holy and the disbelief we breathe in with the air of the times.... "

This statement could not be clearer or more true about O'Connor's aim and works. She wrote of *The Violent Bear It Away*, "A lot of arty people will read it and be revolted. I trust." And, "Nobody would have been found dead writing it but me." Her determination to stick to her last was a matter of intellectual conviction and spiritual certitude, not a matter of pride or pique.

The author of the letters, as of the stories and essays, stands there with Dr. Johnson's *Lives of the Poets* on one hand and the Georgia *Market Bulletin* in the other. She fulfilled the Johnsonian stricture: she cleared her mind of cant. This author would perplex a Van Wyck Brooks and his Highbrow/Lowbrow machine; Philip Rahv would not be able to color her Paleface or Redskin without distorting her own "speckled" shades. We must think of her as she describes herself (newly perched on crutches): "a structure with flying buttresses."

The Flannery O'Connor of the letters can write thus: "... We are not judged by what we are basically. We are judged by how hard we use what we have been given. Success means nothing to the Lord, nor gratefulness. ... The violent bear it away." Sally Fitzgerald has assembled the letters so that we may see the rigor of Flannery O'Connor's sincerity.

March 16, 1979

The Sage's Progress

Samuel Pickering Jr.

There is a class of ailments which, like the indiscretions of youth, are considered too commonplace to be delved into in the medical journals. Yet these ailments—the occupational hazards, such as tennis elbow and housemaid's knee—are often far from trivial, and, as a survey of academics from Maine to California would reveal, one of them strikes at the very heart of our intellectual life. In the paneled halls of ivy there lurks—pomposity.

Rarely fatal, this virus usually leads to a comfortable mental state in which the sufferer becomes quite inaccessible to thought. Even the brightest, most blue-eyed and fit, young instructor eventually slows, swells, and sickens. No antidote has yet been found for the malign effects of being treated as a sage by undergraduates. The belief that one is Delphic gets under the skin, enters the bloodstream, and becomes incurable.

The disease progresses gradually, going through a series of easily identified stages. The young assistant professor begins to become highly susceptible as soon as his first book meets with friendly critical nods. Giving the lie to the old adage that clothes make the man, the sufferer strides into pomposity's deceptive sartorial stage. Paunching slightly with confidence, he wraps himself in a tattered Afghan coat in winter and lets his toes wiggle through the slits of Rhodian sandals in summer. When reversed, his paisley tie delivers a full-fisted, eyelid-bruising message, matched in its rough whimsicality only by his lavender shorts. To the outsider this would seem to be a young man on the way out. But to the cognoscenti, this is clearly a man on the way up. They know that it is but a short step from romantic Afghan to Brooks Brothers herringbone. Bronzini and Sulka will soon hang from his neck in tasteful grey and blue. The sandals will languish in the closet while those sweet harbingers of spring, Whitehouse and Hardy wingtips, will escort a new associate professor to that tenured land where scotch and water purl against the ice like the Afton flowing gently to the sea.

Not long afterward, our subject becomes "funded" and flies away for a year in the British Museum. A penchant for Gauloises and Harvey's amontillado and the appearance of The Book mark the disease's inexorable progress. After the return from Bloomsbury, *Vanity Fair* prints of willowy John Whistler and languid Lord Leighton decorate the sufferer's office walls, while the poster celebrating the annual rattlesnake roundup in Sweetwater, Texas, curls forgotten in the waste can. On the title page of The Book, L. Stafford Brown rises newborn from the ashes of Leroy Brown Jr.

Elevated to the departmental chair, our sufferer ignores the petty world scrabbling below and nods into greying dignity. Pomposity brooks opposition no longer, and the professor becomes a wonderful old boy in whose presence ideas flap heavily and fall to the ground like dying swans. Alumni recall his incompetence fondly.

His enrollments swell as gentlemanly B's are bestowed with grand largesse. Time seems to doze until one long noon when pipe smoke gathers about the professor like cumulus clouds rolling to a storm. Suddenly there is a puff and he is gone. Some say that he never left, and that his spirit still haunts the university.

Whatever the truth may be, the L. Stafford Brown Reading Room is duly dedicated. From above the mantlepiece, a mantlepiece on which Dr. Johnson once rested a weary elbow while expostulating with Boswell, stares the professor himself. He is portrayed walking across the Cotswolds. Sheep frisk behind him, while in his right hand he carries The Book. In his left hand he holds a pipe. There are always students drowsing in the room. Soon it is known as the Cave of the Old Sleeper.

September 28, 1979

Maoism Is Dead

Francis B. Randall

Several worlds ago I had the astonishing good fortune to be one of the first twenty Americans allowed into Russia after Stalin's death. I have now just returned from a journey to China that began about a month after Mao died. Everything was the same and everything was different.

Both trips were Philosophical voyages, on which the traveler must be gripped with his encounter with the most alien societies on the planet, and with his own inmost values. Old Russia and Old China were both glorious, insofar as they survived, and both tragic in their ruin. And Communism? What can one say? It was and is simultaneously a wonder, a horror, and a farce—and no part of that paradox can ever be argued away. And the future of Communism? When Stalin died that question was the life and death of the whole world. It may still be the greatest question. But I think I saw the end of the Chinese Revolution.

Mao Tse-Tung

After forty years of yearning to go to China, Marco Polo's, Ibn Battuta's, and every traveler's ultimate dream, I walked across the bridge at Shumchun, north of Hong Kong, and entered the forbidden empire on the other side of the world— and I had the overwhelming feeling that I had been there before. The neatly manicured rice paddies of Kwangtung outside the immigration halls were quite different from the gloomy pickle marshes that greeted me near Leningrad a generation earlier, but everything that the Communists had done was almost identical.

The bureaucratic buildings were of the same grayish, Romanish, Stalinist style. The rooms were plastered and pine-floored in the same way, with the same tall, dirty windows, hung with the same coarse lace curtains, while the same Victorian Stalinist furniture was decorated with the same coarse lace doilies, and the lamp shades were similarly fringed. Quite similar edifying slogans of the Communist gods were presented in the same carved, gilded letters (or characters) on the same red boards. And the gods themselves, Marx, Engels, Lenin, and the deeply beloved Stalin, joined in China, of course, by the supreme god, Mao, glared down from the same three-quarter-face busts in the same frames. And after quite similar bureaucratic formalities, we were fed, in very different cuisines, a similarly cold, greasy, and abominable Communist lunch.

But is China (was Russia) the True Paradise or one vast slave camp? Can any traveler, carefully herded by innumerable agents of a huge Communist bureaucracy practiced for decades in the bamboozling and propagandizing of foreign innocents, succeed in breaking through to "the real Russia" ("the real China")? (I gratefully remember my own guides—you, Elena, and you, Tamara, you, Mr. Ch'en, and you, Miss T'ang, all more bamboozled against than bamboozling, who arranged, guided, lectured, and scolded me so patiently, and who worked so mightily to gain so many of my requests from your own maddening bureaucracies.)

Yes, a traveler can. Communists can at most build Potemkin villages, not Potemkin Moscows and not Potemkin Chinas. One can't do everything. When I noticed after Stalin's death that our guides only took us around western Moscow, which was, Lord knows, poor enough, I simply walked over to eastern Moscow—no one stopped me—to see the ghastly slums in which most Muscovites lived. And *all* Chinese streets, off the main show boulevards, are scenes of Asian poverty that makes Moscow look like Bronxville.

I have now traveled from end to end of China. I know they have lots of tractors—I've seen them being made in an East-Is-Red tractor factory. But they are clearly too precious to use very often. In one commune in Honan I saw two tractors leveling the ground on one lot, breaking an otherwise perfect record of thrillingly beautiful agrarian landscapes peopled by peasants out of Sung paintings bent double over rice, millet, or cabbages, men hauling immense loads, women staggering under the great weight of two baskets hanging from yokes across their bent necks. If they let you into their countries at all, Communists cannot herd and bamboozle you away from seeing how their serfs live. Scholars may argue whether the Chinese peasants now eat more or less than they did in 1937, but China really is a horribly poor Asian country, about on the level of Java, in which I had traveled the month before.

If poverty is a horror (and the Communists, after all, did not invent poverty in Russia and China), foreign visitors are relieved by plenty of farce. It was side-splitting to hear grown men and women repeating all over the Soviet Union, "As the great Stalin, genius leader of the peoples of humanity, taught ..." followed by some manifest falsehood or blithering cliché. It is very hard to keep from exploding with giggles when adult Chinese recite, in every heavy industrial plant, "Chairman Mao says, 'Iron and steel are the heart of our metallurgical industry.' " In every commune, "Chairman Mao says, 'Take grain as the key link in agriculture.' " Anywhere in the Yellow River provinces, "Chairman Mao says, 'Do everything connected with the Yellow River with care.' " Apropos of anything, "Chairman Mao says, 'We must learn to walk on our own two feet.' " Apropos of nothing, "Chairman Mao says, 'Take class struggle as the key link.' " "We increased production in this factory threefold by arming the workers with Chairman Mao's Thought." Chairman Mao says, war is peace. Chairman Mao says, Queen Anne is dead.

Even more ludicrous are the passing political campaigns, whose slogans are mouthed with unbelievable intensity for some fleeting period. My group kept hearing, in factories, schools, women's meetings, railroad stations, and even in Buddhist caves, "The important tasks confronting the Chinese people [workers, students, women, or whatever] are to deepen criticism of Teng Hsiao-p'ing's reactionary attempts to reverse the correct decisions of the Great Proletarian Cultural Revolution, to rejoice in the frustration of the plots of the Anti-Party Gang of Four in Shanghai, namely Chiang Ch'ing, Chang Ch'un-ch'iao, Wang Hung-wen and Yao Wen-yuan, and warmly congratulate Chairman Hua Kuo-feng on his assumption of the Party Chairmanship, the Premiership, and the Chairmanship of the People's Military Commission."

This was quite a mouthful of a slogan to repeat syllable by syllable all over China! So the effect was hysterically goofy. But that was a few weeks ago; the line has changed again; I hear that nobody criticizes Teng Hsiao-p'ing any more; he is coming back, again, and soon they will all be warmly congratulating him on his assumption of blah blah blah blah blah, again.

March 4, 1977

The New Boys in the Bunker

Robert S. Strother

The Marxist revolutionaries now occupying the bunker of ousted President Anastasio Somoza in Nicaragua are not given to mirth; but when they pause in their authoritarian work they must, like Stalin looking up from a satisfactory death list, allow themselves a faint sardonic smile.

As guerrillas flying a bogus banner of human rights, they succeeded, with the support of one of the world's most impressive dictators, in bringing an elected government friendly to the United States crashing down in a storm of fire and a torrent of blood. Better yet, some of their prospective future targets had eagerly helped them win. All very amusing indeed, from the viewpoint of the victors.

Some of the leaders of this socialist revolution had feared that non-Communist countries might recognize and oppose a replay of the well-thumbed script used by Fidel Castro to conquer Cuba almost 21 years ago; but their fears proved groundless, and the plan is running like clockwork.

Fidel Castro

The Free World is rushing to supply money for reconstruction and for new weapons, along with diplomatic recognition and an honored place in that great forum for peace and justice, the United Nations. All in all, a positive riot of laughs for Moscow....

Newsweek recently sent two writers to interview Tomás Borge, Nicaragua's new Interior Minister, apparently with the purpose of removing roadblocks to socialist revolution in Central America. The chat ended on a charming note:

Q: "Why is it that at times you sound more like a poet than a revolutionary?"

A: "All true revolutionaries are poets."

The hairy gunmen in the bunker must have laughed aloud at that one.

November 23, 1979

The Light from the East

John Lukacs

The Pope arrived in the United States on the first day of October. Forty years earlier, on the first day of October in 1939, in Poland the crackle and the boom of guns stopped. That day the last Polish soldiers, begrimed and ragged, dropped their arms. The pall of death spread over that melancholy country. The Germans, a new, brutal breed of Germans, had conquered it. Their then allies, the Russians, a new, brutal breed of Russians, poured in from the east. Between them they divided Poland. In Cracow, the sacramental city, the German viceroy of Poland, Hans Frank, set up his retinue and palace. The Russians would deport thousands of Poles. The Germans would tell them that they were slaves, close their schools and most of their churches, for the purpose of starving their spirit, and not only their flesh, into submission. Karol Wojtyla, a plain Polish draftee from around Cracow, was among those millions of potential slaves.

Forty years later he is the Pope, the ruler of the Catholic Church, the Bishop of Rome, the only remaining true monarch in the world. Now he arrives in the United States on a triumphal visit. He lands in Boston, the hub-city of the American intellectual tradition, seat of the richest and most famous university of the globe, repository and representative of the scientific view of the world, according to which the economy of man is determined, his biological evolution ineluctable. Oh you ghosts of President Conant, Justice Holmes, Professor Skinner, watch the Polish Pope flying in from the East.

How strange and miraculous this is! A century ago the Pope was the prisoner in the Vatican, suspected and shunned by the government of Italy, a man in a gilded cage in Rome. During the last world war no one dared to touch him, not even Hitler. In 1943 Hitler said to his confidants that there were three powers in Rome: Mussolini, the King, and the Pope, and that the Pope was the most powerful of them all. In the midst of Hitler's Europe the Vatican was a safe house and an island of flickering light.

Today many people see in the Pope the last real monarch in the world, the last King of the West. And he comes to America from the East, a witness to certain truths, like Aleksandr Solzhenitsyn—the erstwhile Polish draftee and the erstwhile Soviet captain. *Ex oriente* and from a portion of the world where not so long ago many intellectuals had chosen to see the new light of egalitarian justice for the masses.

In the darkening evening, I listen to the radio station which is tidying up the news of the Pope's day in Philadelphia. The newscaster mentions the long duration of the Mass and the length of the Pope's homily. A priest at the microphone comments: "Yes, it was very long. He brought in everything, didn't he? It was a little heavy for people who were standing there for hours."

How about the Pope? Wasn't it heavy for him? I had been there, a bit bone-weary, straining to hear his sermon as it came cracking and fading through the megaphones. Indeed he spoke about many things: Philadelphia, the Declaration of Independence, the Liberty Bell. The people clapped at times—an odd custom during a sermon—as he spoke. I, too, thought that perhaps he should not have talked about all of those things; it had a touch of the expected routine of a foreign dignitary on his visit to Philadelphia. But then I changed my mind. That distant figure on the platform, white but far from being spectral, robust and fatherly, kept on speaking in his booming, slow, careful way. Now he was speaking to these thousands of people against the kind of freedom that is, in reality, a kind of slavery, the very opposite of personal integrity and of independence: against the pursuit of material happiness, against the pursuit of sexual license, against the pursuit of the self-degrading preoccupation of the self.

How tired he must have been, after these interminable long hours, traveling, preaching, praying, traveling, preaching, again! But he was compelled to go on, to speak about these things, to try to exhort people to lead a better and more honest life, returning to this theme again and again. He did not demand these things from his listeners; I felt, deeply, that he was demanding this effort from himself, sacrificing his remnant strength for us, this Father.

There were beautiful things this day: the sudden coming of a golden autumn afternoon after a morning of dark, miasmatic rain; the gentle billowing of the pure and radiant vestments on the podium in that blessed breeze; the silent southwest flight of 13 wild geese suddenly crossing the canopy of the blue sky during Mass, after the whirr of the police helicopters had died away; above all, the white figure with his eloquent hands, this personal presence of the Vicar of Christ.

He was not speaking for himself. He was speaking to us.

To us ... but who are we? His divisions, his *franc-tireurs*, his guerrillas? His subjects, his followers, his children? How many of us will hear, listen, remember? And is it a matter of numbers?

It is not given to us to know everything.

October 26, 1979

The Best of Men

Russell Kirk

In the park of his enchanted palace of Balcarres, near the end of last year, there died David Robert Alexander Lindsay, 28th Earl of Crawford, 11th Earl of Balcarres, Baron Wigan, Baronet of Haigh, Knight of the Thistle. He was Premier Earl on the Union Roll and, among his many other distinctions, a clan chief—though he never wore kilts. His like will not be seen again.

Our words "aristocracy" and "aristocrat" signify "leadership by the best." The Earl of Crawford was the best of Scots in this century. More than anyone else I ever encountered, David Crawford was suffused by what Edmund Burke called "the unbought grace of life." For nine centuries, the great family of which he was the head for 35 years, "the light Lindsays" ("light" means debonair), had been soldiers and statesmen and poets.

Lord Crawford, despite his grand station and his remarkable personal talents, was a marvel of courtesy and generosity. He seemed to know everything worth knowing. (His classical Greek, for instance, was better than that of most professors of Greek.) He was the best speaker in the House of Lords—the best since Lord Rosebery, the Sheriff of Fife told me. In his prime, when first I met him, he was the handsomest man in Scotland.

He knew more about paintings and books than did the most exalted art critics and librarians. He was chairman of the National Trust, of the Royal Fine Art Commission, of the National Art-Collections Fund, of the National Library of Scotland; rector of St. Andrews University; a most active trustee of the Pilgrim Trust, the National Gallery, the British Museum, and several other important institutions and associations. In effect, Lord Crawford was the guardian of culture in Britain.

Though endlessly busy at his responsibilities, writing thousands of inimitable letters, speaking everywhere—still, at his ancient country house of Balcarres he seemed to find infinite time for his guests. One might meet anyone in that rambling tall mansion of black stone, crammed with rare books and with marvelous works of art. Eliot told me once that Lord Crawford was the finest example of his class, as "class" is described in *Notes toward the Definition of Culture*.

For 27 years Lord and Lady Crawford were kind to me; I spent whole summers at Balcarres, the Countess and I pruning the yews round the roofless Gothic chapel, the Earl and I talking of everything in heaven and earth, while time seemed to stand still at Balcarres. They lived frugally amidst artistic splendors. Mary Crawford, a Cavendish, with charming simplicity of manners, usually did her own pleasant cooking. Cleaning women came by the day, but most years no servant slept under those roofs.

Once, at dinner there, I ventured to remark that it must be melancholy to speculate on the prospect of continuity at Balcarres—a continuity of high culture that the Lindsays had maintained century upon century. "There is no expectation of continuity here," said Lord Crawford, with a faint smile, "or almost none." Though a witty and humorous man, he could never escape from the oppression of living in a bent world. All about him a civilization was disintegrating; he knew that like the Celts of the Twilight, he went forth to battle, but not to victory.

In manners, in taste, in integrity, in talents, the Earl of Crawford and some others of his class were the flowering of many generations of growth. Now that class is being extirpated by an envious egalitarianism. And as that class and its culture disappear, the greatness of Britain runs down the drain.

Russell Kirk

What he might do to redeem the time, the Earl of Crawford did. To everyone who met him, there seemed to pass, by a kind of osmosis, some touch of David Crawford's high rectitude and kindness: his magic was more powerful than that of his ancestor the alchemist earl, whose book of formulas he showed me once. His ashes are buried by the wall of that Gothic chapel, in the perpetual shade of those yew trees. But such natures, working upon the community of souls, are made for immortality.

June 25, 1976—From the Academy

Goodnight, Ladies: Five Obituaries

I. Martha Mitchell, R I P

During the early days of the Nixon Administration, Martha Mitchell struck everyone—regardless of ideology—as an enormous relief. In that peculiarly constricted milieu she risked spontaneity. In, ironically enough, her Watergate apartment, she was a charming hostess and an amiable friend to many, though the surrounding tone of the Administration, from the President himself on down to the lower levels, suggested that almost everyone had somehow internalized Bob Haldeman's "zero defect system"—which, not surprisingly, turned out to have a few defects. Nixon himself, like LBJ before him, presented to the world a transparently fictitious persona, a sort of Madame Tussaud's waxworks image of a human being. Within the White House and the Executive Office Building, though there were exceptions, the tone was set by buttoned-up functionaries and tense beavers who seemed to have modeled themselves on B. F. Skinner's superego.

Martha Mitchell brought to this scene a welcome touch of zaniness and genuine good humour. Seizing on a rare good thing, the press tended to exploit her. What originally had been innocent japes became media events. During the Watergate furor, her abortive TV career proved to be another and finally pitiable example of the capacity of the media to exploit and consume the vulnerable.

It may be incorrect to describe her as a victim of Watergate, in the wake of which so many lives, careers, and marriages lie wrecked upon the shore, but surely she, like many other individuals, had no inkling of what lay in store for her when she journeyed to Washington in 1969 with the incoming Nixon Administration.

—Jeffrey Hart
June 25, 1976

II. Margaret Mead, R I P

"A general in the army of feminism," a crusader for clean air, mental hygiene, nuclear disarmament, and women's careers, a thrice-divorced pundit of "social change"—full of compassion for the victims of the world and withering scorn for the complacent and the rich—so the media ushers its Loved One through the portals of Whispering Glades where many a Mr. Joyboy plies his journalistic mortuary goo and paints a sweetly sappy *non nisi hokum* smile on the fierce visage of Margaret Mead.

Miss Mead was no rigorous thinker, and she reveled too much in her role as *Redbook* orator on every issue from Watergate to water pollution. As she grew older she increasingly left her anthropology behind and took up with new trends and fashions. But she was also a genius, and though most of her current advocates prefer her best-selling juvenalia and her late-blossoming TV prattle, in 1949 she summed up her decades of anthropological experience in *Male and Female*, which for all its impressionistic faults, is an extraordinary work of the social sciences. From a perspective of intimate study in nine different cultures, she revised and amended many of her most quoted views from earlier works and developed a comprehensive vision of human culture and sexuality that is deeply conservative in its implications. Human culture is "infinitely fragile," she wrote. Our "humanity depends not on individual instinct but on the traditional wisdom of society." Ironically enough, among the necessities of civilization, Miss Mead believed, was the sanctity and permanence of marriage and the maintenance of clear sex roles, and no one has written so eloquently about the innate differences between men and women.

Even in her final years, when she was being flaunted as "a general in the army of feminism," she described "as flawless in its argument" Steven Goldberg's anti-feminist book, *The Inevitability of Patriarchy*, which feminists had repeatedly cited early works of Margaret Mead to deride and denounce. Gathering a wealth of anthropological and biological material, Goldberg demonstrated that male dominance was the result not of "discrimination," but of changeless physiological and psychological differences. While liberals called him a "fascist" and the Sisterhood ranted, and virtually no prestigious voice rose in his defense, Margaret Mead—perhaps remembering at last her learning rather than her life—calmly wrote that he was absolutely right. Miss Mead had her weaknesses—a fickleness and a desire to please—but she deserves better than she is getting from her friends and Whispering Glades.

— *George Gilder*
December 8, 1978

III. Golda Meir, R I P

Behind her desk in her office—surely the most tatterdemalion of any occupied by a chief of government anywhere in the world—were two pictures, one of Richard Nixon (the year was 1972), one of John Lindsay. On being asked about the criteria for qualifying to have one's picture on her wall, she chuckled and said that the President of the United States (whoever he is) is regularly there. As for John Lindsay, then mayor of New York, she said she loved him, and indeed that she had got him elected in 1969 during his crisis with the Republican Party. "Yes," she said, "I did it," and chuckled. "I get along very well with American politicians. I make it my business." Asked about McGovern, she warned of the implications of his anti-Defense Department policies. Why didn't she speak out to world Jewry on the subject? Well, she agreed she was chief of government of a Jewish state, but she wasn't going to start giving Jews orders whom to vote for in American elections. Israel needed U.S. good will and U.S. support, but Israel would otherwise look after itself. There was no alternative. "I was in the Waldorf Astoria when at the Security Council they were talking about a cease-fire resolution, and the talk talk talk went on for three days, and before they got to the resolution, India had overrun East Pakistan. And you know what the delegates were doing? While Pakistan was going down the drain? They were laughing! It could have been Israel." She leaned back and lit another cigarette and talked about the reluctance of Israel to give up the captured territories in the absence of believable guarantees, nowadays defined as guarantees with a higher Moody rating than those we gave to Taiwan. "You know, I just love American Presidents. They are so nice to me. But"—her laughter, though coarse, was infectious—"you know, I have *yet* to find a U.S. President who has offered me command of the Sixth Fleet." Golda looked after her people with ruthless disregard for lesser matters. And all other matters were lesser matters. If she had been President of the United States, we'd have had peace in Indochina, in the Mideast, in the Far East; and Moscow, a quaint duchy in the heartland of Asia, would be exporting wheat and importing Jews. God be with her. She will look after Him.

—William F. Buckley Jr.
January 5, 1979

IV. Mamie Eisenhower, R I P

Mamie was quite splendid. She constructed no particular philosophy around her intuitive decision that she and Ike would be happier if he attended to world wars, she to home—that was, quite simply, the way it turned out, and both of them were happier for it. The notion that this made her a human wallflower confounded anyone who had the least acquaintance with her (e.g., this obituarist). In a casual encounter several years ago at Gettysburg

College she spoke quite frankly about "Ike," whose memory she treated with affection, but also with detachment. "Very few people really knew him," she said, broadly implying that even she did not know him completely. She remarked the irksomeness of some of the details of post-presidential life without presidential resources. "But he got used to it. Good for him," she smiled quickly, then stopped, bowed her head—someone was saying grace. Her reflexes were instinctive, and decent, and endearing. Like Bess Truman, she was loyal, understood power, but didn't particularly seek it out. And, in retirement, she retired, but she brightened what company she held.

—William F. Buckley Jr.
November 23, 1979

V. Mae West, R I P

Mae West specialized in tight slinky gowns, blondness, a languid and sultry voice, a swaying strut, and a figure that made Dolly Parton look like Twiggy. Ostensibly a seductress—"Come up and *see* me sometime"—her effect was, paradoxically, the opposite. By kidding sex, by exaggerating sex, she really communicated a kind of relief from it—a useful thing to do.

She had a rich wit, and many of her remarks became legendary: "The man I don't like doesn't exist." "Too much of a good thing can be wonderful." And some of her funniest lines, ad libs, ended up on the cutting-room floor ("Do you have a gun in your pocket, or are you just glad to see me?").

From St. Paul through de Sade and Freud to Masters and Johnson—and despite the different attitudes taken—we are instructed that sex is Very Serious Stuff. Mae West offered some relief from the heavy view, finding the humor in sex, and also communicating a robust camaraderie. Everyone got the point, and got into the act. During World War II, the RAF named its inflatable life-jackets "Mae Wests," and the U.S. Army did the same for its twin-turreted tanks.

A great entertainer and—in a way—a force for sanity.

—Jeffrey Hart
December 12, 1980

A Man in the Subway

D. Keith Mano

Description of place. Grand Central: uptown IRT station. 2 A.M. approx. Present: six or seven male persons, black and Hispanic; an injured, bewildered man (Caucasian); myself.

The man: circumstantial evidence. An eminent moralist once said, "Babes, if you're gonna fall down in New York, you better be very well dressed." And the man is: we're not tinkering with a derelict here. More than that: he is thoroughly beautiful. Looks like John Lindsay: the Lindsay of those first, optimistic mayoral campaign posters: WHEN EVERYONE ELSE IS TIRED, HE'S STILL FRESH. Something, however, has come down on the man. Namely, a wicked contusion across his right cheekbone: half clot-busy blood; half the blue-crimson of crushed, in-shock capillaries. It has a great and even more colorful future, this wound. Note also: four knuckles shredded to their white cartilage on each large, handsome hand: sixty hard seconds with a small-gauge potato grater would've done about as much damage.

Reasonable conclusion. He has gone necklong, in the last minute or so, perhaps down a full and 18-edged stair flight: impact taken particularly by face, by shut fists.

Speculation: the man's state of mind. Crashed, totaled: on something more than liquor. This is new and fearful: the head has been screening bleak-wild footage. An unfamiliar trip (LSD, angel dust, who can say?) with no courier to make connections for him. The man will walk in over-emphatic, looping—yes, funny—strides: as if he could put space between himself and hallucination; as if the trite mechanics of movement alone could reassure. The mouth is active: it grimaces: sign language rather than word. Gorilla, chimp: they mouth at us so. He is abruptly animal, dumb: and afraid.

Assumption: the others, what they feel. Unease certainly. The track has been making advances: his dice-toss, compulsive lurch will flirt with it. Death by IRT local doesn't grab even your most diligent New York morb: it throws too much skin around. And authentic concern. Twice they proffer counsel: Sit down, Mister; Mister, you'll hurt yourself. But the responsibility devolves on me: we are white together. They have done a quick character work-up: clothing and demeanor set him apart, above. They can't, by canon, lay hands on him: it would hole the social weave. They are worldwise. The rose-flip is stark, and anyhow motives can get misunderstood: they, East-Harlembound, couldn't shoulder him to Sutton Place. It'd have the structure of a mugging.

Reasons for help.

a) *Curiosity.* Who-is-that-and-how/why-did-he-get-this-way? This is of minimal weight.

b) *The Christian, prescriptive.* "A certain man went down from..." But in New York you'd never move from Point X to Point Y on the Samaritan principle, strictly construed. Bum, panhandler, whore, addict, shopping-bag woman. Which of us, seeing some wino asleep on a subway grate, doesn't consider him inanimate, nonhuman? Doesn't consider him. Still the parable can't be horsed around with: it is absolute. And this wasn't a wino. I felt substantial guilt: apparently not substantial enough.

Description (Cont.): final encounter. My, our train grinds steel in. Some narrow fault has opened between the figment and figment: he will fall-run, all things are downhill; through it, through a door, sidelong, not much clearance in the thronged mind. He can't dare sit. His last struggle to erect posture, I think, had probably been more traumatic than australopithecus' first. Fiftieth Street: one stop: my chance is blown. Sidelong again, tough rushing yardage, through a closed-off tackle hole. As the train pulls north, I watch him bound, momentum is important, upstairs, face-on into NO EXIT ironwork. His nose snorts blood out. And gone.

Some reasons for not helping the man.

a) *Inconvenience.* Reject: it was late, but I had no momentous commitment elsewhere.

b) *His size.* True: there were tactical misgivings. He stood six-one, possibly over two hundred. Manhandling that would have been like pulling your Christmas tree down a long U-shaped corridor with sconces on the wall. Inept charity is worse than none.

c) *Lack of caring.* Reject again. I was anxious for him; remain so. Here I've taken a thousand words to cauterize the event.

d) *Respect.* The determining factor, I guess. This was not a man—we all felt it—to whom one could lightly say, "Excuse me, but you're not capable of walking." He didn't solicit attention: at that moment, with a big assist from his whacked-over mind, the occasion was still private. He had to work it out for himself. An offer of help would have made the scene public: objective, not subjective: humiliating.

For further study: a few questions. The conservative Christian must operate in a paradox. On average, I suppose, we are as charitable as any, still we honor self-reliance. "Forgive seventy times seven" will conflict—should conflict ad infinitum—with "go and sin no more." We do expect a fair return on capital invested: improvement, relief: we externalize a healthful pride. After all, there is just so much cash, time, emotional revenue on hand. And, in the welfare state, theft of charity has become our one go-go small business. Yet we are meant to be fools, suckers for Christ: to be taken in gladly. Can it be measured? For whose benefit do we give: ours, theirs, His? I leave that to you.

And, yes, it goes without saying, I should have helped the man.

March 17, 1978—The Gimlet Eye

Delectations

At Home

Nika Hazelton

I've always liked to entertain, which, to me, means having people in for meals. But my attitude toward entertaining has changed in the course of my life and, I am happy to say, has become much more reasonable. When I was young, I sought perfection, with a vision of myself as an exquisitely groomed hostess—her brow serene, her movements soft, her table and food things of beauty in every detail. Now that I am no longer young, I know that this kind of perfection and serenity can be achieved only by a hostess with a large, well-trained staff. People like me, who do everything for themselves with little help, cannot be perfect.

Two verities that life has taught guide me in my entertaining. The first is that guests, however inconvenient, must be honored; the second is that one should never as a hostess wear the patient air of a tired saint. To me, the best way of honoring guests is to feed them properly, because, even if they came to the house with side thoughts, they also came to eat. So, in order to avoid weary saintliness, I serve food that needs only a few finishing touches at serving time. I also concentrate on dishes that do not have to be eaten at a precise moment. This means no soufflés or fried foods. It also means that things like beef bourguignon, chicken fricassee, and even roasts have to be somewhat undercooked to emerge nicely rather than as mush when the time comes. The one vegetable that goes with the main dish (more than one is a waste, because people don't notice them unless, like asparagus, they are served as a separate course) is pureed and kept warm in a double boiler. Pureed vegetables don't fade in color and flavor, which is why so many restaurants serve them that way.

Recently, after a trip to France, I solved the problem of the salad. Served after the main course, a salad means new plates and forks and the consequent getting up of the hostess-waitress. The French taught me to serve it as a first course, which kills, so to speak, two birds with one stone, since first courses are a dicey proposition: dicey because they have to be light but tasty, and interesting to boot, as well as being simple to make. The salad as first course should be a little more interesting than the usual tossed salad, though one does not have to go to the length of filleting roasted duck breasts and serving them with truffles on a bed of endive (a salad I ate in France). Thus my entertaining menus are simple: a salad to start with; a main dish of meat (generally a roast) with a few potatoes or some other starch, and a vegetable; cheese, if people are devoted to it; and dessert.

Never believe people who say they don't eat dessert. With a lovely concoction such as chocolate mousse in front of them, or a roulade or cake, or fruit tarts, 99 per cent of them will first have a soupçon and then come back for more. Chocolate is a sure-fire winner, and I usually also serve something made with fruit. Choice is always nice when it comes to sweets, I've found.

Always seat people, even if there are only six at the table. Never invite more than one star at a time. Never, but never, allow a guest to get up from the table to help you clear unless he/she has been specifically asked to do so. If you aren't firm about this your party will be a shambles because other guests, feeling guilty, also will get up. Don't delay dinner too long. Serve wine that is good, though not necessarily rare, and plenty of it (at least half a bottle per guest). This animates people without getting them sloshed and will carry them on after the dinner, whereas too many cocktails and too little wine make for that horrid after-dinner silence/slump. Happy holidays!

January 4, 1980

Abroad: Sicily

Nika Hazelton

The loveliest of the baroque towns I saw in Sicily were Palazzolo Acreide, Noto, and the old part of Syracuse, the island of Ortygia. Syracuse is the most touching of cities; all the historical layers are even more open to view than in other parts of Sicily (and one of Sicily's great charms is that its history, from the pre-Greek era to the Bourbons, is so visible). In most Sicilian towns you find the baroque churches, big, splendid, frequently with imposing flights of stairs leading up to them. But *all* of Palazzolo Acreide and of Noto is baroque: besides the churches, there are ochre-colored two- and three-story palaces, with the balconies bulging at the bottom to let ladies in crinolines stand on them and look down. The ironwork is beautiful, and even more beautiful are the carved details on the supports of the balconies, the pillars, the drain pipes. All these palaces and houses are lived in—in contrast to Palermo, whose magnificent baroque edifices decay in the city's old section. And the churches, especially those of Noto, are grand and sure of themselves. In this southeastern part of the island dwelt the great baronial families who built their elegant towns, living in formal splendor, fed by their "*monzus*" (as the French chefs were called: a local pronunciation of "*monsieur*").

In Syracuse, the cathedral made from the temple of Athena is flanked by baroque palaces; the Fountain of Arethusa, where Hannibal watered his troops, is not far from a Norman castle; Greek and Roman buildings and artifacts turn up wherever the archaeologists dig; the food is marvelous; and in February the almonds blossom for miles around. That was another unexpected Sicilian impression: the afterglow of the glory that was Greece—in Agrigento, in Selinunte, and among the Doric columns of the cathedral, *née* temple of Athena, praised by Cicero for its golden and ivy portals.

December 10, 1976

Film: Two Reviews by John Simon

The Cheap Detective

A different backward glance is taken by *The Cheap Detective*, Neil Simon's new film, directed, like his *Murder by Death*, by Robert Moore. This is a parody of Humphrey Bogart movies—chiefly *Casablanca* and *The Maltese Falcon*, spiced with added allusions to *The Big Sleep* and *To Have and Have Not*. The problem is evident: the political pieties and bittersweet romanticism of *Casablanca* are a far cry from the private-eye toughness of *The Maltese Falcon*. Parody, a small, precise genre, demands perfect accuracy and self-control: to swat with different implements at diverse projectiles is, like trying to play tennis and hockey simultaneously, a mess.

The execution, moreover, is a tangle of self-indulgence. One corpse discovered in the exact position it assumed while alive is funny; a whole series of such corpses is not. Naming all three policemen after Italian-American baseball players is too much or, depending on how you look at it, too little. Having a character's name turn out to be something else every few seconds is a running gag that soon runs out of steam. Everything here is milked to the point where, if it were a cow, it would trample the dairymaid to death.

This is not to say that there are not, as always with Simon, a few funny sight gags and one-liners. Yet even they are rare here, and suffer from the weight of the all-encompassing heavy-handedness. James Coco and John Houseman in particular are victimized by a lack of funny material; Dom DeLuise, despite a pretty good take-off on Peter Lorre, has for his comic mainstay the fact that he exudes an unbearable stench. A character in a Feydeau farce can turn bad breath to good comic account; stinking all over is considerably less funny. The parodist, mocking vulgarity, must not himself fall into worse vulgarity.

Among the generally undistinguished performances, Louise Fletcher's Ingrid Bergman take-off is particularly disconcerting: a character meant to be boring is played quite literally boringly. The very Hispanic Fernando Lamas is unintentionally ludicrous as a Frenchman; his prototype in *Casablanca*, Paul Henreid, was not very French either, but this is hardly a subtly ironic jab, only Hollywood's perennial insensitivity to telling details. Peter Falk is insufficiently inventive as a comedian to carry the main role, and I wish that his baby-talk version of Bogey's speech would stick in his craw instead of mine.

A final example of the prevailing sloppiness. The song that haunts Simon's lovers is not the nostalgic "As Time Goes By," but the bouncily silly "Jeepers Creepers." Now, good satirical parody would intensify the nostalgia to absurdity, not simply substitute its opposite—a cheap effect typical of a cheap film.

August 4, 1979

American Gigolo

W e come now to the notorious Paul Schrader's latest: *American Gigolo*, a recasting of that hoariest of clichés, the whore with a heart of gold, into the male hustler with a heart of gold. We need not dwell on the simplistic pseudo-intricacies of the plot, which record the activities of Julian (Richard Gere), a highly paid but still rising Los Angeles gigolo, among whose valuable services are proficiency in several languages, access to the L. A. Country Club, intimacy with the maitre d' of the Polo Lounge, a wardrobe designed by the celebrated Giorgio Armani, and unequaled gifts for soft talk and hard loving.

Julian is conned into a kinky S & M job of a sort he otherwise would not stoop to, and is promptly framed for the murder of a masochistic wife by her sadistic bisexual husband. The latter is in cahoots with a black pimp who has it in for Julian, and with Senator Stratton, whose beautiful but neglected wife, Michelle (Lauren Hutton), has fallen helplessly in love with our hero. Michelle's love, whose very existence, let alone magnitude, the film is unable to make credible, pursues Julian like a combination Hound of Heaven and Daddy Warbucks. When Julian is finally apprehended for the supposed S & M murder as well as the defenestration of the pimp, of which he is the accidental cause, Michelle fights everyone and everything for him: her jealous and powerful husband, the law, and Julian's own deep-seated resistance to any love that is not bought. At last—need I tell you?—love triumphs as Julian sobs into the little window through which, an imprisoned Pyramus, he must communicate with his Thisbe; sobs about why it took him so long to accept the gift of love. I wish I had his exact words, but I was too convulsed with laughter to get them down.

Schrader is that sinister figure Hollywood turns out intermittently: the hack with a dangerous bit of learning. Equipped with a smattering of literature, philosophy, art history, and theology, he clearly thinks that he has created in Julian (whose full name is Julian Kay, a probable allusion to Kafka's Joseph K.) an existential hero for our times out of Camus, Celine, and Dostoyevsky.

Actually, he has written and directed something out of Kerouac with a touch of watered-down Colette. Julian emerges, first of all, as stupid. When, during body-building exercises, he is learning Swedish from phonograph records, he repeats not only the Swedish phrases but also the English ones! (He may, of course, need to build up his English, too.) When he first meets Michelle in the Polo Lounge, each pretends to be French and fools the other, despite a command of Racine's tongue that would hardly pass muster in Racine, Wisconsin.

Now for a sample of Julian's sexual spiel: "I can make you relax, relax like you've never relaxed before. Make you aroused like you've never been aroused before. Excited. I know how to touch you. Where to touch you..." And so on. If this is high-class gigolo talk, what could the diction of medium-priced lovers be like? Grunts, I daresay. But the Armani *couture* is *haute* enough, and Schrader's camera lovingly pans across well-stocked closets and drawers filled to bursting. Julian's other worldly goods are likewise scrutinized (expensive car, various electronic gadgets, etc.), but the seamier side of his trade is cravenly elided. We never see him escorting a truly old or ugly woman, and we see him in bed only with Lauren Hutton, which would present no problems even for the rankest amateur.

As *American Gigolo* would have it, Julian's troubles stem only from that one kinky trick he was tricked into turning—the kind of trivial misstep a reputable writer might make by publishing once in the wrong magazine. The moral questions of Julian's existence are never even remotely confronted, and his defense of his calling (bringing joy to the needy) is written, staged, and photographed for maximum persuasiveness. Toward Michelle, he comports himself like a perfect, albeit loveless, gentleman, preferring to sacrifice his freedom and very life perhaps rather than involve her in any way, a veritable Sir Kay of Arthur's court. No wonder, then, that his redemption is brought about as gratuitously and unconvincingly as his previous gallantry was sentimentally contrived. If you take also Gere's superficial performance and Hutton's better but still insubstantial one, what have you got? A terrific commercial for Giorgio Armani.

April 4, 1980

Less Is More: Zeffirelli's
Jesus of Nazareth

M. J. Sobran

NBC has rebroadcast Franco Zeffirelli's *Jesus of Nazareth*, and its very excellences point up its failure. Nearly everything about it is fine; I don't expect ever to see a better version of the Gospel story; but somehow it doesn't work.

Part of the problem is that it's one of those Who's Who spectaculars: a synod of great actors in great cameos—Ustinov, Plummer, Olivier, Richardson, Mason. Ustinov, as Herod, is a terrifying figure, all right, not because of any royal grandeur but precisely because he embodies pure petulance liberated by absolute power, raging with violent self-pity at the rumor of a *baby*. But then he's gone, and it's somebody else's turn to be memorable for a minute. By the time Ernest Borgnine and Anthony Quinn turn up, it's wearing pretty thin. The big names flashing by have the unfortunate effect of emphasizing the discontinuity of the Gospels, especially when they are conflated to get all the facts in. The acting, the dusty visual beauty, the pungent Jewishness of the intimate scenes—these are undermined by the attempt to be comprehensive.

It seems cruel to dispraise Robert Powell's Jesus, a noble and tasteful effort, neither saccharine nor sanctimonious; but avoiding vice isn't the same thing as achieving virtue. Often he is lovable; always he is inoffensive—which is the trouble. Jesus went around shocking as he healed, performing miracles to stave off enemies for a while, withholding claims more shocking than the ones he made publicly. And even his confidants were shocked by his confidences. Powell gives us a Jesus who is too easily taken for granted, a conventional Jesus. He should have reminded us how strange the convention itself is. As lawyers say, one needs a certain "standing" to forgive sins: you must be either the victim of particular sins, or else God. A man who without explanation tells people that their sins are forgiven is on the face of it annoying at least. The saner he seems, the more outrageous. Nobody but a villain could feel the urge to humiliate and kill a nice British gentleman like Powell's Jesus. But we shouldn't be permitted to feel so superior to those who hated Christ; and this production lets us feel superior even to the disciples.

Of course we have an unfair advantage over them to begin with: we know how the story comes out. But that very fact turns the story into ritual, whereas the point of a dramatization is to dramatize, to immerse our emotions in the flow of events. Jesus has to be made more vivid than an icon and we must at least be made to feel why people no worse than most of us could marvel, wonder, be troubled and antagonized by him. We aren't innocent enough to react that way to this story; for us the Good News is stale news. The dramatist must help us to approach it freshly, like a little child. Anthony Burgess' script spares us the rod and spoils us with grown-up familiarity.

Burgess himself is a lapsed Catholic, he says, and this has one good effect: he left his faith at once rather than by the liberalizing degrees that so often reduce the Gospels to a de-supernaturalized husk before they are finally discarded; so, while treating it as fiction, he allows the story its integrity. But this also causes him to tell it with a nostalgic reverence that ignores its urgency, its challenge, its danger to those who hear it. So he avoids inventing dialogue for Jesus, and Powell must speak like a walking Bartlett's, while those around him are free to talk politics and weather and ask where the men's room is.

In this solemn isolation the invented contexts are too artificial, the Word lacks flesh, and his give-and-take with the world becomes pure sermon-*cum*-soulful-gazing rather than mutual provocation. To be flesh is to be commonplace and therefore to have frequent occasion to say less than eloquent things; the real challenge of portraying Jesus is to show him between his miracles of act and word. If we can see him eating, we should be able to hear him asking for butter and commenting on the food. Otherwise his great utterances can't surprise: and we know that every time Powell opens his mouth we are about to hear something we already know. The Gospels do not present a Jesus of aloofness and taciturnity; they are deliberately concentrated and stylized, but their Jesus is a *presence*—which Powell must attempt futilely to convey, in between the red-letter speeches, with looks of pensive kindliness. What we want is fiery love; and this is falsified by reverent silences.

May 11, 1979—Television

Vladimir Nabokov, R I P

T he cover of this magazine had gone to press when word came in that Vladimir Nabokov was dead. I am sorry—not for the impiety; sorry that VN will not see the cover, or read the verse, which he'd have enjoyed. He'd have seen this issue days ahead of most Americans, because he received NATIONAL REVIEW by airmail, and had done so for several years. And when we would meet, which was every year, for lunch or dinner, he never failed to express pleasure with the magazine. In February, when I last saw him, he came down in the elevator, big, hunched, with his cane, carefully observed by Vera, white-haired, with the ivory skin and delicate features and beautiful face. VN was carrying a book, which he tendered me with some embarrassment— because it was inscribed. In one of his books, a collection of interviews and random fare, given over not unsubstantially to the celebration of his favorite crotchets, he had said that one of the things he *never* did was inscribe books.

Last year, called back unexpectedly to New York, I missed our annual reunion. Since then I had sent him my two most recent books, and about these he now expressed hospitable enthusiasm as we sat down at his table in the corner of the elegant dining room of the most adamantly unchanged hotel in Europe: I cannot imagine, for all its recent architectural modernization, that the Montreux-Palace was any different before the Russian revolution.

He had been very ill, he said, and was saved by the dogged intervention of his son, Dmitri, who at the hospital ordered ministrations the poor doctors had not thought of—isn't that right, Vera? Almost right—Vera is a stickler for precision. But he was writing again, back to the old schedule. What was the schedule? (I knew, but knew he liked to tell it.) Up in the morning about six, read the papers and a few journals, then cook breakfast for Vera in the warren of little rooms where they had lived for 17 years. After that he would begin writing and would write all morning long, usually standing, on the cards he had specially cut to a size that suited him (he wrote on both sides, and collated them finally into books). Then a light lunch, then a walk, then a nap, and, in nimbler days, a little butterfly-chasing or tennis, then back to his writing until dinner time. Seven hours of writing and he would produce 175 words. [What words!] Then dinner, and book-reading, perhaps a game of Scrabble in Russian. A very dull life, he said chortling with pleasure, and then asking questions about America, deploring the infelicitous Russian prose of Solzhenitsyn, assuring me that I was wrong in saying he had attended the inaugural meeting of the Congress for Cultural Freedom—he had never attended *any* organizational meeting of anything—isn't that right, Vera? This time she nods her head and tells him to get on to the business of ordering from the menu. He describes with a fluent synoptic virtuosity the literary scene, the political scene, inflation, bad French, cupiditous publishers, the exciting breakthrough in his son's operatic career, and what am I working on now?

A novel, and you're in it.

What was that?

You and Vera are in it. You have a daughter, and she becomes a Communist agent.

He is more amused by this than Vera, but not all *that* amused. Of course I'll send it to you, I beam. He laughs—much of the time he is laughing. How long will it take you to drive to the airport in Geneva?

My taxi told me it takes "un petit heure."

Une petite heure [he is the professor]: that means fifty minutes. We shall have to eat quickly. He reminisces about his declination of my bid to go on *Firing Line*. It would have taken me *two weeks* of preparation, he says almost proudly, reminding me of his well-known rule against improvising. Every word he ever spoke before an audience had been written out and memorized, he assured me—isn't that right, Vera? Well no, he would answer questions in class extemporaneously. Well *obviously*! He laughed. He could hardly program his students to ask questions to which he had the answers prepared! I demur: his extemporaneous style is fine, just fine; ah, he says, but before an audience, or before one of those ... television ... cameras, he would freeze. He ordered a brandy, and in a few minutes we rose, and he and Vera and I walked ever so slowly to the door. "As long as Western civilization survives," Christopher Lehmann-Haupt wrote in the *Times* last Tuesday, "his reputation is safe. Indeed, he will probably emerge as one of the greatest artists our century has produced." I said goodbye warmly, embracing Vera, taking his hand, knowing that probably I would never see again—never mind the artist—this wonderful human being.

William F. Buckley Jr.
July 22, 1977—Notes & Asides

The Style of E. B. White

Donald Hall

I learned a few things, reading E. B. White's *Letters*. The first thing I learned was where *The New Yorker*'s style came from. I don't mean the magazine's dear eccentricities of content—Ivy League football columns, racetrack chit-chat, thickets of factual data on *anything*; those large qualities came from Harold Ross. I mean instead *The New Yorker* tone of voice—at once self-mocking and self-assured, witty through comic juxtaposition, ironic and modest and uppity all together—which characterizes "Talk of the Town," and which the whole staff caught like a communicable disease from E. B. White. When Thurber caught it he added his own grand touches, but he needed to catch it before he could begin to be Thurber. Wolcott Gibbs caught it, anonymous drones who churned out Talk pieces caught it—and John Updike in one of his incarnations, and Brendan Gill.

One sees the start of The Style in White's *Letters*, in letters written before Ross called *The New Yorker* into existence. By this time, the familiar *New Yorker* style has dispersed itself among hundreds of writers not clever enough to write for the master's magazine. The Style turns up in the *Turnipgrower's Gazette*, looking slightly shifty-eyed. If he wades around in the monthly journalism of our day, White must feel at times like an imperfect Typhoid Mary, seeing so many weak imitations of the disease he carried.

But we must not blame him if his genius was semi-communicable. Most of his influence has been benign, for the elements of his style are elegant and forceful, brief, idiomatic, rhythmic, particular, and pointed. White's principles of prose resemble Ezra Pound's or George Orwell's—three rather different writers—but beyond the principles there is a cadence of feeling in White's work that pervades and identifies him specifically. The Style is the man, and the man comes to seem The Style.

But when he went to Maine, E. B. White began—it turns up in letter after letter—to look outside the coziness of his monoclass world, into the world of rural people among whom class is insignificant. More important, White and his beloved wife, Katharine, began to suffer—as we shall all suffer, if we do not kill ourselves earlier—the gradual debilitations of body, day to day, over the long road through aging toward death. As he and his wife suffer infirmity, pain, and the loss of their bright talents, acknowledged suffering enters White's prose. The style enlarges, self-mockery is no longer possible, and he joins a dance of dying which unites him with the rest of humanity. Compassion and empathy become him; he is a noble and fine old man; and his firm and scrupulous language leaves him not at all, but serves us all.

June 10, 1977

Brief and Peppy

John Greenway on Michael Harrington

Michael Harrington (*The Vast Majority*, Simon & Schuster) returned from his Third (and Fourth) World tour with the revelation that we Americans, not satisfied with having invented the plagues of profit, poverty, oppression, capitalism, nationalism, colonialism, multinational capitalistic economic imperialism, slavery, well-poisoning, pollution, genocide, anthropology, and procrastination, devised out of our surfeit of innocent maliciousness such things as Tanzanian fanaticism, filariasis, schistosomiasis, prostitution in Tiajuana (sic), chewing gum for beggar children in Mexico City, and a socio-economic system "that makes children leprous in Bombay, furrows the foreheads of women in Kenya, and turns Indians in Guatemala into drunkards." And if we don't quit it in less than no time, our misbehavior "will be a crime against billions of men, women, and children, including millions of the halt, the blind, and the maimed." Shees. It's enough to furrow your forehead and make you fall to the ground and bite sticks.

February 3, 1978

David Evanier on Lillian Hellman

Pages 11 (where Maybe, *by Lillian Hellman starts) to 18:* There was this and there was that and it's nuts to think about it because you can't really know anything anyway. Sarah Cameron was part of it but she wasn't, because I don't remember much of it. She didn't matter to me and I didn't matter to her, because that was the way it was. I met her or didn't at a *New Yorker* thing given by Wolcott Gibbs. She always denied this, but that was Sarah. "Sarah is Sarah" her husband said and I turned away from that kind of crap talk.

Pages 18 to 41: Ferry Dixon asked me about my first love, but it was so boring talking to a drunk that I kept ordering the best oysters and caviar, but there weren't anymore, though you keep hoping. Yes, she was right, I remembered Alex. He kept asking me if I wanted to take a bath. Why, why, I asked, do you keep asking me that? It's your odor, he said. Years came and went and 15 years later I was gratified to see Alex in bad shape on Fifth Avenue, punished by life as I had hoped he would be.

When I got married my husband told me I took three baths a day and I said what he was saying was nuts. Something was wrong, very wrong. I sent a cable to my father. The bath stuff was there. I finally asked my husband if I smelled. He said no. But I smelled myself all the time, everywhere. I took trips, slept with an Englishman. Years passed.

I was sick of this nut stuff and walked. There was a lot of talk, but I don't remember it. In the morning I awoke in a field and crawled to the hotel where I ordered a raw egg, double sherry, and Worcestershire sauce.

Well, I told Ferry I'd had enough of this rich bitch nonsense, just sick of it and had to go.

I've gotten you to page 41, so you don't need to read that part, and from here you can work your way to page 102, where it stops. Many blank pages follow, thoughtfully provided by the publisher for your note-taking.

What else is there to this thing? Gourmet food, name-dropping (Sam Goldwyn, "Willy" Wyler). The gangster with the heart of gold is Frank Costello, who plunks down five thousand clams because "many good folk had been trapped by the victorious Franco fascists. . . ." And there is the humble, tough Aunt Hannah, salt of the earth, with the sum of the world's wisdom, out of old Hellman melodramas.

[Miss Hellman should] not get off the hook for foisting on the public this non-book of incidents dimmed at the time they happened by alcoholic haze. Having no book to write, she has made an event of that dismal fact.

August 22, 1980

Murray Kempton on Evelyn Waugh

Waugh is more mysterious than most of our great novelists because their disguises so often cover their sins, while his mask his virtues. He seems almost to have preferred his conversion to Romanism to be assigned to an ambition to be identified with the recusant aristocracy; to have it thought otherwise would have betrayed the desperation of his hunt for grace and forgiveness. ("I am wrestling with Father D'Arcy on love ... a subject on which I am grossly ignorant.") He was, in fact, wildly romantic and so hopelessly sentimental that he had a lifelong vulnerability to the appeal of the higher pathos.

Murray Kempton

For all the persistence of his attempt to estrange us, Evelyn Waugh ends up endearing himself to us. How sad it is, however, to think how hard his habit of mistaking his virtues for vices made it for him to endear himself to himself.

March 30, 1979

Evelyn Waugh on Chesterton

"Chesterton," Evelyn Waugh wrote in a letter to WFB, "was a lovable and much loved man abounding in charity and humility. Humility is not a virtue propitious to the artist. It is often pride, emulation, avarice, malice—all the odious qualities—which drive a man to complete, elaborate, refine, destroy, renew, his work until he has made something that gratifies his pride and envy and greed. And in doing so he enriches the world more than the generous and good, though he may lose his own soul in the process. That is the paradox of artistic achievement."

November 14, 1980—Notes & Asides

Guy Davenport on the Incendiary M. Sartre

I have assisted in extinguishing Jean-Paul Sartre when he was on fire. Pete Maas and I, in our salad days, were at the Deux Magots of an evening. "Guy," said the affable Pete, "that old wall eye over the way put his lit pipe in his jacket pocket awhile ago and in just a bit will be in flames, wouldn't you say? Go tell him."

We tried out various phrases, selecting *Monsieur, vous brûlez* as the most expressive. Pete is a more forward person than I, and it was he who went over, begged the pardon of Sartre, and told him that his jacket pocket was on fire. Nothing happened. The conversation raged on, arms flailing, Existentialism as thick in the air as the smoke from Sartre's *confection*. Sartre did not deign to notice Pete, though Pete ventured a polite tug at his sleeve. Nor did Monsieur Camus or Monsieur Richard Wright give the least heed. Whereupon I offered Pete our carafe of water, and this he poured into the philosopher's pocket, which hissed.

July 7, 1978

Epilogue

Anniversary Salute

George F. Will

(An address by George F. Will, speaking on behalf of the ailing Senator Barry Goldwater who with Clare Boothe Luce and Roger Milliken sponsored NATIONAL REVIEW'*s 25th Anniversary Dinner in the Grand Ballroom of New York's Plaza Hotel on December 5, 1980, just one month after Ronald Reagan's election to the Presidency.)*

In your program it says that at this point you're to be addressed by the senator from Arizona, the man who bore into electoral politics the banner bearing the words he took, I believe, from General Douglas MacArthur, "There is no substitute for victory." I am acutely aware that there is no substitute for Barry. I will, however, say a few words about Barry Goldwater, and about the magazine, the fate of which has been entwined with his and with the conservative movement.

I cast my first vote for President at Princeton University as a graduate student, in 1964, for Barry Goldwater. That was the year in which the Princeton faculty voted, my research tells me today, 93 per cent for Johnson, 4 per cent for Goldwater, and 3 undecided. Thus giving fresh meaning to the generic Ivy League ballad, "Don't send my son to Princeton, the dying mother said."

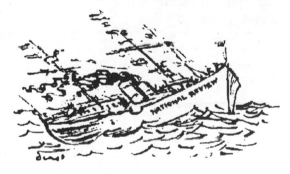

It took approximately 16 years to count the votes in the 1964 election, but finally they all came in, and Goldwater won. He won in two senses. He won in the sense that he sealed, with his triumph in capturing the nomination, the civil war that had simmered and occasionally raged within the Republican Party since the split of 1912 between William Howard Taft and Teddy Roosevelt. After Goldwater's nomination, the Republican Party was a conservative party. Second, he won in the sense that, cleverly taking down to defeat a number of Republicans with him, he broke what had existed in the Congress since 1938, which was a basically conservative legislating majority. For two years thereafter, the Democratic Party was cursed with the principal curse in politics, which is too much opportunity. And they enacted what was to be called, first with high hopes, and then with the taste of ashes, the "Great Society." And there began, I believe, the undoing of the modern liberal agenda. And by 1980 the American people turned round with regard to the liberal agenda and those who advocated it, and paraphrased Dr. Johnson's remark about a manuscript that was sent to him. Dr. Johnson said, "Your manuscript is both good and original. But the part that is good is not original, and the part that is original is not good."

What happened in 1980, I believe, is that American conservatism came of age. In 1964 Barry Goldwater made the Republican Party a vessel of conservatism, and, starting before that and particularly after that, NATIONAL REVIEW magazine has filled that vessel with an intellectually defensible modern conservatism. Now, the principal architect of this achievement of course is William F. Buckley Jr., the Pope of the conservative movement, operating out of a little Vatican on 35th Street. I have in mind with Bill a particular Pope: Urban IV, who, when he entered the room, chose to be addressed by his aides, *"Deus es, Deus es,"* which means, roughly, "Thou art God, Thou art God." Urban IV said, "It is a trifle strong, but really quite pleasant."

But all the great Biblical stories begin with Genesis. And before there was Ronald Reagan there was Barry Goldwater, and before there was Barry Goldwater there was NATIONAL REVIEW, and before there was NATIONAL REVIEW there was Bill Buckley with a spark in his mind, and the spark in 1980 has become a conflagration.

Those of us who are privileged to have worked at NATIONAL REVIEW, and have graduated from that exacting school, know that Bill will be known to history as Priscilla Buckley's brother. Priscilla, aided by Bill, has made NATIONAL REVIEW an instrument of making the Republican Party—for the first time since 1912, when Woodrow Wilson eclipsed Teddy Roosevelt as the animating force of our politics—the principal party of ideas in the United States. And what the Republican Party's success indicates, and no doubt in some future event the resurgence of some other party will indicate, is that history is still the history of mind. It is the history of ideas. We have been plied and belabored for more than a century by bad nineteenth-century ideas, deriving from or attributed to, Darwin or Marx or Freud, all of which purport to show that we are passive instruments of vast impersonal forces. It seems to me that what NATIONAL REVIEW shows is the power of the little platoon, the power of the individual mind, in a century otherwise dominated by large forces. Now, in a way, it is against the conservative inclination to devote as much time to politics as conservatives have had to do in this century. John Adams, the great conservative of the American Revolution, said: "I study war so that my children can study politics, so that their children can study poetry." A civilized hierarchy of values: expressed, perhaps, with more concision by Oscar Wilde, who said, "The trouble with socialism is, it takes too many evenings."

And so I do believe that NATIONAL REVIEW's stupendous success is a peculiarly American story. As Yogi Berra said when told that a Jewish gentleman had been elected mayor of Dublin, "Ah, only in America!" But it is not the last 25 years that we should be concerned with, but the next 25 years. It was five years ago in this room that Governor Ronald Reagan of California gave a stirring address featuring a somber and sobering quotation from the works of Whittaker Chambers, contemplating the perishable nature of Western values. Ronald Reagan's campaign, if it were to be reduced to a single sentence, is the assertion that, evidence to the contrary notwithstanding, the trajectory of American history has not passed its apogee.

I think his spirit is the spirit of the first Republican President, who, on the eve of going to Washington to take power, gave an address in which he told the story of the Oriental despot who assigned to his wise men the task of finding a sentence to be carved in stone, to be ever on view, and always true. The wise men came back with the sentence, "This too shall pass away." "And yet," Lincoln said—"And yet, if we attend to the cultivation of the physical world around us, and the moral and intellectual work within us, perhaps we shall endure."

NATIONAL REVIEW has endured for 25 years and will for 25 more. And that is one reason why the United States shall endure and prosper.

December 31, 1980

About the
Authors

John Brennan (1924-   ) was a psychological services official in the Boston public school system, and a political satire writer who was a regular contributor to NATIONAL REVIEW, *Sting, Conservative Digest* and *Status*.

Colm Brogan (1903-1977) was a regular contributor to NATIONAL REVIEW, a former schoolteacher in Scotland, and a writer on British politics. He was the author of *Our New Masters*.

Richard S. Brookhiser (1955-   ) is a senior editor of NATIONAL REVIEW and a columnist for *The New York Observer*. His books are *The Outside Story* and *The Way of the WASP*.

F. Reid Buckley (1930-   ), President of The Buckley School of Public Speaking, is the author of *Speaking in Public*, and of two novels, *Eye of the Hurricane* and *Servants and Their Masters*.

Priscilla L. Buckley (1921-   ) is a senior editor of NATIONAL REVIEW and the editor of *The Joys of National Review*.

William F. Buckley Jr. (1925-   ) is the founder and former editor of NATIONAL REVIEW; he is currently its editor-at-large. He is also a syndicated columnist, host of the long-running television series *Firing Line*, and author of numerous books, including *God and Man at Yale, McCarthy and His Enemies, The Unmaking of a Mayor, Saving the Queen, Who's on First, Stained Glass, Overdrive, Atlantic High, WindFall, Happy Days Were Here Again,* and *A Very Private Plot*.

James Burnham (1905-1987) was a founding editor of NATIONAL REVIEW and wrote a regular column, "The Third World War" and "The Protracted Conflict" in every issue of the magazine from 1955 to 1978 when he retired. He is the author of *The Managerial Revolution, The Machiavellians, The Coming Defeat of Communism, Containment or Liberation, Congress and the American Tradition, Suicide of the West,* and a number of other books.

John Chamberlain (1903-   ) was a daily book reviewer for the *New York Times*, an editor of *Fortune, Life,* and *Barron's*, Managing Editor of *Harper's*, book editor of *Scribners*, senior editor of *The Freeman*, and NATIONAL REVIEW, and for many years a daily columnist for King Features. Among his books are *The Root of Capitalism, The Enterprising Americans, A Life with the Printed Word,* and *The Turnabout Years*.

Whittaker Chambers (1901-1961) was a senior editor at NATIONAL REVIEW and *Time*. He is the author of *Witness*.

John S. Coyne Jr. (1935-   ) is a NATIONAL REVIEW contributing editor and an executive communications consultant with a major corporation in Chicago. He served as speechwriter for Spiro Agnew, Richard Nixon and Gerald Ford. He is author of *The Qumquat Statement, The Impudent Snobs: Agnew vs. the Intellectual Establishment, The Big Breakup* and *Fall In and Cheer*.

Guy Davenport (1927-   ), a Rhodes scholar who was educated at Duke, Harvard and Oxford, was a professor of English at the University of Kentucky. He is the author, among many other works, of *Da Vinci's Bicycle, Geography of the Imagination, The Mimes of Herondias, Anakreon*, and *Belinda's World Tour*.

Joan Didion (1934-   ) is author of the novels *Run River, Play It As It Lays, A Book of Common Prayer, The White Album*, and of a book of essays, *Slouching Toward Bethlehem*. A one-time columnist for *The Saturday Evening Post*, she has also written a number of screen plays, among them *The Panic in Needle Park, A Star Is Born*, and *True Confessions*.

John Dos Passos (1896-1970) was a renowned novelist who frequently contributed to NATIONAL REVIEW. Among his works are *The Theme Is Freedom* and his novels: *Three Soldiers, Manhattan Transfer*, the famous *U.S.A.* trilogy, composed of *The Forty-Second Parallel, 1919*, and *Big Money*, and a second trilogy, *District of Columbia*.

William H. von Dreele (1924-   ) is a contributing editor of NATIONAL REVIEW and a retired editor of IBM's international newsletter. His verse appears regularly in NATIONAL REVIEW, *The Litchfield Times*, and *The New York Observer*. He is the author of *If Liberals Had Feathers*.

David Evanier (1946-   ) was fiction editor of the *Paris Review*. The author of *The One-Star Jew: Short Stories* and *Red Love*, his work was featured in *Best American Short Stories, 1980*. He was an official with the Anti-Defamation League.

John Greenway (1919-1991) was professor of anthropology at the University of Colorado. He is the author of numerous books, including *American Folk Songs of Protest* and *Down Among the Wild Men*.

George Gilder (1939-   ) is a senior editor of *Forbes*, a contributor to NATIONAL REVIEW, and a fellow of the Discovery Institute. He was a speechwriter for Richard Nixon and Bob Dole, and is the author of numerous books, including *Sexual Suicide, Naked Nomads, Wealth and Poverty*, and *Life After Television*.

Donald Hall (1928-   ) is a poet, author, playwright, and essayist. He was a professor at the University of Michigan and the poetry editor of the *Paris Review*. An editor of many poetry anthologies, his own works of verse include *Exiles and Marriages, A Roof of Tiger Lilies, The Happy Man, The One Day*, and *Old and New Poems*. Among his numerous other writings are two memoirs, *String Too Short to Be Saved* and *Remembering Poets*.

Norman B. Hannah (1919-   ) is a retired Foreign Service Officer, a frequent contributor to NATIONAL REVIEW and author of *The Key to Failure: Laos and the Vietnam War*.

Jeffrey Hart (1930-   ) is a NATIONAL REVIEW senior editor, a syndicated columnist, a retired professor of English at Dartmouth College, and author of *From This Moment On: America in 1940, When the Going Was Good: American Life in the Fifties*, and *Acts of Recovery: Essays on Culture and Politics*.

Nika Hazelton (1908-1992) was NATIONAL REVIEW's "Delectations" columnist from the mid Sixties until her death. She is the author of dozens of cookbooks and of the autobiography *Ups and Downs: Memoirs of Another Time*.

Aloïse Buckley Heath (1918-1967) was a frequent contributor to NATIONAL REVIEW and author of *Will Mrs. Major Go to Hell?*

Elspeth Huxley (1907-   ) was for many years NATIONAL REVIEW's African editor and is author of *The Flame Trees of Thika* and *The Mottled Lizard*, stories of her Kenya childhood.

David Johnston (1951-   ) was a high school student in California when he wrote for NATIONAL REVIEW about campaigning for Barry Goldwater.

Murray Kempton (1918-   ) is a Pulitizer Prize-winning columnist who writes for *Newsday*. His books include *Part of Our Time, America Comes of Middle Age, The Briar Patch*, and *Rebellions, Perversities, and Main Events*.

Willmoore Kendall (1909-1967) was a political scientist and founding editor of NATIONAL REVIEW. A professor at Yale University and the University of Dallas, he is the author of several books, including *John Locke and the Doctrine of Majority Rule*, *The Conservative Affirmation*, *Democracy and the American Party System*, and a work on baseball, *How to Play It and How to Watch It*.

Hugh Kenner (1923-   ) is Franklin and Callaway Professor of English at the University of Georgia in Athens. He has been a frequent contributor to NATIONAL REVIEW, and is the author of numerous books, including *Mazes*.

John Keefauver (1923-   ) is a writer of satire, humor, and short fiction who was a regular contributor to NATIONAL REVIEW. A former reporter at several newspapers, his freelance work has appeared in *Playboy*, *Omni*, the *New York Times*, the *Christian Science Monitor*, *The Sewanee Review*, and other publications, and he has contributed to a number of mystery anthologies. He is the author of the juvenile novel *The Three Day Traffic Jam*.

James Jackson Kilpatrick (1920-   ) is a syndicated columnist, a TV commentator, and the retired editor of the *Richmond News-Leader*. Among his works are *The Sovereign State*, *The Smut Peddlers*, *The Foxes' Union*, and *The Writer's Art*.

Nicholas B. King (1923-1992), journalist and diplomat, worked for United Press in London and Paris and subsequently for the *New York Herald Tribune*. He served as a U.S. Press Attaché in Paris and at the United Nations and headed the USIA Foreign Press Center.

Russell Kirk (1918-1994), author, philosopher, teacher, and critic, created NATIONAL REVIEW's "From the Academy" column. He was a professor at Michigan State College, a nationally syndicated columnist, and founder and editor of *The University Bookman* and *Modern Age*. In addition to *The Conservative Mind: Burke to Eliot*, his numerous other books include *Academic Freedom*, *The Roots of American Order*, *The Politics of Prudence*, *Randolph of Roanoke*, and *The Sword of Imagination: Memoirs of a Half-Century of Literary Conflict*.

Sir Shane Leslie (1885-1972) was the author of numerous books, including *The Anglo-Catholic*, *The Epic of Jutland*, *The Oxford Movement*, *Men Were Different: Studies in Late Victorian Biography*, and *Long Shadows*, his autobiography.

Clare Boothe Luce (1903-1987) was a novelist, playwright, social critic and public servant. She was a Republican Member of Congress representing Connecticut and the U.S. Ambassador to Italy. A frequent contributor to NATIONAL REVIEW, she was also author of the noted play, *The Women*.

John Lukacs (1924-   ) has been a history professor at Chestnut Hill College, and has served as a visiting professor at several other universities, including Princeton, Columbia and Johns Hopkins. He is the author of numerous books, including *The Great Powers and Eastern Europe, The Passing of the Modern Age, Outgrowing Democracy, The Duel, Budapest 1900,* and *Confessions of an Original Sinner.*

Sir Arnold Lunn (1888-1974) was a renowned European mountaineering and skiing enthusiast—he is the inventor of the modern Slalom race—a journalist, and author of numerous books, including *The Flight from Reason, Venice, Science and the Supernatural, A History of Skiing, The Harrovians, Spanish Rehearsal,* and *Unkilled for So Long,* his autobiography.

D. Keith Mano (1942-   ) created NATIONAL REVIEW's "The Gimlet Eye" column and is author of several novels, including *Topless, Horn,* and *Take Five.*

Noel E. Parmental Jr. (1927-   ) is a writer and filmmaker who was a frequent contributor to NATIONAL REVIEW. He has come up in the world: once described by Ayn Rand as a "hooligan," more recently he was identified as a "curmudgeon" by *Mirabella,* for which he has also written.

Nathan Perlmutter (1923-1987) was national director of the Anti-Defamation League, a vice president of Brandeis University, and an occasional contributor to NATIONAL REVIEW and other publications. He is the author of *A Bias of Reflections: Confessions of an Incipient Old Jew.*

Robert Phelps (1922-1989) reviewed books for NATIONAL REVIEW and taught at Manhattanville College and The New School. He is the author of a novel, *Heroes and Orators,* and edited a number of books, including *Earthly Paradise: Colette's Autobiography Drawn from Her Lifetime Writings, Belles Saisons,* a Colette scrapbook, *Professional Secrets: The Autobiography of Jean Cocteau, Literary Life: A Scrapbook Almanac of the Anglo-American Literary Scene from 1900 to 1950,* and Ned Rorem's *Paris Diary.*

Samuel Pickering Jr (1941-   ) is a professor of English at the University of Connecticut, and has also taught at Dartmouth College. He is the author of *The Moral Tradition in English Fiction, 1785-1850* and several collections of personal essays, including *Still Life, Trespassing,* and *Let it Ride.*

Francis B. Randall (1931-   ) is a professor at Sarah Lawrence College. He is the author of *Stalin's Russia* and *N. G. Chernyshevskii.* He is the editor of Thomas Hobbes's *Leviathan* and Bernard Pares's *Russia Between Reform and Revolution: Fundamentals of Russian History and Character.*

Joseph A. Rehyanski (1946-   ) is a lawyer, an assistant district attorney in Cleveland, Tennessee, and a retired Army Lieutenant Colonel. He has been an occasional contributor to NATIONAL REVIEW and other magazines.

William F. Rickenbacker (1928-   ) is a former NATIONAL REVIEW senior editor and the author of several books, including *The Fourth House, Wooden Nickels, Death of the Dollar,* and, with Linda Bridges, of *The Art of Persuasion.* He is the editor of *From Father to Son.*

William A. Rusher (1923-   ), former publisher of NATIONAL REVIEW, is a syndicated columnist and a senior fellow at the Claremont Institute. His books include *The Rise of the Right, Special Counsel, The Making of the New Majority Party, The Coming Battle for Media,* and *How to Win Arguments.*

Francis Russell (1910-1991) was a historian and a regular contributor to NATIONAL REVIEW and many other publications. Among his numerous books are *Tragedy in Dedham: The Story of the Sacco-Vanzetti Case, Sacco and Vanzetti: The Case Resolved, The Shadow of Blooming Grove: Warren Gamaliel Harding in His Times, Adams: An American Dynasty,* and *Three Studies in 20th Century Obscurity: Joyce, Kafka & Gertrude Stein.*

William S. Schlamm (1904-1978) was a founding editor of NATIONAL REVIEW and a former aide to Henry Luce. Before coming to America, where he held additional editorial positions at *Time, Fortune, Life* and *The Freeman,* he was an editor in Vienna and Prague for *Weltbuehne,* and the founder and editor of the international affairs journal *Europäische Hefte.* He was author of *This Second War of Independence* and *Dictatorship of the Lie.*

John Simon (1925-   ) is NATIONAL REVIEW's film critic and the theater critic of *New York Magazine.* His books include *Acid Test, Paradigms Lost, Singularities, Something to Declare, Movies into Film,* and *Reverse Angle.*

C. H. Simonds (1944-   ), a former features editor of NATIONAL REVIEW, is now in real estate in New York.

M. J. Sobran (1946-   ), a former NATIONAL REVIEW senior editor and critic-at-large, is a syndicated columnist. He is the author of *Single Issues*.

Lowell Thomas (1892-1981), was a world-famous traveler and journalist and author of *With Lawrence in Arabia*, the story of Lawrence of Arabia's World War II exploits.

Charles Tomlinson (1927-   ) is an English scholar, author and poet. His numerous works include *Collected Poems, Eden: Graphics and Poems, The Flood, Notes from New York and Other Poems, Poetry and Metamorphosis,* and *Some Americans: A Personal Record.*

Ralph de Toledano (1916-   ) is a contributing editor of NATIONAL REVIEW, serving as the magazine's music critic, and a syndicated columnist. He has held editorial positions at a number of publications, including *Jazz Information* and *Newsweek*. He is the author of several books, including *J. Edgar Hoover: The Man in His Time, Seeds of Treason,* and *Hit and Run: The Ralph Nader Story,* and a contributor to *Nixon* and *The Goldwater Story.*

S. L. Varnado (1929-   ) was a NATIONAL REVIEW contributor and an English professor at the University of Southern Alabama. He is the author of *Haunted Presence.*

Evelyn Waugh (1903-1966), the renowned British author, was an occasional contributor to NATIONAL REVIEW. His works include *Brideshead Revisited, Scoop, Vile Bodies, A Handful of Dust, Decline and Fall,* and *Sword of Honour.*

Alec Waugh (1898-1981) was NATIONAL REVIEW's travel editor, and an author of numerous books, including *The Loom of Youth* and *My Brother Evelyn and Other Portraits.*

Frederick D. Wilhelmsen (1923-   ) is emeritus professor of philosophy and politics at the University of Dallas. He is the author of numerous books, including *The Paradoxical Structure of Existence, Omega: Last of the Barques, The Metaphysics of Love,* and *Christianity and Political Philosophy.*

George F. Will (1941-   ) is a syndicated columnist, author, and political commentator. A recipient of the Pulitzer Prize for commentary in 1977, he served as an aide to Sen. Gordon Allott and as NATIONAL REVIEW's Washington editor and book editor. His books include *Statecraft as Soulcraft, Men at Work, Suddenly,* and *Restoration.*

Garry Wills (1934-   ), formerly an editor at NATIONAL REVIEW, is a syndicated columnist, professor at Northwestern University, and an author of numerous books, including *Lincoln at Gettysburg,* for which he won the Pulitzer Prize, *Chesterton: Man and Mask, Nixon Agonistes, Scoundrel Time, Inventing America, Confessions of a Conservative,* and *The Kennedy Imprisonment.*

Peter Witonski (1949-   ) is president of International Corporate Research, and was a former history professor at Harvard University and Washington University. He is the author of several books, including *What Went Wrong with American Education, The Renaissance of Cartography,* and *The American Corporation at Bay.* He is the editor of the four volume series *The Wisdom of Conservatism.*